CASTRO AND THE CUBAN LABOR MOVEMENT

Statecraft and
Society in a
Revolutionary
Period (1959–1961)

Efrén Córdova

UNIVERSITY
PRESS OF
AMERICA

LANHAM • NEW YORK • LONDON

Copyright © 1987 by

University Press of America,® Inc.

4720 Boston Way
Lanham, MD 20706

3 Henrietta Street
London WC2E 8LU England

Printed in the United States of America

British Cataloging in Publication Information Available

Library of Congress Cataloging in Publication Data

Córdova, Efrén.
    Castro and the Cuban labor movement.

    Bibliography: p.
    Includes index.
    1. Trade unions—Cuba—Political activity—History.
2. Central de Trabajadores de Cuba—History.   3. Labor
and laboring classes—Cuba—History.   4. Cuba—History—
Revolution, 1959.   I. Title.
HD6578.5.C67   1987   322'.2'097291   86-28159
ISBN 0-8191-5952-2 (alk. paper)
ISBN 0-8191-5953-0 (pbk. : alk. paper)

All University Press of America books are produced on acid-free
paper which exceeds the minimum standards set by the National
Historical Publication and Records Commission.

TABLE OF CONTENTS

Preface

QUESTIONS CONCERNING THE ORIGINS OF THE CUBAN REVO-
lution have always been both intriguing and critical. Was the
shift to Marxism in Cuba due to external causes or was it
engineered by Castro? Was the establishment of a full-fledged
Communist regime an accident of history or the outcome of
a preplanned operation? Books and articles have been written on the subject but doubts remained and no definitive
answer emerged from the discussion.

Although Castro's consistent behaviour as a bona fide
Communist over the last two decades may have removed
some of the most intriguing aspects of the controversy, it has
not in the least affected its critical implications. For one thing,
the Cuban experience bears a close resemblance to the Nicaraguan revolutionary process, and clear unequivocal replies
with regard to the former may help to evaluate and monitor
the development of the latter. For another, few of the American, European and Latin American writers who felt that
Castro did not envisage at the beginning the establishment
of a Communist regime have publicly recognized that they
were wrong. In fact, there is still a sizeable body of opinion
in academic circles which holds that Castro and his government were pushed into the Soviet camp by the allegedly
myopic policy of the State Department. To some extent, the
debate of the 1960's is still going on.

In this book a different approach has been taken in the
treatment of the subject. Instead of engaging in a general

discussion of the various characters and circumstances surrounding the Cuban Revolution, the answer to the above
questions is rather sought through analysis of a specific set
of events, namely those leading to Castro's takeover of organized labor. The *dramatis personae* is thus largely limited to
the revolutionary elite and the leaders of labor organizations.
The narrative only exceptionally departs from the area of
labor relations and the labor movement. It is hoped that an
in-depth concentration on one particular aspect of the revolution may help to explain and understand its various stages
and perhaps to clarify once and for all questions still being
debated.

The interest of the book goes, however, well beyond the
prospects for finding an adequate reply to the persistent
questions relating to the origins of Communism in Cuba.
Through discussion of the events leading in 1959–61 to
the capture of organized labor by the Castro Government,
the study explores the possibilities of bringing about unanticipated fundamental changes in a society passing
through a turbulent stage. It probes into the resistance
power of an important segment of that society, the labor
movement, and investigates the widening opportunities
for action that control of the state machinery gave to a
determined group of revolutionaries. It may well be that
the study of the contraposition between statecraft and society in Cuba may contain lessons for other similar situa-
tions.

The idea to write this book was born several years ago.
Shortly after I arrived in the U.S., I was impressed by the
degree of misunderstanding about the dynamics of the Cuban Revolution and began to collect material on the subject. Over the years I prepared two texts about the same
topic. One was used to earn a University degree in the area

of industrial and labor relations. The other remained un-published for reasons connected with my work with the International Labour Office, a technical agency of the United Nations from which I recently retired. It is this second text, duly adapted and updated, which I have used for the present publication.

The findings, interpretations and conclusions of this work are exclusively my responsibility and owe nothing to other persons or institutions.

I am most grateful to my former ILO colleague Edythe Epstein for precious editorial help. I am also indebted to Noemí Ofri and David Helfeld for intellectual advice and valuable suggestions.

My gratitude goes finally to my wife Lilia whose untiring collaboration made possible the preparation of this book.

Translations from the Spanish have been made by the author unless otherwise indicated.

E. C.
April 1986

Dramatis Personae

The revolutionary elite

Fidel Castro
Raúl Castro
Ernesto Che Guevara
Camilo Cienfuegos
Carlos Rafael Rodríguez
Augusto Martínez Sánchez
Oswaldo Dórticos
Raúl Roa
Juan Almeida
Celia Sánchez
Antonio Nuñez Jiménez
William Gálvez

The government authorities

Manuel Urrutia
José Miró Cardona
Manuel Fernández García
Manuel Ray
Felipe Pazos
Rufo López Fresquet
Ramón Barquín
Hubert Matos

The old guard of the Communist Party

The Party officials

Juan Marinello
Blas Roca
Salvador García Aguero
Aníbal Escalante
Joaquín Ordoqui

The labor leaders

Lázaro Peña
Fausto Calcines
Ursinio Rojas
Juan Taquechel
Carlos Fernández

The trade union leadership

The old leadership	*The new leadership*
Eusebio Mujal	David Salvador
Angel Cofiño	Jesús Soto
Francisco Aguirre	Octavio Louit
Jesús Artigas	Antonio Torres
Ignacio González Tellechea	Conrado Becquer
	José de Jesús Plana
	Reynol González
	José María de la Aguilera
	O. Alvarez de la Campa
	Noelio Morell
	José Pellón
	R. Iglesias Patiño

Introduction

Theories about the Origins of the Cuban Revolution

EVERY MAJOR REVOLUTION CREATES ITS OWN MYTHOLOGY. The epics of the struggle are magnified; its leaders become legendary figures; its nature and accomplishments are presented in glamorous fashion. Alongside the myths there are the shadowy areas and the deliberately cultivated enigmas, i.e., certain episodes or aspects of the revolution which are purposely shrouded in mystery. Enigmas and shadowy areas may remain as such for indefinite periods or they may give rise to other myths, invariably aimed at enhancing the prestige of the revolution.

The Cuban Revolution was no exception to this rule. In fact one of the most prominent of those enigmas relates to the very origins of the revolution and the role of its leaders in the inception of a Marxist regime. Why is it that the Cuban Revolution turned so rapidly and effectively into a Communist Revolution? Was the revolution pushed towards the Soviet camp by the hostile and short-sighted policy of the U.S. Government? Or did Castro introduce

1

Communism in Cuba in order to realize his own hidden
design, a design that he gradually and skillfully implemented? The response to these questions has touched off
a heated debate pitting U.S. academics and journalists
against each other as well as the bulk of European writers
against the majority of Cuban exiles. Despite the enormous
body of work on Castro, socialism and Cuba, the debate is
still going on and lingering doubts persist.

The idea that the Cuban Revolution was originally intended to be a democratic and nationalistic revolution which
was forced to turn into a Marxist regime because of U.S.
opposition to structural reforms and the expropriation of
businesses belonging to American citizens and corporations has long exerted a strong attraction among scholars.
In its more basic formulation this theory (which could be
called the "reaction theory") seeks to exonerate Castro of
any improper manipulation of the objectives of the revolution against Batista and to blame the subsequent turn of
events on the erroneous policy followed by the U.S. State
Department.

The abolition of the Cuban sugar quota in the U.S., the
refusal to refine Russian oil, the U.S. Government's in-
sistence on obtaining adequate compensation for the expropriated American industries and the support given to
anti-Castro groups in Florida, are accordingly seen as the
main factors leading to the radicalization of the revolution.

More frequently, however, the reaction theory is coupled with other more complex explanations concerning
the intrinsic inevitability of the revolutionary process. There
is, for example, the notion that the new revolutionary leaders had no preconceived ideas about the ultimate goals of
the revolution and that they learned from their experience
what the revolution might consist of and where it might

go. According to a modified version of this hypothesis, which could be called the "internal forces theory," Cuban socialism was the product of a complex interplay of social, economic and political forces which no one, not even Castro himself, was able to plan or foresee. The establishment of a Marxist regime is thus regarded as an inevitable phenomenon prompted by economic stagnation, social backwardness and political degradation. The advocates of this theory, who seem to follow a Marxist interpretation of history, hold that individual beliefs or deeds take second place to the analysis of the relationship between existing ownership systems and the forces of production and that the real reasons for the Communist revolution are to be sought first of all in the stifling economic situation and the low living standards of the Cuban population.

Whatever the exact wording of these theories, there is no doubt that they have enjoyed wide support in academic circles. Though they were also later accepted *mutatis mutandis* by several foreign observers, their early formulation and strength originated in the U.S. At a critical stage of the Cuban Revolution, when Castro's power was not yet consolidated and premature disclosures could have jeopardized the future of the revolution, a number of American scholars, researchers and writers tried hard to demonstrate that Castro was not really a Communist or that his was a special and unique brand of Marxism.[1] So widespread became the views presented by these authors that they were sometimes taken for granted as the standard explanation of the Cuban Revolution.[2] One author has even suggested that the "conspiracy theory," i.e., the idea that Castro and a small group of followers had planned in advance the inception of Communism, offends common sense and displays an attitude towards the Cuban people

bordering on contempt.[3] European writers of socialist or
social democratic orientation followed the U.S. example
and contributed to disseminate both the established reaction theory and the internal forces version of the origins
of the revolution.[4] Neither subsequent developments nor
the testimonies of well-informed members of the revolutionary elite seemed to affect the momentum of this school
of thought. Recent publications have reiterated the view
that it was the escalation of the American confrontation
which set the stage for the introduction of socialism in
Cuba.[5]

In contrast with the support given to the reaction cum
internal forces explanation, the so called "conspiracy theory" failed at the beginning to attain the same level of
success. First, its very title seemed to suggest cloak-and-
dagger operations with Kremlin agents, and this provoked
a negative reaction among liberal and university people.
Secondly, some early discussions of the theory written by
American journalists[6] were quickly set aside by many academics who regarded them as an oversimplified and superficial presentation of Castro's actions in favor of international Communism. Thirdly, a few first hand reports of
Cuban exiles who had held important positions during the
first stage of the revolution were also discarded out of hand
as biased or insufficiently convincing.[7] A similar fate befell
the testimonies of former members of the U.S. diplomatic
service or CIA agents who had served in Cuba during the
critical years of 1959 and 1960.[8]

Academic circles thus tended to remain by and large
unimpressed by the first batch of incriminating accounts.
The notion that Cuba became a Communist regime as a
result of Castro's design and maneuvers was looked down
on or dismissed with a certain degree of hostility. A myth

was thus beginning to take shape. The Cuban Revolution was to be regarded for some time as a reactive process in which some inner, structural forces also played a role.

There were, of course, some exceptions. Most prominent among partisans of the conspiracy theory (in its broad sense) was Theodore Draper, whose early penetrating analysis of the Cuban Revolution (particularly *Castro's Revolution: Myths and Realities,* 1962) deserved wide recognition. According to Draper's reasoning, a genuine revolutionary leader does not change the fundamental character of the revolution because American oil companies refuse to refine oil or because the U.S. suspended a sugar quota that had been attacked as a symbol of colonialism. But while Draper was thoroughly convinced that the original revolution had been betrayed, he seemed to side-step at times the Communist issue by regarding Castroism as a mere caricature of socialism. Other American authors, from newspaper correspondents stationed in Havana in 1959 to well-known journalists attached to important magazines, have also departed from the conventional reaction-oriented approach and provided detailed accounts of Castro's efforts to bring Communism into Cuba.[9] As the testimonies of Cuban exiles became more refined and well-documented, the conspiracy theory received new impetus. In essence, these authors hold that the establishment of a Marxist regime was envisaged and planned from the outset by the leaders of the revolution, though the plan called for a gradual unfolding of its crucial aspects in order to avoid premature confrontation with anti-Communist forces within and without Cuba.[10]

Other variations of these main hypotheses have also been formulated by scholars in the U.S. and abroad. There is, for instance, the view that Castro's Communism was a way

of securing Soviet nuclear power support and the possibility of spreading the revolution to other countries by
obtaining recognition of Cuba as a member of the socialist
community. Finally a few writers have followed a mid-way
or non-commital approach and content themselves with
indicating that the first stage of the revolution lacked a
well-defined ideology.

Castro himself has contributed to the proliferation of
hypotheses by providing at least two different versions about
the origins of the revolution. One is a prospective view of
what the revolution was going to be according to the promises he held out before the Cuban people. This is the pre-
1959 version, which drew up the outlines of a reformist,
nationalist and socio-democratic revolution. The other is
a retrospective account of the rationale and development
of the revolutionary process, which suggested that a Marxist Revolution had been envisaged from the beginning.

A chief purpose of this study is to put into perspective
the choice between the different hypotheses discussed above
and between the pre-1959 and post-1961 versions given
by Castro, by reviewing the history of the relationship between Castro and the Cuban labor movement during the
first three years of the revolution. The role of the latter
during a revolutionary process is no doubt a critical and
eventful one. Indeed, as the following chapters will suggest, the major battles concerning the establishment of a
Communist regime in Cuba were not waged in the Bay of
Pigs invasion or in the hit-and-run attacks of Cuban exiles
but in connection with the control of the trade union
movement.

Aside from choices and theories there is the underlying
contraposition between statecraft and society. The particular circumstances created in Cuba after Batista's downfall,

i.e., a political vacuum similar to the one that was to obtain in Nicaragua in 1979 (and which incidentally was not present in Chile during the Allende administration) offered ample possibilities for the manipulation of state's powers and resources. As we shall see in the body of this study, such possibilities were thoroughly, skillfully and unscrupulously used by the people in power in accordance with their particular goals and ideology. Moreover, resort to statecraft was not circumscribed to the wielding of police power, but reached into the areas of public relations, dissemination of information, employment opportunities and educational facilities.

There were nevertheless limits to the use of state manipulations. One of these limits was represented by the changing character of the state which in the period of 1959–61 evolved from a brief pseudo-liberal phase to a full-fledged totalitarian regime passing through an incipient dictatorship of the proletariat. Another limit was, of course, the need to reckon with the society's reaction to the dramatic changes that were in store. The experience of the Castro Revolution seems to indicate, however, that the resistance power of the Cuban society—as well as that of many other Latin American countries—was not particularly strong. Lack of deeply rooted democratic institutions, a crisis of moral values, the inadequate system of land tenure and the failure of so many previous governments, all this had sapped the capacity of Cuban society to resist change. It is a telling indication of this state of affairs that the most serious challenges to Castro did not come from the middle classes, the Catholic Church, the peasants or the military, but from the wage-earning class. Few people would have expected that in the light of labor's precarious position at the end of Batista's dictatorship. Yet it was from the courage and vitality of organized labor that stemmed—as we shall see—the only serious setbacks to Castro's plans.

Some Basic Questions and a Few Milestones

While the attention of this book is largely limited to the government takeover of organized labor, the discussion will demonstrate that the takeover actually encompasses all the major features, objectives and tactics of the revolution. In a period of severe strain in society, when the country was trying to recover from the turmoil of Batista's dictatorship, Castro and his followers saw fit to use the state apparatus to gain control of the labor movement and eliminate other interest groups. The government determination to emasculate and dominate the labor movement as soon as possible, and reshape it in accordance with its own objectives, can be regarded in retrospect as one of the most relevant threads running through the first three years of the revolution. To achieve the complete subordination of the formerly independent trade unions became a sort of idée fixe on the part of the revolutionary elite. Although employing different methods, Fidel Castro consistently pursued this goal even at the price of creating further disturbances. In fact, the first manifestations of this undertaking can be traced back to the speeches and proclamations that announced the inception of the new government in January 1959.

As developments unfolded in the following months and Castro relentlessly pursued his aim of controlling organized labor, one is entitled to wonder about the rationale of such an endeavour. Why did the emasculation of the labor movement become a major priority of the new regime from its earliest days? Why was Castro so intent on crushing in 1959 the anti-Communist factions within labor? Why did he try to do away from the beginning with the existence of independent labor organizations? Was the notion of a free trade union movement incompatible with Castro's personal philosophy and plans?

The suspicion that an ideological and preconceived blueprint was involved would appear all the more plausible as one considers the other significant developments that were simultaneously taking place in the social area. From the first days of the revolution Castro attempted—sometimes strenuously, sometimes in more subtle ways—to highlight the role of labor, to praise its contribution to the victorious fight and to hold out enormous expectations of power and prosperity for the Cuban workers. The revolutionary leader was obviously seeking to win the allegiance and support of the Cuban working class. That such courting was taking place at the time of Castro's efforts to eliminate the elected representatives of the same class should not come as a surprise. By means of such maneuvers Castro was aiming at building up a strong proletarian constituency whose support to the regime was going to be channelled through the structure previously set up by the old labor movement.

These two developments coincided with another important feature of the first months of the revolutionary process. Although apparently indifferent at the beginning to conventional government positions, Castro was in fact determined from the outset to secure absolute political control of the country. No other political or revolutionary movement was ever allowed to share the exercise of power. Some figureheads were initially appointed to provide a convenient mask during the transitional period, but these were ephemeral and inconsequential arrangements. Castro's own July 26 Movement was permitted to rise in prestige and influence until Castro felt sufficiently secure and then it was quietly disbanded. Castro and his trusted associates gradually monopolized all key posts in the government and the army. By the autumn of 1959 all sources of political power were firmly in their hands. A revolution that had been fought by all Cubans was transformed into a revolution led and controlled by only a few.

Full political power and the capacity to undermine the labor movement from below were then used to eliminate the anti-Communist leadership in all labor organizations. Statecraft was also used to destroy the power of the old bourgeoisie and to promote a close collaboration between government and the rank and file. The basic ingredients of a dictatorship of the proletariat were thus in place by the summer of 1960. A revolution that had been conceived to restore democracy and to introduce political reforms could now be used to serve Castro's personal purposes which, as subsequent developments more clearly demonstrated, were also those of Marxism-Leninism.

The plan and timetable for action to bring about a Communist takeover thus seemed impeccable. It was clear, however, that their smooth or rough implementation depended on the attitude of organized labor. What would be the position of the Cuban working class vis-à-vis Castro's scheme? Would the apparent beneficiaries of the proposed changes prove responsive to the idea of vesting them, more or less effectively, with the power to guide the revolution? Castro was probably counting on the revolutionary potential frequently attached to labor and the lingering influence of the Communist Party. He probably intended to profit also from the confusion created by Batista's downfall as well as from the divisions afflicting the existing central workers' organization. But signs of resistance appeared and there was room for uncertainty. Would labor have sufficient grasp of events and enough inner vitality to mobilize its forces in order to mount an opposition to his plans? The trade union elections, the purges and the persecutions of trade unionists discussed at some length in this book provide answers to these questions.

These three developments, i.e., the search for absolute power, the domination of the labor movement and the enticement of the working class, are obviously interconnected. To treat them as separate, discreet phenomena would have little purpose. Each one of them would only acquire its full significance in the context of all three. Only by bringing them together in a coherent fashion, would it be possible to demonstrate that the shift to Communism was not due to external causes, as so many scholars believed, but actually engineered by Castro.

Another dimension should be added to this new facet of the Cuban revolutionary process. As it happened later with other countries of Latin America, the Cuban leadership pretended for a while that its ideology was a hybrid and pragmatic one and that it was unique to the Cuban situation. Several European and American writers lent credence to this pretension and wrote high-brow, intellectually profound interpretations of the sources of the revolution. As everybody knows by now, the façade of humanism and the claim of a third position quickly crumbled in the face of Castro's unveiling of his Marxist aims. But even before the relevant announcements were made by Castro and his associates, there is sufficient evidence to show that while the initial misrepresentation of the pur-

poses of the revolution may have fooled other segments
of public opinion it could have hardly deceived those within
the labor movement who were confronted with the stark
reality of the government's daily attempts to impose its
Communist objectives. One is entitled to ask, nonetheless,
whether elements of deceit, duplicity and fraud were instrumental in the success of the revolution. Inward im-
pulses were indeed essential to the process, but the question arises: Were they represented by deterministic forces
relating to material conditions of life or by the implacable
resolve of a group of dedicated, unorthodox Marxists?

These are some of the major questions which the following chapters will try to answer. These questions are
basic to a thorough understanding of the origins of the
revolution. As the rest of this book will try to demonstrate,
they are probably more pertinent and important than the
oft-repeated ones concerning the choices open to the revolutionary elite with regard to external alignments, or about
the need for drastic changes in the framework and composition of the Cuban production process.

Areas of Investigation

The study of unions and labor relations offers a fertile
area of investigation, particularly suitable for testing the
validity of existing hypotheses and the two Castro versions.
Not only is the government-trade union relationship of
critical significance during the early stages of any revolution, but the whole area of labor constitutes a sensitive
domain liable to reflect the aims and ideological orientation
of the revolutionary leaders. Given the nature of a Com-

munist-oriented regime and its twofold objectives of em-
bodying the interests of the working class and abolishing
private property, there is little doubt that the analysis of
the relationship between government, employers and labor
during the first transitional years becomes particularly il-
lustrative and may even be regarded as indispensable for
any serious study of the initial character of the revolution.
Since the Cuban labor movement had a long history and
was regarded as a formidable power within Cuban society,
there is every reason to believe that the Castro Revolution
attached particular and early importance to its dealings
with organized labor. The attitudes of revolutionary leaders and their cohorts as reflected in their speeches, statements and actions, the government policies vis-à-vis the
trade union leadership and the rank and file, and the
changes in the institutional framework of labor relations,
thus acquire notable significance and may serve to identify
trends and patterns of conduct.

It is hoped that the analysis of the events regarding the
wooing, infiltration and eventual takeover of the labor
movement by the Revolutionary Government will shed further light on the shadowy critical area concerning the origins
of Communism in Cuba and set the record straight as
regards the real objectives of Castro's revolution. The following chapters will seek to demonstrate in this respect
that the conspiracy theory provides the only plausible explanation of the Communist character of the revolution.
It may be noted from the outset, however, that the term
conspiracy theory is used in this book in the sense that the
establishment of Communism responded to a design that
Castro had in mind before January 1959 and that he proceeded to implement from the beginning of the revolution.
By way of corollary, the book also seeks to dispel the wide-

spread and, in the author's view, rather naive notion that the existence of a Marxist-Leninist regime in Cuba was the result of U.S. blunders and misjudgements.

One additional word about the selection of the 1959–61 period. The socialist character of the revolution was officially proclaimed in April 1961 and the so-called Marxist-Leninist speech in which Castro admitted that his Communist views dated back to before his victory was delivered in December 1961. The two preceding years were thus formative ones and witnessed critical developments concerning the shaping of the final course and nature of the revolution. For all practical purposes, the 1959–61 period may thus contain the key to explaining the origins of the Cuban Revolution.

The table of contents of the book follows a historical and analytical approach. Castro's conflicting versions about the purpose of the revolution are presented in the first chapter. Another preliminary chapter (II) provides a short description of the setting, i.e., the position of the labor movement and Cuban society on the eve of the revolution. The historical account is developed in some detail in Chapters III to XI. Chapter III starts with the analysis of the general strike of January 1959, and goes on to discuss a series of events that took place during the first tumultuous weeks of the revolution. The reader is also introduced to some of the main characters of the *dramatis personae*. A detailed discussion of the strategy followed from the beginning by Castro and his colleagues to woo Cuban workers and to establish a special relationship between the revolutionary leadership and the labor movement is contained in Chapter IV. There is also in this chapter a reference to the attitudes of the revolutionary elite vis-à-vis industrial disputes and seizures of enterprises. Such attitudes throw

light on the early orientation of the Castro Government
with regard to eventual state management and control of
the means of production as well as to Soviet style ways of
disposing of labor disputes. Chapter V discusses the anti-
Communist reaction and pays special attention to the trade
union elections that were held in the summer of 1959. A
growing realization that something unusual was taking place
began to set in among the leaders of labor organizations.
Their reaction related at this point to the increasing as-
cendancy of the old Communist leaders, but the result of
the elections also meant that Castro's plans towards complete subordination of organized labor were not going to
materialize without a serious challenge. Chapter VI con-
cludes the discussion of what could well be regarded as
the first stage of the revolution by describing at length the
proceedings of the fateful Tenth Congress of the Cuban
Workers' Confederation. Particular importance is attached
to Castro's speeches, their influence on the adoption of
resolutions and the election of leaders and the feelings that
prevailed among the delegates. A completely different
strategy was adopted by the Castro Government after the
congress and this is discussed in Chapter VII, which provides an account of the way in which the Revolutionary
Government resorted to more direct measures to control
organized labor. Emphasis is placed on the process of
purges of the trade union leadership that occurred at the
end of 1959 and in the first half of 1960. As Castro moved
ahead with his plans to capture the labor movement, Chapter VIII discusses the various measures adopted to consolidate his grip, namely workers' militias, the labor census,
the promotion of workers' contributions and the switch to
a productionist policy. Attention is paid in the next chapter
(IX) to the accelerated process of changes in workers' at-

titudes and trade union functions that took place during 1960 and to the series of government actions that led to a new structuring of labor-management relations. The discussion focuses chiefly on the emasculation of collective bargaining and the dismantling of tripartite machinery but there is also a reference to the nationalization of business enterprises and the links of the Cuban labor movement with the international trade union centers. Chapter X goes on to discuss the last vestiges of resistance to Castro's plans and again analyzes the methods used to quell such resistance and the reasons given to justify government action. With the success of the second stage of the revolutionary strategy, the transition comes to an end, culminating in the Eleventh Congress of the Cuban Workers' Confederation. Chapter XI provides an over-all view of the drastic ideological reorientation of organized labor that came about in the two years that had elapsed since the Tenth Congress and which found reflection in the speeches delivered at the Eleventh Congress by Castro, Guevara and the Minister of Labor, Augusto Martínez Sánchez. Finally, Chapter XII seeks to establish some conclusions as regards the two major versions about the origins of the revolution and the plausibility of the conspiracy theory. Appropriate comparisons are made in this connection with the Soviet model. A discussion of the roots of Castro's Communism is presented in the last section of this chapter.

No attempt will be made to ascertain with absolute precision whether Castro became a Communist while fighting in the Sierra Maestra or during his prior Mexican sojourn or in jail or even earlier. What is important is to demonstrate that the design to implant Communism in Cuba was already in Castro's mind in January 1959, and that everything he did afterwards corresponded in one way or another to that design. Nor will this study retrace the full history of Cuba during the period 1959–61. Stress is laid on the relationship between Castro and the trade union movement, although some references to political developments and their international ramifications will also be included in order to provide a better understanding of the revolutionary process.

The author has relied basically on primary sources, i.e., official or semi-official publications containing legislation, data, speeches and statements made by Fidel Castro and his colleagues, Cuban newspapers such as *Revolución, El Mundo, Hoy, Havana Post, Diario de la Marina, Avance* and *Información* and periodicals such as *Bohemia, Trabajo, Vanguardia Obrera* and *Verde Olivo*. Extensive use was also made of the wealth of published material available. Primary and secondary information are sometimes coupled with the author's eyewitness accounts.

The significance of ascertaining the real causes of the Cuban Revolution is apparent. History should have no place for myths or enigmas, no matter how cleverly elaborated and how high the level of their scholarly support. There are also the moral and political implications of the debate. Cuba was presented as an example of the dilemma between social progress and U.S. foreign policy. Because the U.S. refused to accept social progress, it was alleged, Castro was forced to look elsewhere for desperately needed help. The argument has by now a rather familiar ring, as it has repeatedly been raised in the case of other Latin American countries. Perhaps it is high time to look again into the plausibility of its first application in Cuba. If Castro did not plan to introduce Communism and was on the contrary thwarted in his reformist or democratic revolutionary endeavours by U.S. policy, then American oppo-

18   *Efrén Córdova*

sition to the new regime and its support for anti-Castro activities was morally wrong and politically unwise. But if Castro was, on the contrary, intent from the beginning on furthering a Communist revolution in Cuba, then guilt complexes should give way to the realization that a more determined and consistent policy should have been followed to deal with the establishment of a Communist regime in the very heart of the American sphere of influence. It is suggested that an analysis of the origins of Cuban Communism, i.e., the first three years of the revolution, is essential for understanding the intricacies of the U.S. predicament during those years as well as more recent political processes in that country and elsewhere in the region.

NOTES

1. See, for instance, C. Wright Mills, *Listen Yankee*, (New York: Ballantine Books, 1960); Herbert Mathews, *The Cuban Story*, (New York: G. Braziller, 1961); Warren Miller, *90 Miles from Home: The Face of Cuba Today*, (Boston: Little, Brown, 1961); Leo Huberman and Paul M. Sweezy, *Anatomy of a Revolution*, (New York: Monthly Review Press, 1961); J.P. Morray, *The Second Revolution in Cuba*, (New York: 1962); Maurice Zeitlin and Robert Scheer, *Cuba: Tragedy in our Hemisphere*, (New York: Grove Press, 1963); and James O'Connor, *The Origins of Socialism in Cuba*, (Ithaca, N.Y.: Cornell University Press, 1970).

2. Martin Kenner and James Petra, eds., *Fidel Castro Speaks*, (New York: Grove Press, 1969), p. 74.

3. O'Connor, *op.cit.*, p. 4.

4. See, for instance, Claude Julien, *La Révolution Cubaine*, (Paris: Julliard, 1961); Dudley Seers, *Cuba: The Economic and Social Revolution*, (Chapel Hill, N.C.: University of North Carolina Press, 1964); and K.S. Karol, *Les Guerrilleros au Pouvoir*, (Paris: Robert Laffont, 1970).

5. See, for instance, Maurice Halperin, *The Taming of Fidel Castro*, (Berkeley, California: University of California Press, 1981) and David Detzer, *The Brink: Cuban Missile Crisis*, (New York: Thomas Y. Crowell, 1979).

6. See Daniel James, *The First Soviet Satellite in the Americas*, (New York: Avon Books, 1961); Nathaniel Weyl, *Red Star over Cuba: The Russian Assault on the Western Hemisphere*, (New York: Devin-Adair, 1960); and J. Monaham and K.O. Gilmore, *The Great Deception*, (New York: Farrar, Strauss and Company, 1963).

7. See, for instance, Manuel Urrutia, *Fidel Castro and Company*, (New York: Frederick Praeger, 1964) and Rufo López Fresquet, *My Fourteen Months with Castro*, (New York: The World Publishing Company, 1966).

8. See Paul Bethel, *The Losers*, (New Rochelle: Arlington House, 1969) and Howard Hunt, *Give Us the Day*, (New Rochelle: Arlington House, 1973).

9. See, for instance, Ruby Hart Phillips, *The Cuban Dilemma,* (New York: I. Obolensky, 1962) and Lionel Martin, *The Early Fidel: Roots of Castro's Communism,* (Secaucus, N.J.: Lyle Stuart Inc., 1978).

10. See, for instance, Boris Goldenberg, *The Cuban Revolution and Latin America,* (New York: Praeger, 1965); Samuel Farber, *Revolution and Reaction in Cuba,* (Middletown, Conn.: Wesleyan University Press, 1976); and Mario Llerena, *The Unsuspected Revolution,* (Ithaca, N.Y.: Cornell University Press, 1978).

I

Two Different Versions

Castro's Views Before 1959

Prior to the Moncada Assault

FIDEL CASTRO WAS NOT KNOWN AS A COMMUNIST BEFORE January 1959. The son of a Spanish immigrant who became a relatively wealthy sugar cane grower in the Oriente Province and "a Cuban woman who entered the Castro house as a cook,"[1] Castro was educated by the Jesuit fathers in two well-known schools of Havana and Santiago. When Fidel and his brother Raúl were still at the primary school, their illegitimate origin was removed in accordance with Cuban legislation, as a result of the marriage of their father, by then a widower, to their mother.

While a law student at the University of Havana, Castro was involved in revolutionary activities and became a member of a terrorist organization called the Revolutionary Insurrectional Union (UIR), which was never accused of Communist links.[2] Although UIR's objectives were subversive, its views on sociopolitical issues were never clearly expounded; the organization was headed by Emilio Tro, a veteran of the Second World War who was allegedly suffering from war psychosis and had at any rate a marked penchant for violent action. This group clashed frequently and violently with other terrorist organizations, including the Socialist Revolutionary Movement (MSR) led by Mario Salavarría and Rolando Masferrer, the latter also a gunman who had fought on the Republican side in the Spanish Civil War.

As a politician during the early 1950's, Castro belonged to the reformist and nationalist Cuban People's Party (PPC), also known as Orthodox Party,[3] where he was generally regarded as a young and ambitious radical without definite ideological coloration. In 1952, Castro was a PPC candidate for Congress from the Havana province, but the election was never held because of General Fulgencio Batista's coup d'état. The future revolutionary leader remained a full-fledged member of this Party until March 1956. A few months earlier, however, he sent a message to the Orthodox Party Congress indicating that he had founded his own July 26 Movement,[4] which was not a mere faction within the party, but the revolutionary apparatus of "chibasismo."[5] According to this message, the Movement would not include big landowners (latifundistas), magnates, powerful lawyers, stock market operators or incompetent politicians. While the language of this document sounded radical it was in fact the kind of jargon frequently used at that time by populist movements in Latin America. Similar words can be found, for instance, in the Declaration of Principles made in October, 1945, by the founders of the Peronist Movement in Argentina.

Though Castro's activities before 1959 included some subversive ones, such as participation in the abortive 1947 invasion of the Dominican Republic and the Bogotá riots of 1948, no ostensible connection with national or international Communism has ever been established. To the general public, Castro appeared to be an "activist" beset by a nebulous history of gangsterism and who operated on his own, outside the influence or control of the Communist Party.

Castro's writings and public statements seemed to corroborate that impression. Six days before the Batista coup d'état of March 10, 1952, the future Prime Minister wrote an article for a Havana newspaper decrying the crisis of authority of the Carlos Prío Socarrás administration and accusing the President of buying off criminal gangs with bribes and government positions.[6] There was a reference to the different treatment accorded to those who stole private monies and those who embezzled public funds, but no other social issue or anti-capitalist denunciation was mentioned. A similar concern for political problems permeated the brief lodged by Castro before the Court of Appeals on March 24, 1952, two weeks after the infamous coup d'état staged by General Fulgencio Batista. In it Castro pointed out his attachment to the 1940 Constitution and asked the Court to put Batista on trial for the crimes of treachery and sedition. The whole text was based on the application of existing laws, though he also rejected the notion that the Batista insurrection was a source of law by stating that "without a new conception of the State, society and juridical order based on deeply rooted historical and philosophical principles, there is no revolution generating rights."[7]

Before the assault led by him on the Moncada army barracks in Santiago de Cuba on July 26, 1953, the future revolutionary leader prepared a manifesto (intended to be broadcast after victory) in which he mentioned as ideological sources of his movement the ideals of José Martí, the hero of the Cuban War of Independence, and the revolutionary programs of three nationalist movements: Young Cuba, Radical ABC, both founded in the 1930's, and the Orthodox Party.[8]

The attack was carried out by some 180 people of very mixed ideological orientation. Most were students, blue collar workers, office employees and members of the youth section of the Orthodox Party, who dreamed of a democratic society and were aroused by Batista's dictatorship. Others including Jesús Montaner, Abel Santa María, Boris Santa Coloma, Melba Hernández and the Castro brothers, were activists who had no doubt more profound disagreements with the existing social and political structures. Yet despite their advocacy of left wing views and their contempt for conventional politics, they had never been clearly identified as members of the Communist Party.

Between Moncada and the Sierra Maestra

While the Moncada operation failed, it made a lasting impact on public opinion and catapulted Castro into the category of a national celebrity. During the subsequent trial Castro delivered in his defense a speech that he later refined in prison and that came to be known as *History Will Absolve Me*. The speech contained a populist program couched in relatively restrained and rather ambiguous terms. To be sure, it included a few tirades against capitalist exploitation, but the essence of the program was non-Communist in character. Suffice it to indicate that the three revolutionary laws that Castro envisaged enacting in the social field if his movement were to obtain political power related to granting ownership of the land to cane planters, leasers and sharecroppers who occupied small parcels, the workers' right to participate in 30 percent of the profits of the large industrial, commercial and mining concerns and the right of sugar planters to share with the owner of the mill the net yield in sugar produced by the cane.[9]

Castro was sentenced to 15 years' imprisonment but was set free in 1955 following a general amnesty decreed by Batista. In his correspondence from jail, one may find a few intriguing statements about the way of overcoming Cuba's social and political problems[10] as well as some expressions of admiration for Marx and Lenin and their works.[11] However, these letters were addressed to trusted friends and did not become available to the general public until late in 1959 or 1960.

Immediately after his release from prison, Castro resumed his contacts and activities with a view to planning another military operation. He lived for a few months in Havana, visited the U.S. and settled down in Mexico where he met Ernesto Guevara, by then an independent Marxist and virulent anti-imperialist who had acquired valuable experience during the Arbenz episode in Guatemala. Together they organized a group of Cuban exiles who began to train for guerrilla action under the guidance of Colonel Alberto Bayo, a veteran of the Spanish Civil War.[12]

Castro's written work also included a number of articles published during this period between his release from prison and the beginning of the guerrilla fight. The first of these articles published in newspaper *La Calle* during his brief stay in Havana in 1955 were forcefully ringed with patriotic and anti-Batista overtones. Other subsequent pieces contained a blistering criticism of Cuban politicians and a denunciation of what the revolutionary leader called "the campaign of defamations and plots of the spokesmen of the regime" against him. In one of them Castro expressed his intention "to invite our compatriots to stand behind the ideal of full dignity for the Cuban people, justice for the hungry and forgotten and punishment for the truly guilty."[13] Another article published in *Bohemia* was primarily designed to deny any links with the Cuban Communist Party (PSP).[14] It is true that social implications kept cropping up in these articles and that the July 26 Movement was therein regarded as "the revolutionary organization of the humble" and "the only hope of redemption for the Cuban working class,"[15] but it is no less certain that the solutions proposed by Castro were eminently political and related in particular to the overthrow of the regime and the establishment of a "more dignified public life."[16]

The revolutionary leader was also personally involved in the drafting of the "Mexico Program" of the July 26 Movement, published in 1956, when preparations for the Sierra Maestra operation were already advanced. The Program rejected economic determinism and affirmed, *inter alia*, that the Movement was guided by the ideals of democracy, nationalism and social justice.[17]

A few months later, in order to erase further any possible doubts about his future political endeavours, Castro included the following words in a 1956 statement also issued in Mexico:

> No one in Cuba is unaware of my position toward Communism, for I was a founder of the Partido del Pueblo Cubano along with Eduardo Chibás who never made dealings or accepted any type of collaboration with the Communists.[18]

During the Sierra Maestra Guerrilla Fight

The story of the Sierra Maestra guerrillas has been told many times and need not be recounted here. For the purpose of this book it is more useful to focus on the composition of Castro's forces and their ideological position. Unlike the anti-Batista underground movement in the cities which was predominantly composed of democratic-minded middle-class people, the guerrillas were more heterogenous in character. Castro started up the fighting with a few dozen people who sailed to Cuba from Mexico in the Granma[19] yacht. This group included a number of idealistic and anti-totalitarian revolutionaries like César Gómez and Fernando Sánchez Amaya (who were later called upon to hold important posts in the Department of Labor), together with Raúl Castro, Ernesto Guevara and other Castro associates of more radical views. The small, initial group grew slowly and eventually attracted some support from unhappy peasants of the area and other people of humble origin. At no point, however, were the guerrillas a peasant army or a proletarian contingent. Nor was it a Marxist-oriented military outfit. Marxian tenets were, in fact, alien to the thinking of the great majority of these people and the possibility of a Communist regime did not even cross their minds.

A curious phenomenon also occurred with regard to the final composition of the guerrillas. Batista's police was implacable in the cities while the army was totally inept on the battlefield.[20] The mountainous regions of the Oriente province thus became almost a haven for the underground militants fleeing the cities. White-collar employees, members of the liberal professions and students, together with rank and file activists of the nationalist parties joined the guerrillas and reinforced their middle-class components. If there were also a handful of affiliates of the PSP, their presence was hardly noticed until September, 1958, when the top PSP theoretician Carlos Rafael Rodríguez also joined the armed struggle. Less visible, but more important was the presence of a number of unconditional and obscure pro-Castro officers (Calixto García, Juan Almeida, William Gálvez, etc.) who only later were identified as Communists. However, towards the end of the fighting, Marxism seemed to gain some subtle momentum, particularly among the highest level of the leadership where Raúl Castro and Ernesto Guevara exerted an undeniable influence. But Fidel Castro managed to place himself above ideological definitions and emerged simply as the charismatic leader of a growing and militant anti-Batista movement.

During the period of the Sierra Maestra fight, Castro's non-Communist views were formulated—and widely publicized—in clear and unequivocal terms. In his first full manifesto addressed to the Cuban people from the Sierra Maestra, for instance, he reaffirmed his liberal convictions and underscored the need to re-establish the principles of trade union democracy which had been neglected during the Batista regime.[21] The Economic Thesis of the July 26 Revolutionary movement, in turn, was a "developmentalist" document which stressed economic growth and paid little attention to structural changes.[22] According to the Thesis, the correct road for Cuba was to establish a rational plan of economic development with strong citizens' support in order to increase national production, develop the Cuban economy, offer full productive employment and finally raise the standard of living of the population, without excluding appropriate social justice measures.[23] The Thesis listed the proposition that Cuban labor legislation blocked economic development as the first fallacy that should be dispelled and contained some vague generalities about wage increases and the promise that "the right to strike would be guaranteed." Finally, on the occasion of a labor congress held in the mountains a few months before his victory, the revolutionary leader pledged to institute a system of four shifts of six hours each in the sugar industry in place of the existing three shifts of eight hours.[24] The new system was intended to benefit the numerous sugar workers and to combat unemployment by creating thousands of jobs.

A few months before victory, Castro emphasized his democratic and non-Communist views to various American journalists, including Herbert Mathews, Robert Taber, Andrew St. George, Homer Bigart and Jules Dubois. These interviews were published by some of the most important newspapers and periodicals of the U.S. and were fully or partially reproduced by the Cuban press.[25] In the course of the interview given to Jules Dubois, Castro mentioned the need to promote "free enterprise" and made it clear in most categorical terms: "I am not and have never been a Communist. If I were one, I would have the courage to proclaim it;" and he added, "Never has the July 26 Movement talked of socialism or nationalization."[26]

To the Cuban people, the above excerpts and indications represented the salient points of the economic and social thought of Fidel Castro as it was known and had been widely disseminated before the triumph of the revolution. Other statements of a political nature, issued during the final days of the war and at the beginning of 1959, seemed to indicate that a future government led by Castro was to pursue a nonaligned foreign policy, to encourage a quick return to democracy and to establish a mixed economy. It

was all in all a moderate and liberal program anchored in
the progressive Constitution of 1940 and based on the
recognition of a pluralist society. It was thus eminently
acceptable to the whole spectrum of society.

True, other documents corresponding to this period
contained unexpected and somewhat alarming passages.
For example, in a letter of June 15, 1958, addressed to his
close confidante Celia Sánchez, Castro indicated: "When
the war is over, a much wider and bigger war will com-
mence for me; the war that I am going to wage against
(the Americans). I am saying to myself that this is my true
destiny."[27] However, these documents were not published
until after the victory.

Other bewildering developments also came to be known
later. But for every suspicion of Communist links, there
was always a countervailing proof, an excuse or an appropriate denial. Raúl Castro, for instance, had some connec-
tions with front organizations related to international
Communism and had apparently applied in 1953 for admission to the youth section of the PSP.[28] However, in an
interview given to Jules Dubois in July 1954, the younger
Castro admitted that he had attended a World Youth Congress held in Vienna in 1953 and visited various Eastern
European countries, but insisted, not without a certain logic,
that this did not necessarily mean that he was a Communist.[29] Guevara was also an obvious Marxist sympathizer,
but he belonged to a new breed of independent Communists who refused formal affiliation and was consequently in a position to claim repeatedly and without hesitation that he was not a member of the party.

Castro's Statements After the Establishment of Socialism

In contrast with the preceding indications, there are other statements made by Fidel Castro after the consolidation of his victory, which offer a completely different view of the revolution.

The Marxist-Leninist Speech

On December 2, 1961, for instance, almost three years after his accession to power and seven months after the proclamation of the socialist character of the revolution, Castro delivered a speech before the People's University in one of Havana's television stations. This speech, which later came to be known as the Marxist-Leninist speech, included a historical account of Castro's background and the different stages of his struggle for power.

The Marxist-Leninist speech was the first occasion on which Castro publicly portrayed himself as a convinced Marxist and vowed to remain a Communist until the day of his death ("I am a Marxist-Leninist and shall be until the day I die"). As it was only natural to expect, the Marxist-Leninist speech contained an impassioned defense of Marxian tenets and their application to the Cuban revolutionary process. The text also included, however, some unanticipated references to Castro's personal history vis-à-vis the Communist ideology. The Prime Minister said, for instance, that during his years as a student at the University of Havana he was not a Marxist because he was "influenced" by imperialist and reactionary propaganda.[30] But he added that by 1953, i.e., at the time of the Moncada attack, his political thinking "was more or less what it is today" (1961). Replying to his own questions, Castro further volunteered the following information: "Did I believe in Marxism on January 1st (1959)? Yes I did. Did I believe on July 26 (1953)? Yes I did. Did I understand Marxism as I do today after ten years of fighting? No I did not. Did I have any prejudices? Yes, I did have some prejudices."[31] Though Castro also indicated that in 1953 he was not yet a complete revolutionary and that it was only after he came to power that he fully developed into a Marxist-Leninist, he also made clear that "all the ideas that I have today were already in my mind on January 1st (1959)."[32]

These personal indications were capped by a famous phrase in which the Prime Minister candidly recognized that his identification with Marxism had so far been kept undisclosed for political reasons. In Castro's own words: "We have hidden our belief in Communism from the Cuban people for years because otherwise we might have alienated the bourgeoisie and other forces which we knew would eventually have to fight."[33]

The Marxist-Leninist speech was closely connected in its tone and contents with another important address made by Fidel Castro a few days earlier, at the closing ceremony of the Eleventh Congress of the Cuban Workers' Confederation (Confederación de Trabajadores de Cuba, CTC). A detailed analysis of this speech is contained in Chapter XI. It might be useful to recall here, however, that in his address Castro chastised the "myopic labor leaders" who failed to understand that the revolution aimed from the beginning "at the abolition of the propertied classes." He also stated in categorical terms:

The Revolution was forced to move ahead cautiously during its first stages because the balance of power was different and the working class was still placed in a dangerously weak position. It was then difficult to visualize the bright future that was ahead for the working class. Many workers who contented themselves at that time with securing certain demands were actually renouncing the elimination of employers and were consequently giving up the task of replacing them in the control of government. How admirable was, therefore, the instinct of those in the working class who understood the Revolutionary Government and had faith in it.[34]

The Lockwood Interview

In 1965 Castro gave a marathon interview to the American journalist Lee Lockwood.[35] He had already been interviewed in 1962 by Daniel M. Friendenberg and in 1963 by the ABC-TV and by Congressman Charles O. Porter, but his conversations with Lockwood were particularly detailed and comprehensive. Questions about Castro's beliefs in 1959 and the existence of a hidden design to socialize Cuba were raised and Castro's answers, though basically similar to the 1961 Marxist-Leninist speech, were somewhat more ambiguous. Castro's words were addressed here to an American audience and this apparently required some changes in the content and tone of his statements. He portrayed himself throughout the interview as a "revolutionary leader" who came to power with a "revolutionary platform" influenced by Marxist-Leninist ideas and determined to carry it out "in a revolutionary way." He took pains, however, to state that he was not, in 1959, a "classic" Marxist or Communist. Castro recognized that he "could have drawn up a socialist Constitution in January 1959" but indicated that this would have resulted in aligning against the revolution "all the more reactionary forces, which were then divided."

After discussing at length his initiation to Marxist readings during his university years and providing information about the gradual radicalization of his thinking, he nevertheless stated: "If you asked me whether I considered myself a Marxist-Leninist or a Communist when I was in the mountains I would say no. I did not consider myself a classic Communist. Today, yes." He proceeded later to point out that: "I was not a member of any Marxist party (in 1959) but my ideas were very much influenced by Marxist-Leninist theory. I was not a disguised or infiltrated agent or anything like that." Castro immediately acknowledged however that his brother Raúl was more formally connected with international communism as a member of the Communist Youth, although he made clear that Raúl was no longer an active member of it at the time of the Sierra Maestra war. He also considered that Guevara was more mature and advanced in his Marxist convictions but insisted that they did not discuss ideology in Mexico, nor in the Sierra Maestra mountains, because they were involved full-time in the revolutionary struggle against Batista. Speaking of the Moncada attack (1953), Castro said that there were other "people of the left" involved (Abel Santamaría, Montané, Ñico López, etc.) and that "we read books by Marx, Engels and Lenin" but stopped short of considering themselves real Communists. He also indicated that the program contained in *History Will Absolve Me* would not be regarded as Marxist by a true Communist and added that "the degree of development of the people's revolutionary consciousness was then much lower than what it was when we came to power." Then he asserted: "During the subsequent years of prison, of exile, of war in the mountains, the correlation of forces changed so extraordinarily in favor of our movement that we could set goals that were more ambitious." He finally sought to establish some linkages between the final outcome of the revolution and the composition of his forces by saying that 90 percent of those who fought in the Sierra Maestra were workers and farmers. While this was no doubt an exaggerated and distorted picture of the guerrilla mix, it served nevertheless to highlight the differences between Castro's alleged 3,000 guerrillas in the mountains[36] and the innumerable people that fought Batista in the cities.

The 1975 Report to the Communist Party

The speeches delivered at the Eleventh Congress and on December 2, 1961, and the interviews with American journalists are not the only evidence available in this respect. Though the Prime Minister later preferred to be more reserved on this particular question—probably realizing that his 1961 confessions did not contribute to enhance his image—there are other statements which could also be included in Castro's second version of his pre-1959 plans and objectives. Particularly on the occasion of revolutionary celebrations, when the atmosphere was conducive to personal reminiscences, the Cuban Prime Minister saw fit to provide further glimpses of his old ideological leanings.[37] In October 1973, for instance, the Cuban Prime Minister declared:

> Even before March 10, 1952, some of us had become in-
> timately convinced that the only solution to the problems
> of Cuba had to be revolutionary, i.e., that at a given moment
> we had to take power by force of arms and with the masses
> and that the *objective must be socialism.* (Author's italics.)[38]

It was not, however, until 1975 that Castro felt it opportune to make another explicit reference to his alleged
pre-1959 Marxist-Leninist feelings. The occasion chosen
this time by the Prime Minister was a historical one, namely
the First Congress of the Cuban Communist Party held in
Havana on December 17 and 18, 1975. His statements were
contained in a lengthy report submitted to the congress,
which Castro read out during an eight-hour-long speech.

Castro's speech included an introductory part dealing
with the historical analysis of the revolution. Following a
Marxist interpretation of the Wars of Independence and
the first decades of the Republic and after repeated references to "the role played by the hideous yankee imperialism" and the "combative and dedicated platoon of Cuban
Communists," he proceeded to discuss the events related
to the fight against Batista and the first months of the
revolution. Castro made a distinction between the "old
Communists" and the "new Communists" and indicated
that the latter took upon themselves the responsibility of
leading the revolution for the simple reason that they were
not known as Marxists while the former were suffering
from isolation and prejudices.[39] He then acknowledged
that Marxism-Leninism was not the predominant ideology
of all the guerrillas engaged in the Sierra Maestra war but
made it clear that it was the accepted credo of its "main
leaders."[40]

Referring to the Sierra Maestra struggle, Castro stated

that the proclamation of socialism during the period of the guerrilla fight "would not have been understood by the people and would have led to a military intervention by the imperialist forces."[41] As regards the conduct of the whole revolutionary process he said that it required both determined action and a measure of "astuteness" and "flexibility."[42] Objectives were therefore set and accomplished at each stage according to the priorities of the revolution and the maturity of the people. This he added, led to some confusion and misinterpretation but it was the price to be paid for the success of the revolution. The revolutionary leader also recognized that while the overthrow of Batista and the "Moncada Program" met with the approval of everybody, other subsequent objectives became more controversial and led to internal strife and accusations. As the Prime Minister put it, however:

> When later on the victorious and mighty Revolution did not hesitate to move ahead, some people said that it had been betrayed, without realizing that the real treason would have been to stop half-way the revolutionary process. To shed the blood of thousands of humble people just to maintain the imperialistic and bourgeois power and the exploitation of man by man would have been the most outrageous treason, both for the cause and for all those who fought since 1868 for justice and progress and the future of the country.[43]

A few final words about the saga of Castro's admissions and denials. The revolutionary leader's acknowledgements of his old Marxist leanings did not end with the 1975 report. Eight years later, in a 1983 interview with the Spanish

Television, he insisted that he was a Communist since 1953, i.e., since the Moncada assault, although he added that he was not then a card-carrying member of the PSP. More recently, in the course of his conversations with the Brazilian friar Frei Betto, Castro reiterated that his spousal of Marxism had already taken place at the time of the Moncada assault. In the first round of these long conversations, held in May 1985, Castro more specifically indicated that his Communist background started from his university days. He added that his determination to carry out the revolutionary struggle step by step and his conviction that capture of political power was necessary for the establishment of a Communist regime, also date back to the period 1950–53.[44] Other similar statements will no doubt come up in the future. It is already noteworthy that Castro has maintained his second version for almost a quarter of a century.

The Problem of Choice

Although the then Prime Minister has always been a prolific and long-winded orator, his other references to the crucial question of whether or not he had preconceived the introduction of socialism have been rather scanty or vague. Nor can one find in his speeches any denial of the Marxist-Leninist story nor any different version about the date of his acceptance of the Communist philosophy. Apparently he has preferred to leave this question in a limbo of shadowy or elliptical statements.

The two versions stand, however, on their own and in evident contradiction. The pre-1959 statements present the picture of a non-Communist revolutionary who sought to carry out institutional changes within a liberal and democratic framework. The Marxist-Leninist speech, the Lockwood interview and the First Congress report point to a Marxist believer who deliberately concealed for some time his convictions until he felt it appropriate to reveal the real objective of his revolution.

As mentioned in the *Introduction*, the choice between these two accounts has plagued observers of the Cuban Revolution for many years. Some experts profess to remain skeptical about Castro's credibility and question the validity of the conspiracy statements. Others argue that such assertions were prompted by Castro's urge to obtain credentials as a Communist and to secure the support of the Soviet Union. Still others feel that the conspiracy assertions do not necessarily eradicate the possibility that Castro and various important associates of his believed in the feasibility of structural changes in the Cuban society without a complete transformation along Communist lines. Relatively few observers have been inclined to take Castro at his word in his assertions of 1961 and later.

The mystery surrounding the ideological origins of the Cuban Revolution contains two known elements which are apparently opposed and actually refer to two different periods. One is the period prior to the victory of the guerrillas and the other is the period following the declaration of the Socialist Republic. It is suggested that the analysis of the intervening years (1959–61) might serve to interrelate these different periods and to fill some of the existing gaps in the history of the Cuban Revolution. Before doing that, however, it may be useful to summarize the background history of the Cuban labor movement and to describe the setting in which the initial stages of the revolution were to unfold.

NOTES

1. Herbert Mathews, *Revolution in Cuba* (New York, Charles Scribner's and Sons, 1975), p. 42.

2. See Andrés Suárez, *Cuba: Castroism and Communism* (Cambridge, Mass.: MIT Press, 1967), pp. 14 and 15; Paul D. Bethel, *The Losers, op.cit.*, p. 57; Mario Llerena, *The Unsuspected Revolution. The Birth and Rise of Castroism, op.cit.*, chapter 1 and J. Alvarez Díaz et al., *Cuba: Geopolítica y pensamiento económico* (Miami, Fla.: Duplex, 1964), pp. 467–469.

3. The Orthodox Party was set up in the late 1940s by dissident members of the then ruling Cuban Revolutionary Party, who complained about lack of morality in the administration of the state. PPC and PRC are the Spanish initials of these two parties.

4. July 26 was the date of the assault on the Moncada barracks that will be discussed below.

5. A doctrine derived from the name of the founder of the Orthodox Party, Eduardo Chibás. The term was seldom used in Cuba.

6. Fidel Castro, "El derrumbe constitucional." *Alerta* (Havana), March 4, 1952, p. 2.

7. "Brief to the Court of Appeals" in Rolando E. Bonachea and Nelson P. Valdés, eds., *Revolutionary Struggle, 1947–1958*, Volume I of the Selected Works of Fidel Castro (Cambridge, Mass.: MIT Press, 1972), p. 151.

8. "Manifiesto a la nación de los asaltantes al Cuartel Moncada," p. 1. The full text is available only at the Revolutionary Archives in Havana. Excerpts appear in K.S. Karol, *Les guerrilleros au pouvoir, op.cit.*, p. 163, and Jules Dubois, *Castro: Rebel, Liberator or Dictator?* (Indianapolis, New York: The Bobbs Merrill Co., 1959), p. 82.

9. Fidel Castro, *History will Absolve Me* (Havana: Güairas Book Institute, 1967), pp. 64 and 65.

10. As, for example, the one contained in a letter dated

15 April 1954 in which he said: "I would be willing to earn the hatred and animosity of a few thousand (Cubans) for the sake of securing the happiness of the whole country." See *Diario de la Revolución Cubana* (Barcelona: Ediciones Du Seuil and Ruedo Ibérico-Eduardo R. Torres, 1976), pp. 98–99.

11. Some relevant quotations: "a political genius" and "a redoubtable polemicist" (Marx); "true prototypes of revolutionary" (Marx and Lenin). The works of Marx and Lenin were in turn regarded as "the result of a scientific and realistic perception of history." See the letters of 27 January, 15 March and 4 April in *Diario de la Revolución Cubana, op.cit.*, pp. 90–91, 92 and 97.

12. Bayo was only a captain at the beginning of the Spanish Civil War when he was entrusted with the responsibility of invading Mallorca, a major military operation involving 10,000 people. The expedition was a complete fiasco and Bayo's competence was subjected to investigation and preliminary trial. He was nevertheless acquitted and transferred to headquarters duties; he subsequently finished the war as lieutenant colonel. According to some Spanish historians, Bayo had become by then aligned to the Communist Party. See, for instance, Vicente Guarner, "La expedición republicana a Mallorca," *Historia y Vida* (Barcelona), No. 91, October 1975, p. 103.

13. "Frente a todos." *Bohemia* (Havana), January 8, 1956.

14. Fidel Castro, "Basta ya de mentiras." *Bohemia*, July 15, 1956, p. 84. PSP were the Spanish initials of the People's Socialist Party, the name given to the Communist Party during the Second World War.

15. "El Movimiento 26 de Julio." *Bohemia*, April 1, 1956, p. 71.

16. *Ibid.*, pp. 54 and 70.

17. The Mexico Program appeared in Enrique González-Pedrero, *La revolución cubana* (México: Escuela de Ciencias Políticas y Sociales, 1959), p. 89.

18. *Bohemia*, July 1, 1956, pp. 61 and 62.

19. Although the Greek word Gamma (letter) is spelled with two m's the name of the yacht was wrongly spelled or derived from a different word.

Efrèn Córdova

20. Twice during a period of twenty years (in 1933 and in 1952) Batista's coups d'état had decapitated the army depriving it of its best officers.

21. Quoted by Juan Antonio Acuña, *Cuba: Revolución Frustrada* (Montevideo, 1960), p. 53.

22. *Political, Economic and Social Thought of Fidel Castro,* (Havana: Lex, 1959), p. 123. The Economic Thesis was written by Felipe Pazos and Regino Boti with the approval of Castro. Pazos and Boti later became members of the so-called "liberal" Cabinet appointed by Presidents Manuel Urrutia and Oswaldo Dorticós in 1959.

23. *Ibid.*, p. 125.

24. See Mario Barrera, "Metamorphosis of the Cuban Labor Movement." *Inter-American Labor Bulletin*, Vol. XII, No. 8 (August 1961), p. 2.

25. The interviews with Mathews and Bigart were published by the *New York Times;* the *Chicago Tribune* (and several Latin American newspapers) carried the article by Dubois and *Coronet* published St. George's piece. Taber's report was broadcast by CBS.

26. See Jules Dubois, *Castro: Rebel, Liberator or Dictator? op.cit.*, p. 263. The interview was first published in May 1958. Excerpts can also be seen in *Diario de la Revolución Cubana, op.cit.*, pp. 443–445.

27. *Diario de la Revolución Cubana, op.cit.*, p. 471.

28. See Hugh Thomas, "Middle Class Politics and the Cuban Revolution" in Claudio Veliz, *The Politics of Conformity in Latin America* (London and New York: Oxford University Press, 1967), p. 258.

29. Excerpts of the interview appear in *Diario de la Revolución Cubana, op.cit.*, p. 532.

30. "El programa del partido unido de la revolución socialista será un programa ajustado a las condiciones objetivas precisas de nuestro país." Speech at the People's University of December 2, 1961, *Bohemia*, Year 53, No. 50, December 1, 1961, pp. 54–55. Castro's speech also appeared in *Revolución* (Havana), De-

cember 2, 1961, p. 1, and *Verde Olivo* (Havana), Vol. 2, November 10, 1961. Excerpts were published in the *New York Times* of Sunday, December 3, 1961, pp. 1 and 4. The following citations will be from the *Bohemia* text.

31. *Ibid.*, p. 55.

32. *Ibid.*

33. *Ibid.*

34. *El Mundo* (Havana), November 29, 1961, p. 7.

35. The interview was published verbatim in Lee Lockwood, *Castro's Cuba. Cuba's Fidel.* (New York: The Mac Millan Company, 1967).

36. In fact the strength of the guerrillas (including all different fronts and groups) probably did not exceed 2,000 people. (See Boris Goldenberg, *The Cuban Revolution and Latin America*), *op.cit.*, p. 159.

37. See, for instance, Fidel Castro, "El VIII aniversario de nuestra Revolución." *Cuba Socialista* (Havana), Year VII, No. 65, p. 28.

38. Fidel Castro, "Nuestra estrategia política." *Bohemia*, Año del XX Aniversario, October 10, 1973, p. 3.

39. "Informe central al Primer Congreso del Partido Comunista de Cuba. Rendido por el Comandante en Jefe Fidel Castro, Primer Secretario del Comité Central del Partido Comunista de Cuba, los días 17 y 18 de diciembre de 1975." *JR* (Havana), December 1975, p. 4.

40. *Ibid.*

41. *Ibid.* p. 5.

42. *Ibid.*

43. *Ibid.*

44. *Fidel y la religión. Conversaciones con el Sacerdote Dominico Frei Betto.* (Santo Domingo: Editora Alfa y Omega, 1985), pp. 157, 164 and 169.

II

The Labor Movement and the Larger Society on the Eve of the Revolution

The Setting

Batista's Downfall

BATISTA'S DICTATORSHIP ENDED IN SHAME AND DISGRACE ON December 31, 1958. An incompetent, corrupt and unpopular ruler, Batista's somber shadow covers a long period of the recent history of Cuba. His 1952–58 dictatorship originated in a sneaky and totally unjustified coup d'état which threw the country into the throes of uncertainty, anger and confrontation. Because he was never able to attain legitimacy and resorted instead to growing repression, Batista's regime set the country on a dangerous course with unforeseeable consequences.

The downfall of Batista created in effect a political vacuum of immense proportions. Not only was the army defeated and the police and other enforcing agencies totally disbanded, but the Congress was abolished, the elected local and provincial authorities deposed "en masse" and the high-ranking officers of the public administration removed from their posts. The only piece of the state machinery which remained was the judiciary and this was also going to be subject to a drastic reorganization.[1] Two additional circumstances contributed to dramatize the situation. Seven years of Batista's dictatorship, on top of decades of unfortunate political history, had left the country deeply shocked and disturbed. People were anxiously looking for something to cling to when all other leaders and political parties had been shattered. While a deep sense of frustration permeated all levels of society, the victorious issue of the guerrilla war[2] had at the same time created "an extraordinary mood of hope, confidence, enthusiasm and comradeship."[3]

With the temper of the people so favorably disposed, Fidel Castro emerged from the Sierra Maestra as a truly charismatic personality. He had been the leading force, guide and spokesman of the armed struggle; he was also particularly suited for the role of leader of a mass movement. The rebel chief possessed the ability to fascinate audiences of ordinary people, the gift of arousing instant feelings of enthusiasm, fanaticism or hatred, the capacity to blend subtly patriotic and demagogic themes and the power to inspire devotion to the revolutionary cause. A shrewd agitator, Castro knew the political uses of social inequalities, resentment and poverty. Moreover, he was fully possessed by a sense of mission and exhibited an enormous capacity to pursue relentlessly his personal goals and ambitions. Small wonder that some authors contend that the Cuban Revolution should actually be called the Castro Revolution and that others were later inclined to characterize his regime as a "personal autocracy."[4]

A political vacuum, a sort of chiliastic state, and a charismatic leader constitute an unusual set of circumstances which rarely occurs in the history of a country. In January 1959, Fidel Castro could no doubt count on those propi-

tious circumstances to carry out his objectives whatever
they may have been. Many experts have also felt that any
possible radicalization of the revolution was inevitably
going to be favored by the then existing conditions of
poverty and exploitation.

Yesterday's Cuba: Some Social and Economic Indicators

The fact is, however, that while Cuba was still, in 1959,
an underdeveloped country, it was not the impoverished,
primitive and exploited nation that subsequent propaganda would be intent on depicting. In 1958, Cuba's gross
national product per capita was the fourth highest in Latin
America and had been increasing since 1941 at a rate of
almost 9 percent per year.[5] Both the structure of the national income and the increase in monetary and real income pointed to the emergence of a modern economy in
which non-agricultural production, domestic trade and
building construction played important roles. After World
War II, Cuban investors were strong enough to buy a substantial share of U.S.-owned sugar production which fell
from 75 percent of the total at its highest point in the
1930s to about 35 percent in 1958. As regards the industrial non-sugar sector, recent studies of the 1930–58 production index point to a substantial growth during the
period immediately preceding the revolutionary takeover
and cast serious doubts about the validity of the Cuban
economic stagnation hypothesis.[6]

A number of social indicators also showed that Cuba
ranked among the top three Latin American countries in
such outward signs of modernization as caloric intake,

number of motor vehicles, estimated circulation of newspapers, mass media (TV and radio), extent of transportation systems and educational facilities.[7] Moreover, the
1933 Revolution had brought about a far-reaching social
legislation which enhanced labor's share of the national
income to the point where two-thirds of it was paid out in
wages and fringe benefits.[8] True, there were still beggars
in the streets and slums in Havana, Santiago and other
large cities, while in the countryside, dwellings were for
the most part primitive and health care failed to meet
adequate requirements. But widespread destitution of the
character and magnitude that one sees today in many less
developed countries was hardly visible.

The country also differed from most underdeveloped
nations in that it was no longer a predominantly rural
society. According to the 1953 Census, the majority of the
population lived in towns and cities and were employed in
the secondary and tertiary sectors. Nor was Cuba particularly revolution prone as a result of racial tensions, religious differences or class hatreds. Its 1959 social mix has
actually been regarded as among the most homogenous in
Latin America.[9]

But over-all economic and social indicators do not tell
the whole picture of Cuba's development, as there is little
doubt that substantial disparities existed in 1959 between
the urban and rural sectors, both in working and living
conditions. Urban life was by and large modern and middle
class oriented; rural life was tougher and more primitive.
Even within each of these two main sectors there were
striking differences among various subsectors. Not only
did the growing middle class groups differ in attitude and
standard of living from the working class but even the
latter included within itself rather different social groups.

At the top of the spectrum among these groups there

appeared the *industrial proletariat,* numbering over half a million people,[10] and beneficiary since 1933 of a long series of protective labor legislation measures. Minimum wages were fixed for this group at reasonable scales which started in 1958 at $85 per month.[11] Prevailing wages were considerably higher as shown by a survey conducted by the National Association of Manufacturers (ANDI) a few weeks after Castro's victory which indicated that the mean monthly salary of an industrial blue-collar worker was $210 and that of an office worker $271.[12] Social benefits such as a one-month paid vacation, a 44-hour week with 48-hour pay, sickness benefits, special summer holidays, workmen's compensation, social security and maternity protection were generally applied several years before the Castro Revolution.[13] Moreover, in the area of protection against unjustified dismissal the 1934 and 1938 legislation has been regarded as a landmark in the development of job security provisions throughout the world.[14] There was also a considerable degree of collective bargaining which helped to increase the official level of wages for certain strategically located sectors, to improve other minimum standards of working conditions and to introduce a number of additional fringe benefits. In fact, the volume of social benefits granted to the urban workers group was such that a report prepared in 1951 by an international body expressed some reservations about the impact of Cuban labor legislation on the country's economic development.[15]

At the other extreme of the spectrum, there were the *landless peasants, squatters, small tenants and sharecroppers* who led for the most part a life of poverty and dejection. Though these groups were not entirely cut off from the mainstream of Cuban society, they could be regarded as the Cuban equivalent of the fringe social groups or "marginados" still

visible in most Latin American countries. Yet few would
consider this group as a potentially revolutionary one, in
view of its relatively small size, geographic dispersion and
lack of class conscience.

Between these two extremes there were two important
groups that occupied strategic positions in the Cuban social
spectrum. *Sugar and tobacco wage-earners* had always performed essential functions in the Cuban economy due to
the paramount significance of these two industries. Those
working in the tobacco industry had enjoyed since the 19th
century a considerable degree of organization but were
affected by the market constraints of a shrinking industry.
Those that belonged to the sugar industry did not attain
adequate social recognition until the 1930s but had benefited since then from the slow recovery of Cuba's first
industry. Because both industries involved an agricultural
and a manufacturing phase, there existed within each of
them a clear distinction between the industrial workers,
who could be assimilated in many respects to the urban
industrial sectors, and the plantation workers who remained rural in character and outlook. The latter group,
numbering some 400,000 workers, had experienced a
gradual improvement in their conditions of work as a result
of the extension to the rural areas of most (but not all) of
the protective labor legislation and social security measures
and the introduction of unionization and collective bargaining practices. However, they continued to suffer considerable hardship and insecurity due to the cyclical nature
of their work; only a small percentage of plantation workers had permanent jobs and the others were forced to
perform odd jobs during the slack season or to find refuge
in subsistence agriculture. No sustained improvement of
their living conditions had consequently been achieved;
many workers continued to live in miserable barracks or

primitive huts; moreover, medical services, school facilities and other social services were still utterly deficient.

Finally, there were the *jobless workers,* a fluid and changing group which included the outright unemployed, the underemployed and the poorly self-employed. Unemployment rates for the whole country fluctuated sharply according to seasonal variations: in 1958, for instance, the unemployed represented only 7 percent of the labor force (155,000) in March, and as much as 16.8 percent (372,000) towards the end of the year.[16] Underemployment was concentrated in the agricultural areas and the services sector and was calculated to affect 13 percent of the over-all labor force in the 1950s.[17] Many urban workers scraped a living by joining an informal market of street vendors, shoe-shine boys, parking attendants, sellers of lottery tickets and performers of sporadic jobs. Because the latter group had been exposed to the amenities of modernization without being able to secure an adequate share of them, it probably exhibited the highest potentiality for revolution. Until 1959, however, the unemployed remained quiet, probably because of their lack of organization, the dispersion of the rural workers concerned and the fact that many urban unemployed belonged to the secondary labor force, i.e., were not heads of households. As we shall see later, a substantial proportion of the revolutionary militias came from this group, who also provided a ready "claque" for political gatherings.

The picture of Cuba in 1959 exhibited other shortcomings but they stemmed largely from the inefficiency and corruption of its public administration. Despite the relatively large sums allocated to the Department of Education, the country still showed a lamentable rate of illiteracy. Notwithstanding the sizeable staff employed by the Department of Finance, tax evasion was rife and the income tax was hardly collected. In spite of the Constitutional provision against latifundia, Congress failed to restrict or take any other action in respect of the big holdings that still characterized the land tenure system. The 1940 Constitution also provided for the establishment of labor courts but the Department of Labor was unable or unwilling to draw up the relevant bill. This meant that settlement of even minor disputes over rights were first submitted to the Department of Labor and went later, on appeal, to the ordinary courts, thereby entailing long delays and unnecessary expenditures.

Other failings of pre-Castro Cuba were grossly exaggerated later by a well-orchestrated propaganda. Havana, for instance, was depicted as a decadent and sinful city where US organized crime and corrupt government officials profited from drugs, gambling and prostitution. While there were some elements of truth in this, the real picture was considerably different. Consumption of hard drugs was a relatively rare occurrence, the city never played a major role in drug trafficking and smuggling or peddling marijuana was severely penalized. Gambling had traditionally taken place only in three famous night clubs until Batista permitted it also in a few hotels. However, only two hotels were built for tourists and gambling purposes during this period (Capri and Riviera). (A third one, the Havana Hilton, where gambling was not allowed, was incidentally built with money provided by the Hotel and Restaurant Workers' Pension Fund.) Finally, as in any other port city, Havana had its share of prostitution and pornographic shows but a "red light district" located near the center of the city was closed down during the Grau administration (1944–1948) and what remained was no more and no less than what can be found in other Latin American cities of similar dimensions.

All these were, at any rate, political deficiencies, the correction of which called for strictly political measures. Except for the PSP, no other political party of major importance ever advocated a social revolution or a drastic structural change as a suitable means of overcoming such deficiencies.

The Target: The Cuban Labor Movement

A balance sheet of the Cuban labor movement before Castro shows a striking mixture of strengths and weaknesses. On the one hand, trade unions were able to play a leading role at the level of the enterprise and in the national scene. On the other hand, they suffered from several serious shortcomings which affected their image and tended to sap their power of resistance.

Quantitative and Qualitative Strengths

That organized labor was a major force in Cuban society appears to be beyond any doubt. Not only was the labor movement the largest voluntary organization in the country, with one out of every five Cubans belonging to workers' organizations but it also enjoyed a tradition of nearly one hundred years of struggle.[18] So powerful was the labor movement that during the 1950s it almost had a stranglehold on the government; the Prío Socarrás administration (1948–52) gave practically free rein to the Cuban Workers'

Confederation (CTC) as if it were a sovereign power within the state; the Batista dictatorship, in turn, found it advisable to run the country by means of an alliance with organized labor.[19]

Various features of the Cuban labor movement contributed to enhance its power. To begin with, it was a relatively independent, class-oriented interest group which had managed to be recognized by employers and to take root in Cuban society without establishing permanent organic links with political parties. Though Cuban trade unions had successively been under anarchist, Communist and nationalist revolutionary ("auténtico") influences, their strength was not in the least connected with ideologies but rather derived from their own organizational set up and membership support as well as the remarkable ability of their leadership.

The sheer size of the labor movement represented another important factor to its credit. By 1958, almost all organizable sectors had been largely organized and the number of trade union members exceeded the one million figure. While the CTC membership was predominantly made up of industrial, commercial and service workers, it actually cut across the whole labor force, including white collar personnel in banking and other offices and 500 agricultural unions; in point of fact, two of the most influential federations, namely those of the sugar and tobacco workers, grouped chiefly plantation workers. Only government employees, who were prevented by law from forming trade unions, remained outside the CTC field. However, a Cuban Association of Government Employees, set up in 1939 (and later transformed into a Confederation) was informally recognized by Government and, to some extent, functioned as a *de facto* trade union with the support of the CTC.

This impressive number of trade unionists was organized in a three-tiered structure, which included the local
level (usually represented by an enterprise union), industrial federations (which sometimes embraced also provincial federations) and a single national confederation. In
1958, there were 33 federations and some 2,000 unions
grouped under the Cuban Workers' Confederation (Confederación de Trabajadores de Cuba, CTC). A number of
unions and federations were of a craft nature which entailed a certain amount of overlapping; however, dual
unionism, in the sense of two or more unions in the same
factory or plant, was forbidden.[20] Moreover, the principle
of exclusive representation for the majority union was applied both for registration and collective bargaining
purposes.

A third factor accounting for the strength of the Cuban
labor movement can be found in its capacity to develop a
dynamic and competent leadership. Both at the higher
echelons of the trade union movement and at the local or
federative levels, there existed a large staff of officials,
organizers and activists who displayed considerable activity
in their dealings with employers and government officials.
While a substantial number of high-level officials were
tainted with corruption, there were many others who conducted their business with appropriate professionalism.
Moreover, unscrupulous labor leaders managed to obtain
their illicit gains mainly through dealings relating to the
introduction of capital intensive techniques, the relinquishment of make-work practices or the dropping of exaggerated demands. Legitimate rights of the workers were seldom compromised and this enabled such leaders to retain
membership support.

Also instrumental in explaining the effectiveness of the
trade union leadership was the fact that no discrimination

of a racial or other nature was used in selecting officials. White and black leaders shared the most important posts and worked in complete harmony; leadership positions were rarely given to outsiders, and trade union posts actually became an avenue for workers of all races to move upwards on the social ladder. This policy of promotion from within, together with a relatively satisfactory degree of literacy among urban workers, explains the existence of a reservoir of potential labor leaders among the rank and file of most unions.

A more important factor to be considered in examining the power of the labor movement was the significance acquired by business unionism. While it is fair to say that the Cuban labor movement was progressive in its social thinking, it is no less certain that its main concerns were job security and the continued improvement of working conditions for its members. Only after those two aspirations had been satisfied did trade union leaders concern themselves with broader issues, such as the creation of new jobs or the over-all growth of the economy. This explains why the most powerful unions, e.g., sugar, tobacco and port workers' organizations successfully resisted mechanization, bulk loading and other technological improvements as well as the effective campaigns waged by the trade union movement as a whole against greater flexibility in dismissal procedures.[21]

This pragmatic concern for the welfare of the rank and file inevitably brought about both a middle class mentality within certain sectors and the development of collective bargaining methods and practices. Collective bargaining developed first when the CTC was under Communist control (1939–47) and gained momentum during the ten-year incumbency as Secretary-General of Eusebio Mujal, a former Communist of Trotskyite leanings who had switched to the nationalist "auténtico" party in the 1930s. Together with the securing of additional benefits through the decrees and circulars wrung from the Labor Ministry, the negotiation of agreements and the processing of grievances at the enterprise level became the chief functions of labor leaders. So important did these practices become in the 1950s that when the Communists decided to establish, during the Batista dictatorship, a number of semiclandestine organizations, they were not given a political denomination but were rather called Committees for the Defense of Workers' Demands.[22]

Weaknesses

The attachment to business unionism also entailed some serious shortcomings. Neither the leaders nor the rank and file possessed strong beliefs or ideological convictions able to resist the introduction of a new social philosophy. Members viewed trade unions as a service organization run on their behalf by the elected officials who were supposed to secure continued improvements; there was consequently little membership participation in trade union affairs and many members even exhibited a certain reluctance to pay trade union dues.[23]

Unions saw themselves more as parties to labor relations than as a means of mobilizing the masses or transforming society. Their political functions tended to diminish during the late 1940s and 1950s, and their relations with government and their members became agency-like in nature. Political parties lost, in turn, their influence over the labor movement. The PRC (Auténtico) had exhausted its

nationalistic impetus while the Orthodox Party had little
impact on labor unions. Other more traditional parties
had never really appealed to workers although they also
maintained so-called labor sections. Both unions and political parties saw each other as instrumentalities for the
attainment of immediate goals. There was no mutual in-
fusion of ideology and little sharing of long-term objectives. This was probably a sound development in normal
times and as regards the industrial relations system, but it
was not suitable during a period of institutional crisis and
turmoil. For the absence of any well-established
ideology—nationalistic or social democratic for instance—
entailed a weakening of the resistance power of the labor
movement and made it vulnerable to external pressures.

Trade union officials thus developed a pragmatic and
somewhat cynical attitude; they continued to rely on the
Labor Ministry to find a favorable settlement in case of
impasse in negotiations. At the same time, some of them
profited from their growing expertise and full-time devotion to labor matters to squeeze employers with a view
to improving both the workers' lot and their own fortunes.

This crisis of moral values reached its culmination during the Batista dictatorship. Following a weak attempt to
thwart the military coup d'état with a general strike, Mujal
and his colleagues of the CTC Executive Committee
reached an understanding with the military dictatorship,
whereby Batista undertook to respect trade union rights
in exchange for labor's neutrality vis-à-vis the new regime.
Gradually, however, the CTC leadership moved from a
position of neutrality to one of support to the Batista regime. Whether this evolution was a political error on the
part of the leadership or the result of the prevailing economic orientation of trade unions, is difficult to ascertain.
But the temptation is strong to think that business union-

ism and "economist" feelings were of primary importance. During the subsequent seven years of Batista's ruthless dictatorship labor remained, in effect, largely passive, and the only manifestations of protest (the sugar dispute of December 1955, the bank employees' strike of September 1955 and the railway dispute of November 1956) were related to economic demands.[24] Moreover, the various appeals for political strikes issued by the Sierra Maestra guerrillas in August 1957 and April 1958 turned out to be complete failures.

The July 26 Movement had nevertheless organized underground cells in many unions throughout the country. In 1958, when the opposition to Batista reached critical dimensions, labor leaders of the July 26 Movement succeeded in setting up a clandestine national organization called the National Workers' Front (FON). This group, led by David Salvador, merged in October with the Committees for the Defense of Workers' Demands and the non-Communist Workers' Revolutionary Directorate (DOR), and gave rise to the United National Workers' Front (FONU). This leadership apparatus provided a sort of shadow cabinet or replacement team that was intended to ensure the continuity of the CTC. Because they represented an all-out opposition to the government and the official leadership controlled by Mujal, the new leaders were placing themselves in a position to take over the top level offices in the central labor organization and to cleanse its executive body of some of its most glaring stains.

Outside organized labor, other less known events also took place during the last days of Batista's dictatorship. A so-called National Congress of Sugar Workers, which actually gathered only a limited group of agricultural wage earners, was hastily convened in December 1958 in the small town of Carrillo in Las Villas Province, in what was

already called "liberated territory."[25] Another workers'
congress had been previously organized in the northern
region of the Oriente Province. While the holding of these
congresses hardly transpired to the public opinion, they
seemed to convey to the workers involved and to certain
segments of the labor movement a special message of interest and concern. It is also noteworthy that it was in Las
Villas where Guevara was operating at the end of the war,
together with one of the few rebel military chiefs (*comandante*) affiliated to the PSP, Felix Torres. The Northern
region of Oriente corresponded in military terms to the
Second Front headed by Raúl Castro.

NOTES

1. See Blas Roca, *Los fundamentos del socialismo en Cuba* (Havana: Ediciones Populares, 1960), p. 120. See also Fidel Castro, *Humanismo revolucionario* (Havana: Editorial Tierra Nueva, 1959), p. 70.

2. While the Sierra Maestra guerrillas captured the imagination of many people, one should not overlook the important part played by the opposition in the cities ("el Llano") mainly composed of students, professionals and white-collar employees. Not only did the urban underground help support the guerrillas but it also carried out its own actions which were many times more daring and risky than the guerrillas' operations.

3. Hugh Thomas, *The Pursuit of Freedom* (New York: Harper and Row, 1971), p. 1,065.

4. See Ward M. Morton, *Castro as a Charismatic Hero* (Lawrence: University of Kansas, Center of Latin American Studies, 1965), pp. 7–8. See also Andrés Suárez, "Leadership, Ideology and Political Party" in Carmelo Mesa Lago, ed., *Revolutionary Change in Cuba* (Pittsburgh: University of Pittsburgh Press, 1971), pp. 4 and 13.

5. See Cuban Economic Research Project, *A Study on Cuba* (Coral Gables, Fla.: University of Miami Press, 1965), p. 620.

6. See Jorge F. Pérez López, "Cuban Industrial Production, 1930–1958," *Caribbean Studies* (Río Piedras, P.R.), Vol. 14, No. 1, April 1974, p. 168.

7. See United Nations, *Statistical Year Book 1959* (New York, 1959), pp. 298, 332, 578, 548 and 586. Some authors even argue that Cuba should not be considered in the category of an underdeveloped country; see, for instance, Ruby Hart Phillips, *Cuban Dilemma, op. cit.*, Chapter I, and Theodore Draper, *Castro's Revolution, Myths and Realities* (New York: Praeger, 1962), p. 21.

8. See International Labour Office, *Yearbook of Labour Statistics, 1960* (Geneva, 1960), pp. 395–398.

9. Richard Fagen, "Revolution for Internal Consumption

Only," in Irwing Horowitz, *Cuban Communism* (New Brunswick: Aldine Publishers Co., 1970), p. 38.

10. According to the 1953 Census, 327,208 Cubans were economically active in manufacturing, 395,904 in services, 232,323 in commerce and 104,063 in transport—a total of 1,059,438 which contrasted with the 818,906 engaged in agricultural activities. A considerable part of the latter were "colonos" and renters of farms of middle class status.

11. See Efrén Córdova, *La nueva tarifa general de salarios mínimos* (Havana: Editorial La Milagrosa, 1958).

12. See *Havana Post*, May 17, 1959, p. 1. The ANDI survey covered a sample of 5,429 workers in 40 different industries.

13. For a summary of Cuban labor laws before 1959 see Philip C. Newman, *Cuba before Castro* (New Delhi: A Foreign Studies Institute Publication, Prentice Hall, 1965). A more detailed account can be found in Efrén Córdova, *Derecho laboral cubano* (Havana: Editorial Lex, 1957), Vol. 1.

14. B. Hepple, "Security of Employment," chapter 22 in R. Blanpain, *Comparative Labour Law and Industrial Relations* (Deventer, New York: Kluwer Law and Taxation Publications, 1985), p. 495.

15. International Bank for Reconstruction and Development, *Report on Cuba* (Washington, 1951), p.381.

16. See Consejo Nacional de Economía, *Empleo y desempleo de la fuerza trabajadora*. Informes técnicos, Nos. 1–12, January-December 1958 (Havana, 1958); see also James O'Connor, "The Labor Force, Employment and Unemployment in Cuba, 1957–1961." *Social and Economic Studies* (Kingston, Jamaica), Vol. 15, No. 2, June 1966, pp. 87–88.

17. See Carmelo Mesa Lago, *The Labor Force, Employment, Unemployment and Underemployment in Cuba: 1899–1970* (Beverly Hills, Cal.: Sage Professional Papers in International Studies, 1972).

18. See Efrén Córdova, "The Cuban Labor Movement: Survey and Interpretation," MS Thesis (Cornell University, 1967).

19. See Hugh Thomas, *The Pursuit of Freedom, op. cit.*, p. 1,173; see also Jay Mallin, *Fortress Cuba* (Chicago: Henry Regnery Comp., 1965), p. 25.

20. See Fausto Clavijo, *Los sindicatos en Cuba* (Havana: Editorial Lex, 1954).

21. Protection against arbitrary dismissals was so rigid that, except for certain agricultural workers, it was extremely difficult to fire an employee even when fair grounds were invoked for the termination.

22. For a discussion of the organization and functions of these committees, see Blas Roca, *The Cuban Revolution*, Report to the 6th National Congress of the People's Socialist Party (PSP) (New York: New Century Publishers, 1961), p. 37.

23. It was probably as a result of this situation that a compulsory check-off system was instituted in 1955.

24. See "Huelgas obreras socavaron los cimientos de la tiranía," *Revolución* (Havana), July 26, 1959, p. 4.

25. Carlos del Toro, *XX Aniversario del Granma"* (Havana: Talleres del CC-PCC 1976), p. 19.

III

January 1959

The General Strike

ONE OF FIDEL CASTRO'S FIRST DECISIONS IN THE EARLY MORN-
ing of January 1st, 1959, only a few hours after Batista had
fled from Havana, was to call a general strike. The strike
call, which was immediately supported by the National United
Workers' Front (FONU), effectively paralyzed the country
for almost five days and was followed by mass demonstrations
in various cities.

The purpose of the strike was to ensure military victory
and to signal Castro's refusal to accept the junta regime
headed by a Supreme Court Magistrate and General Eulogio
Cantillo. As the junta regime lasted only a few hours and
the rebels secured almost instant control throughout the island, it may be wondered why the strike was maintained
until January 5th.[1] The question has been raised by some
observers who noted the severe economic effects of the work-
stoppage and were intrigued by its prolongation.

Teresa Casuso, for instance, suggested that the strike was
called to demonstrate Castro's personal power and to even
the score of his previous unsuccessful appeals for a general
strike, but professed ignorance as to the satisfaction that the
new leader could have derived from maintaining the strike
order for five days.[2] Edwin Tetlow pointed out that Castro

wanted to make sure of the loyalty of the mass of workers in the capital, but added that there was no valid reason for prolonging the strike.[3] Samuel Farber considered the strike as almost superfluous and aimed against no one in particular, because Batista and his cohorts had already fled the country and no one else dared to challenge Castro.[4]

One might attempt to explain the January general strike on the basis of Castro's intentions to introduce drastic changes in the political set-up of Cuba. By calling a general strike, Castro was first giving the working class the opportunity to participate in the revolutionary process in which, up to that moment, organized labor had played only a very minor role.[5] A massive and prolonged involvement of workers in the strike was thus designed to associate the labor movement with Castro's cause and to trigger a sense of participation, after the disastrous experience of previous general strike attempts. The revolutionary chieftain was thus using the strike as a means of awakening and politicizing the working classes; he probably knew that the massive intervention of the pro-letariat in the 1933 general strike had led to its rapid politicization[6] and he wanted to provoke similar results. He was also sure that the massive walk-out and the ensuing turmoil would contribute to the enlargement of the political vacuum and emphasize the rejection of the then existing authorities.

There is little doubt that the revolutionary leader attached a special significance to the role of a general strike in the revolutionary process. The second Manifesto of the July 26 Movement to the Cuban people issued in 1956 indicated that workers must be organized from the bottom in revolutionary groups in order to declare a general strike.[7] A similar reference to the setting up of committees "in every labor and industrial center" with a view to supporting a general strike is contained in Castro's message to the Junta de Liberación

of Miami, dated 14 December 1957.[8] In August 1957, when
a spontaneous protest erupted in Santiago over the killing
of the young leader Frank País, the Sierra Maestra leaders
decided to declare a general strike, which eventually failed
to spread throughout the island.[9] Several months later, when
Castro called the April 1958 general strike, a circular issued
from the Sierra Maestra and signed by the rebel leader and
political organizer Faustino Pérez regarded the work-stop-
page as the basis of the final decisive stage of the revolutionary process.[10] Even more significant was the language of
the general strike proclamation issued by Fidel Castro on
January 1, 1959. In it the rebel leader called the strike "general and revolutionary," urged the Cuban workers "to organize in all factories and working centers in order to bring
the country to a standstill," and took pains to impress upon
labor that "this is the moment for you to ensure the victory
of the revolution."[11]

That the wording of the proclamation was not of a conventional, stereotyped nature may be seen by the subsequent
appraisals of the general strike made by the revolutionary
leaders. Only a few months after the strike, the Prime Minister was able to proclaim before a national workers' congress
that "it was the general strike declared by the working class
which gave the *coup de grâce* to the dictatorship and attributed
all the power to the revolution."[12] At the following national
labor congress, Castro expressed the view that the victory of
January 1st meant that the working class itself was writing
the history of Cuba.[13] Fourteen years later, the Prime Minister was still maintaining the same position when he asserted
before the First Congress of the Cuban Communist Party
that "the working class with its general revolutionary strike
made in the last battle a decisive contribution to victory."[14]
President Oswaldo Dorticós, in turn, pointed out at the Elev-

enth Congress of the CTC the significance of the work stoppage, in the following words:

> When it seemed that the great insurrection, at the end of
> its great victorious march, was endangered by a possibility
> of frustration, the leader of that insurrection, fully aware
> of the historic role of the Cuban proletariat, did not hesitate
> to call on January 1, 1959, the general strike that prevented
> a military coup or any attempt to crush the Revolution.[15]

Finally, Ernesto Guevara asserted some time later that
the first step in the struggle for the liberation of Cuba was
to incorporate the workers as a social element in the revolution.[16] This assertion coincided with Castro's statement
in his December 2, 1961, speech that he had complied with
the first revolutionary principle, namely to take power with
the masses.[17] Clearly, the obsession with the general strike
that Castro and his colleagues displayed goes well beyond
their natural desire to use all possible means to win the
war.

Marxism-Leninism has always emphasized the significance of mass mobilization techniques and the role of strikes
in a revolutionary takeover. While the idea of a general
strike falls short, in Marxian theory, of the "social myth"
advocated by Georges Sorel and the French syndicalists, it
is nevertheless regarded as a possible means of propelling
labor to power at an instant of political crisis. Lenin, in
particular, had predicted that a united, prestigious proletariat would be able to lead the peasants and the petty
bourgeois groups through mass revolutionary movements,
including strikes. Moreover, the Russian Revolution was
actually aided by general strikes in Moscow and Petrograd

in 1917. In Cuba some workers' soviets were set up in 1933
following the general strike that toppled the Machado
regime.

But to promote the Cuban working class as the leading
force of the revolution it was first necessary to magnify
its role in the war of liberation and to enhance its political
influence. This was all the more urgent in view of the poor
performance of the proletariat during the guerrilla fighting. As a Communist leader of the old guard, Blas Roca
put it in 1959: "The armed struggle had been begun by
the middle classes. For several reasons, the working class
never played a decisive part."[18] Such a situation was not
compatible with the role that Castro had envisaged for the
proletariat and called for an early redress. This was accomplished by the January 1st, 1959, strike, which also
served to mobilize labor and to stimulate its class consciousness. A semi-official organ of the Revolutionary Government was thus able to say in 1961 that the general strike
was "a step towards the organization of the masses," "a
means of promoting class struggle."[19] An essentially non-
proletarian and definitely non-Communist revolution was
thus deftly turned by Castro at its very beginning into a
social movement involving organized labor.

It should be added that other general strikes of a political
nature were declared during the transitional period of the
revolution (1959–60). In the course of 1959, for instance,
at least four general strikes of shorter duration were organized by the CTC with government support: on January
21, March 13, July 23 and October 25. All these strikes
were declared in order to marshall support for the government in moments of crisis; they all revealed the revolutionary government's interest in identifying itself from
the outset with the working population. In the month of
July, for example, following Castro's resignation as Prime

Minister, a general strike was promptly organized with a view to mobilizing the people of Havana to demand both Castro's return to power and President Urrutia's ouster.

It is also noteworthy that the January 1st strike was vigorously endorsed by the Communist leaders, who participated at a meeting held in Havana's Central Park on January 2, 1959.[20] Moreover, a report submitted at the end of the month to the Central Committee of the People's Socialist Party (PSP) by its Secretary General, Blas Roca, advocated a continuation of the tactic of "calling the masses into action."[21] It is also significant that a city-wide general strike was declared at the end of January in the city of Manzanillo, a traditional stronghold of Communist influence. This strike aimed at protesting against the leniency shown by revolutionary tribunals during the war criminals trials, a pet project of Castro's during the month of January.[22]

Changes in the CTC Leadership

During the general strike and for a few weeks thereafter a struggle for power went on within the trade union movement. The downfall of the dictatorship brought about the removal of the "mujalista" leadership and this created numerous openings at the national and local levels. The CTC's past involvement as a bulwark of the Batista regime broadened the scope of the vacuum and intensified the urge for change. From the top hierarchy of the central confederation to the lowest level of local unions, the trade union movement was apparently destined to undergo drastic changes in leadership and orientation.

Various groups were vying for power: the July 26 Movement labor leaders, the labor section of the Auténtico Party, the Christian youth organizations, the old anarcho-syndicalist militants and the trade union leaders of the PSP. Activists from all these factions, both Communists and non-Communists, swiftly moved in and endeavoured to occupy the offices of various federations and local unions. So-called free trade unions ("sindicatos libres") began to mushroom in a number of sectors. An atmosphere of chaos and revenge appeared to pervade all echelons of organized labor.

The Communists seem to have been particularly active in attempting to capitalize on the initial confusion and restlessness caused by the general strike. Signs of Communist activities were already visible on January 1st, when a group of PSP militants tried to occupy the Workers' Palace, i.e., the headquarters of the CTC in the center of Havana. Though this was probably a spontaneous move, prompted by the sudden realization of the opportunities afforded by the collapse of the old leadership, the attempt to occupy the CTC served to reveal the scope of Communist ambitions and to put other groups on the alert. Other Communist actions were aimed at recovering the control of local unions or federations where they had enjoyed control or support in the past. Finally, a number of PSP militants made a point of appearing at the various labor rallies and mass demonstrations that took place during the first weeks of the revolution.

However, the Communists' early bid for power met with considerable grumbling among the rank and file. Workers resented the Communists' drive to take advantage of the post-civil war situation, accusing them of becoming active only after Batista was deposed and of having been passive during most of the fight against the dictatorship. Andrés

Suárez regarded the opposition to Communism as "virulent" and indicated that it was especially acute in the working class circles of the July 26 Movement.[23] Samuel Farber
observed that the Communist Party's (PSP) prestige was
rather low in 1959.[24] Further, the PSP leadership was also
bidding for power from a position of relative weakness, as
its influence within the labor movement had declined considerably during the 1950s. Many workers who had supported a Communist leadership 12 years before had now
switched allegiances or had simply forgotten their old af-
filiations. For most of them, their loyalties to the former
Communist-run CTC were based more on a service relationship than on ideological commitments. Other workers
who belonged to the Auténtico or Ortodoxo parties identified themselves with the nationalistic ideals of the 1933
Revolution. All of them were thus psychologically prepared to be lured by the July 26 Movement, which offered
new hopes and expectations and appealed to them both
as workers and citizens.

   If Communist control of labor unions in 1959 was not
minimal as some author suggested,[25] it was undoubtedly a
far cry from the privileged position that other writers felt
the Communists had regained at the beginning of the revolution.[26] Zeitlin's assertion that after the purges of 1947–
48 the Communists retained the allegiance of an estimated
25 percent of workers[27] appears somewhat closer to reality,
though it should still be considered on the high side. The
hard core of Communist militants and sympathizers did
not number in 1959 over 15 percent of the trade union
membership.

   Communist strength consisted largely of several unions
in the tobacco industry, some grass roots support in the
sugar industry and in the ports, an important foothold in
the urban transportation industry and a few other unions

in the textile, hotel and restaurant and telephone sectors. As a rule, the Communists' areas of strength reflected the personal influence of particular leaders, who were able in the past to combine charisma with effective organizational drives: Lázaro Peña in the tobacco industry, Jesús Menéndez (shot to death by a military officer in 1946) in the sugar industry, Aracelio Iglesias with regard to port workers and José María Pérez in the Havana transport sector. There were also, of course, a number of Communist sympathizers in many other unions. However, except for the Federation of Hotel and Restaurant Workers, formerly led by officials of Auténtico and independent affiliation, and which was quickly taken over by Alfredo Rancaño, Marxist labor leaders could not recover control of any other national union. Moreover, the most prominent PSP leaders had been away for years and were at the last minute returning from abroad: Lázaro Peña (first Secretary General of the CTC) from Prague, Ursinio Rojas from Mexico and Joaquín Ordoqui from Moscow.

Opposition to the Communists was coupled with the rise of the July 26 Movement leadership as the new dominant force of the labor movement. Though the July 26 Movement lacked enough cadres at the local level, it was able to enlist the support of many former officials or old-hand trade unionists who had not been identified with the dictatorship. Further, the top leaders of the Movement entered trade union politics with impressive credentials earned in the underground fight against Batista. They displayed great diligence during the first hectic days of the revolution and benefited from the prevailing nationalistic mood. The end of the dictatorship had rekindled ardent nationalist sentiments and this attitude, shared by the vast majority of Cuban workers, did not appear to be compatible with the internationalist and class conscious doctrines of the PSP.

Gradually, new *de facto* executive bodies were established at the local level, mostly under non-Communist auspices. The initial confusion was giving way to provisional arrangements whereby new faces, combined with some old ones not accused of collaboration with Batista, took over the posts of command in local trade unions.

At the national level, the initial step taken was the appointment of three trustees (David Salvador, Conrado Becquer, leader of the sugar workers and José María de la Aguilera, of the bank employees' union) to take care of CTC's properties. In practice, trade union affairs were handled during the first three weeks of the revolution by a FONU directorate appointed at a special meeting of the July 26 Movement labor leaders and FONU officials held in Havana in January. The directorate, composed of 21 members, included five associated with the Communist Party, plus an array of leaders of different ideological orientation who claimed allegiance to the July 26 Movement.[28]

As labor resistance to Communist infiltration hardened, the Revolutionary Government decided to avoid a premature confrontation with the rank and file and to move cautiously to consolidate its power. It thus decided to legalize the position of the self-appointed local *de facto* leadership and to recognize a non-Communist directorate at the top of the CTC. To accomplish the first objective, a government decree declared that all prior executive bodies of the labor movement were deposed and that the new National Provisional Committee of the CTC would have authority to designate the provisional executive committees of the various unions and federations, unless the general assembly of the union had met and appointed its own leaders. The new directorates were to remain in office only until free elections were held and new officials elected.[29]

To achieve the second purpose, the National Provisional Directorate was reduced from 21 to 9 members and known affiliates of the PSP were excluded from it. The Committee was, in effect, formed by David Salvador, who was to act as Secretary-General, and the following eight trade unionists proposed by FONU: Conrado Becquer, José M. Aguilera, Octavio Louit, José Pellón, Reinol González, José de Jesús Plana, Jesús Soto and Antonio Torres.

David Salvador had been a member of the PSP in the early 1940s but subsequently severed his Party affiliation and adopted an independent position as leader of the Stewart sugar mill union. He had been extremely active in the anti-Batista underground and emerged as the undisputed leader of the anti-mujalista forces.[30] Two members of the Committee (Plana and González) were Christian Democrat leaders from the Young Catholic Workers Movement, which had also figured prominently in the anti-Batista resistance. Another two members were generally regarded as independent trade union leaders with clean records as opponents of the regime; one of these (Pellón) was an inconspicuous official destined to slip into obscurity; the other, Antonio Torres, was a hard-to-classify left winger who probably had Communist ties but enjoyed a certain reputation of being independent-minded. Aguilera and Louit were ambitious and opportunistic persons capable of acting according to the prevailing winds. Conrado Becquer was in a special position not readily classifiable. He had repeatedly expressed his democratic and independent convictions but he had been elected Congressman in the 1954 elections held under Batista and this made him an easy target for pressures from the top or extortion from the opposite camp. Finally, Jesús Soto was actually of clear

Marxist inclinations, though his Communist links were less
known than his activities as a July 26 Movement official.

What was the government attitude vis-à-vis these changes
in leadership? By and large the reaction of the Revolutionary Government was one of permissiveness and respect
for independent trade union activities. Castro had promised to guarantee freedom of association and he was apparently intent on keeping his word. To buttress further
that impression, the government abolished the compulsory
check-off system established in 1955 and provided that
payment of union dues was thereafter to be a voluntary
affair. Though the Tenth Congress of the CTC held in
November 1959 voted to re-establish a voluntary check-
off, this resolution was never implemented.[31] In terms of
the personalities involved, Castro gambled no doubt on
the composition of the Executive Committee of the
CTC-R but the risks were not exceedingly high, as certain
trusted or potential allies had found their way into the top
hierarchy of the trade union structure.

Government concern with trade union developments
appeared to be confined for the time being to the complete
elimination of the previous leadership. Trade union leaders who were accused of cooperation with the dictatorship
were either ousted, jailed or forced to go into exile. Eusebio
Mujal took asylum in the Argentine Embassy. CTC's Treas-
urer Jesús Artigas and more than 40 leaders were held in
prison for several months without official indictment or
trial. The leader of the maritime workers, Ignacio González Tellechea, who himself had never been a partisan of
Batista, was first arrested, later released and then repeatedly harassed by the government until he went into hiding
and was able to escape from Cuba.[32] The filing of real or
imaginary charges as a pretext for imprisoning trade union
officials who held important posts during the Batista re-

gime became a common practice.[33] An over-all drive to get rid of all the top representatives of the past leadership so as to build the new labor movement from scratch appeared to gain momentum. To dramatize further the change in orientation and the detachment of the new center from the old CTC, the word "revolutionary" was added to the original name and the letter R to the previous initials.

An Atmosphere of Confusion

Outside the labor movement, certain actions and statements of the revolutionary chieftains had created considerable anxiety. Castro's first speech in Santiago on the night of January 1st already contained an attack against the U.S., which was accused of having frustrated the 1895 War of Independence. "This time," Castro promised, "the Revolution will reach its final destination; it will not be like in 1895 when the Americans got in and became owners of the country."[34] This initial charge was followed by a crescendo of accusations. By the middle of January, Castro was asking the U.S. military mission "to pack their bags and leave as soon as possible."[35] A few weeks later he was already saying that "American Ambassadors had been running the country before him."[36]

It is also noteworthy that only a few days after victory the PSP was legalized and its official organ, the newspaper *Hoy*, reappeared. Moreover, the invocation of God was removed from the oath-taking ceremony and a famous Communist poet, Nicolás Guillén, was proclaimed official poet of the revolution. By the end of January, Guevara had started his first indoctrination courses in La Cabaña fortress and delivered a forceful speech before the Marxist *Nuestro Tiempo* organization.[37] Havana newspapers also reported that during the first days of January the files of both the Bureau for the Repression of Communist Activities (BRAC) and the Anti-Communist League were destroyed; according to some observers, this action was taken under Guevara's orders.[38]

At the same time, Castro announced early in 1959 that if anything happened to him the leadership of the revolution and its corresponding political power would be taken over by his brother, Raúl, who had also been his second in command during the Sierra Maestra fight. Since Raúl had been a member of the International Communist Youth and was known for his Stalinist leanings, this announcement provoked further concern. Although Castro had chosen Manuel Urrutia[39] as provisional President of the Republic and José Miró Cardona[40] as Prime Minister, both of whom were respected personalities who inspired confidence, the leader of the revolution shortly proceeded to make clear that their role was a rather limited and symbolic one. Neither Urrutia nor Miró had a political power base and Castro was thus free to undercut their functions at will.

Not surprisingly, these actions abetted the fears of Communism and disturbed some Castro followers. At least on five occasions during the month of January Castro took pains to deny that he was a Communist; on the 7th, in a short statement made in Matanzas en route to his triumphal entry into Havana, on the 15th, in a speech at the Rotary Club,[41] on the 16th, before Eduardo Chibás' grave, on the 22nd, at a meeting with the press in the Havana Riviera Hotel and finally in Caracas on the 24th.

Castro also emphasized on a number of occasions the democratic and nationalistic character of the revolution.

Twice during the first week of January, the newspaper
Revolución—official organ of the July 26 Movement—
categorically denied that Guevara was a Marxist. Repeated
guarantees were given to the public about the non-
totalitarian objectives of the revolution. To allay any fears
of renewed fighting—this time among the various revolutionary groups that had contributed to overthrow Batista—
Castro delivered a conciliatory and democratically-ori-
ented speech at the Columbia military barracks in Havana,
in which he pleaded for the disarmament of all revolutionary factions and asked repeatedly and in the most convincing terms "arms for what?".[42] Employers were told that
they had nothing to fear as long as they paid high wages
and respected the existing labor legislation.[43] Foreign
investors were encouraged to come to the island and
Castro even discussed with some of them the broad lines of
an investment operation.[44] To cap these statements,
Guevara announced in the month of February that Cuba
was about to enter into an era of full capitalism.[45]

Not to be overlooked, however, were the social overtones of other statements made from the outset by the
revolutionary leaders. What had been a strictly political
revolution against a corrupt dictator was apparently being
turned into a social revolution "against all the injustices
and abuses of the past." As early as January 8th, Castro
was already indicating that "in a few years' time, nobody
would be able to recognize Cuba."[46] Next month he made
it clear that "the tyranny had its roots in evils of a social
nature,"[47] and warned the Cuban people that it was also
necessary to fight many other tyrannies, "including mis-
ery, unemployment, illiteracy and lack of hygiene."[48] At
the same time, his brother Raúl suggested that the vested
interests which were at the root of the Batista dictatorship

were even "stronger and more criminal than Batista."[49] A
few weeks later, he stated explicitly that the goals of the
revolution included the destruction of the political and
economic structures of the past.

Some specific social issues were also introduced by the
rebel leaders. Unemployment, for instance, was repeatedly
mentioned as a plague inherited from the previous regimes
which necessitated drastic treatment. Castro, who was by
now called the "supreme or maximum leader" (el máximo
líder) also sought to magnify the dimension of unemployment by offering grim statistics which combined unemployment and underemployment figures or tended to in-
flate the existing rates.[50] Discrimination against blacks and
women also acquired instant priority in Castro's speeches,
despite the fact that such questions were scarcely topical
in Cuba before he came to power.

The frantic tempo of the revolution also contributed to
create a climate of anxiety. Many people had thought that
Batista's downfall and Castro's enormous popularity had
given Cuba an opportunity to relax and enjoy a period of
stability. Yet Castro lost no time in warning his compatriots
mysteriously that "the Revolution begins now. It will be
difficult and full of dangers."[51]

All this created an atmosphere of confusion. There were
no April Theses[52] to define the position of the government
as regards the ultimate objectives of the revolution. The
official ideology was still contained in *History Will Absolve
Me* and the July 26 Movement Thesis, but a number of
actions and statements of the revolutionary government
seemed to depart from the principles embodied in those
pre-1959 documents. The term "Humanist Revolution"
was coined to characterize the aims of Castroism but nobody was able to define it. Castro tried to do so sometime

later by saying that humanism was "the government of the people without dictatorships and without oligarchies," or that it was "freedom with bread and bread without terror," but these statements helped very little to guide government activities. Like his other famous phrase about the olive green colour of his revolution, these statements were actually part of Castro's endeavors to dissipate suspicions by introducing vague notions that tended to suggest a third kind of position. The real aims of the revolution thus remained shrouded in a dense, rhetorical, demagogic style of oratory.

The confusion was indeed so pervasive that it extended beyond social policy and invaded all aspects of life. Many churchmen, including the Archbishop of Santiago de Cuba, Enrique Pérez Serantes, supported the new leaders and even dared to affirm that the principles and ideas of the revolution were in accord with God's words. Here again, Castro's initial statements contributed to increase the atmosphere of confusion and bewilderment. His repeated praise of the cooperation given by Catholics to the revolutionary cause[53] and more particularly his remarks in favor of religious instruction in public school went a long way to dissipate fears about his political objectives. Occasional TV close-ups of Castro and his acolytes also helped, as they showed some reassuring religious medals on their necks. Small wonder that the correspondent of the *The Times* (London) in Havana, was persuaded that Castro was an ascetic and devout Catholic.[54] However, some other foreign observers who had lived through the experience of the Spanish Civil War or a Communist takeover in an Eastern European country, expressed misgivings about the future course of the revolution. A few perceptive Cubans who had fought Batista in order to restore democracy in

Cuba also felt uneasy about Castro's real intentions. For the majority of the Cuban people, however, there was only a vague feeling that the country was moving into uncharted terrain.

NOTES

1. General Cantillo also resigned as chief of the army and was succeeded by Colonel Ramón Barquín. Barquín was a prestigious officer, friendly to the July 26 Movement and who had just been released from jail. His first important decision was to place the Columbia barracks in Havana, i.e., the center of military power, at the disposal of Castro.

2. Teresa Casuso, *Cuba and Castro* (New York: Random House, 1961), p. 140.

3. Edwin Tetlow, *Eye on Cuba* (New York: Harcourt, Brace and World, Inc. 1966), p. 16.

4. Samuel Farber, *Revolution and Reaction in Cuba, 1933–1960, op. cit.,* p. 202.

5. See Ramón E. Ruiz, *Cuba: The Making of a Revolution* (The University of Massachusetts Press, 1968), p. 14.

6. See Luis E. Aguilar León, *Cuba 1933: Prologue to Revolution* (Ithaca and London: Cornell University Press, 1972), pp. 232 and 233.

7. Manifiesto No. 2, "Del 26 de Julio al Pueblo de Cuba," p. 1. Text reproduced in *Trabajo* (Havana), No. 3, March 1961, p. 52.

8. The text of the message is reproduced in Mario Llerena, *The Unsuspected Revolution: The Birth and Rise of Castroism, op. cit.,* annexes.

9. See Robert Taber, *M-26-7: Biography of a Revolution* (New York: Lyle Stuart, 1961), p. 167.

10. *Ibid.,* p. 219 and José Duarte Oropesa, *Historiología cubana* (Los Angeles, 1971), p. 1,387.

11. "General Strike Proclamation," in Rolando E. Bonachea and Nelson P. Valdés, eds., *Revolutionary Struggle, op. cit.,* Vol. I, pp. 448–449.

12. *Dos discursos del Comandante Fidel Castro* (Havana: CTC-R, 1959), p. 8.

13. Fidel Castro, "Discurso de clausura. XI Congreso de la CTC-R." *Revolución,* November 29, 1961, p. 9.

14. *Informe Central al Primer Congreso del Partido Comunista de Cuba, op. cit.,* p. 5.

15. Oswaldo Dorticós, "The Working Class of the New Cuba," *Political Affairs* (New York), Vol. XLI, No. 10, October 1962, p. 37.

16. *Guevara on Revolution: A Documentary Overview* (Coral Gables, Fla.: University of Miami Press, 1963), p. 72.

17. *Revolución,* December 2, 1961, p. 8.

18. *World Marxist Review* (Prague), Vol. II, No. 8, August 1959.

19. *Obra Revolucionaria* (Havana), No. 46, 1961, p. 12.

20. See in *Revolución,* January 13, 1959, the speeches delivered by Alfredo Rancaño, José M. Espino and Jesús Soto (p. 2).

21. "Tesis sobre la situación actual," *Hoy,* (Havana) February 1, 1959, p. 1.

22. See *Havana Post,* January 29, 1959, p. 1.

23. Andrés Suárez, *Cuba: Castroism and Communism, op. cit.,* p. 49.

24. Samuel Farber, "The Cuban Communists in the Early Stages of the Revolution." *Latin American Research Review,* Vol. XVIII, No. 1, 1983, p. 60.

25. See C. Mesa Lago, ed., *Revolutionary Change in Cuba, op. cit.,* p. 211.

26. See James O'Connor, *The Origins of Socialism in Cuba, op. cit.,* p. 189.

27. Maurice Zeitlin, *Revolutionary Politics and the Cuban Working Class* (Princeton, N.J.: Princeton University Press, 1967).

28. See James O'Connor, *The Origins of Socialism in Cuba, op. cit.,* p. 190.

29. Law No. 22 of January 22, 1959 (*Official Gazette,* January 23, 1959). The elections were to be held during a 45 day period beginning 90 days after the law was enacted.

30. See E.P. Wittemore, "Cuba's Unions Come Full Circle," *The New Leader* (New York), February 5, 1962, p. 24.

31. It seems significant to note that according to Communist theory trade unions have no need to institute a check-off system as the unity, self-mobilization and organization of the workers

concerned is expected to provide the necessary financial means. See "Los descuentos. Fragmentos del discurso de Fidel Castro ante la primera reunión nacional de responsables del trabajo de orientación revolucionaria." *Trabajo,* Year II, No. 18, December 1961, p. 16. According to some PSP leaders the check-off practice encouraged the bureaucratization of unions and their dependence on third parties. See, for example, Ursinio Rojas "Cuota sindical obligatoria ¿Para qué?" *Hoy,* June 6, 1959 and Lázaro Peña, "Discutamos la cuota," *Hoy* (Havana), June 9, 1959, p. 1. See also Efrén Córdova, "The Check-Off System: A Comparative Study," *International Labour Review* (Geneva), Vol. 99, No. 5, May 1969, p. 468.

32. González Tellechea was also President of the Interamerican Regional Organization of Workers (ORIT).

33. A final run down of the Executive Committee of the CTC shows that of its 64 members, some 48 went into exile, through diplomatic asylum or other ways; one (Francisco Aguirre) was to die in jail, two others were in prison until recently and the rest remained living on the island after being deprived of their trade union positions.

34. Castro's speech was reproduced in several Cuban newspapers. Its full text also appeared in *Informe central al Primer Congreso del Partido Comunista de Cuba, op. cit.,* p. 5.

35. *Havana Post,* January 14, 1959, p. 1.

36. *Havana Post,* February 5, 1959, p. 1.

37. On January 14 Guevara also launched an attack against the U.S. saying that "The U.S. is to blame for the napalm bombs and strafing which killed so many innocent people and children" (*Havana Post,* January 14, 1959, p. 1).

38. See J. Monahan and K.O. Gilmore, *The Great Deception, op. cit.,* p. 19; see also Hugh Thomas, *The Pursuit of Freedom, op. cit.,* p. 1,078.

39. A member of the judiciary, Urrutia was one of the three judges who tried Castro in 1953. His dissenting opinion in favor of Castro's acquittal and questioning the legitimacy of the Batista regime gave him considerable prominence and apparently earned him the recognition of the revolutionary leader.

40. Miró Cardona was a distinguished university professor and former President of the National Bar Association. He had also been an active opponent of Batista.

41. Castro's words on this occasion were as follows: "I am not a Communist. They call anyone a Communist who is not sold to the Americans." (See *Havana Post*, January 14, 1959, p. 1).

42. See *Revolución*, January 9, 1959, p. 1.

43. See Efrén Córdova, "La legislación laboral del Castrismo," *Cuba Nueva* (Coral Gables, Fla.), Vol. I, No. 4, May 1962, p. 16.

44. These discussions took place on January 12 (see *Havana Post*, January 13, 1959, p. 1). A few days later, however, Castro hit at foreign investments during the mass rally held on 20 January to support the execution of war criminals (see *Havana Post*, January 21, 1959, p. 1). But in April Castro was still saying that "there is total guarantee for capital in Cuba" (see *Havana Post*, April 4, 1959, p. 107).

45. *Havana Post*, February 13, 1959, p. 1.

46. *Revolución*, January 8, 1959, p. 1.

47. See *Political, Economic and Social Thought of Fidel Castro*, *op. cit.*, p. 180.

48. *Havana Post*, March 17, 1959, p. 1.

49. *Havana Post*, February 12, 1959, p. 1.

50. Castro's estimates of unemployment were sometimes put at 500,000 and on other occasions at 600,000 or 700,000. The latter figure appeared, for instance, in *Pensamiento político, económico y social de Fidel Castro* (Havana: Editorial Lex, 1959, p. 38). Not until the February 24, 1960 speech did Castro recognize that his impressive statistics on unemployment also included underemployment figures.

51. Cited by Byron Williams, *Cuba: The Continuing Revolution* (New York: Parents Magazine Press, 1969), p. 158.

52. The theses formulated by Lenin in April 1917 with regard to the establishment of a dictatorship of the proletariat and a Soviet constitution.

53. See, for instance, "Prestaron los católicos de Cuba su co-

operación a la causa de la libertad." *Diario de la Marina,* (Havana) January 7, 1959, pp. 1 and 2A.

54. *The Times* (London), January 2, 1959, p. 1. See also Hugh Thomas, *op. cit.* p. 1,129.

IV

The Development of a Revolutionary Strategy

Direct Contacts and Mass Mobilization

THE FIRST MONTHS OF THE REVOLUTION WITNESSED THE EF-
forts made by the revolutionary leaders to promote closer
communications with the people and, more particularly, with
the labor sector. Though the main figures of the revolution
already enjoyed an enormous popularity, they nevertheless
showed a strong interest in keeping in constant touch with
the masses. To do this Castro and his associates broke from
the outset with the practice of sporadic or indirect contacts
between politicians and the people and introduced a system
of mass meetings and labor rallies at which basic propositions
regarding the future course of the revolution were put before the people for discussion and approval. This system,
which Castro called an exercise in "direct democracy," was
first used with respect to the execution of hundreds of military officers and second-level authorities, whom Castro called,
from the beginning, "war criminals" and was later extended
to all sorts of domestic and international affairs.

For the most part, these meetings took the form of huge
gatherings of people at the Plaza Cívica or in front of the
Presidential Palace, but they also consisted of Castro's ap-
pearances before workers' and peasants' assemblies. During
the first three months of 1959, for example, Castro addressed
personally the sugar workers, the oil workers, the construction workers, the bus drivers, the telephone workers, the

railway workers, the bank employees and the newspaper
workers. In the course of 1959 he spoke at several labor
rallies organized by the CTC-R and participated in the proceedings of a number of federations and local unions. At
the end of 1959 he was able to boast that he had not failed
to attend a single important labor event during the entire
year.[1]

The purpose of these meetings and contacts was twofold:
on the one hand, Castro sought to build up a personal following directly with the masses, and on the other, he wanted
to flatter the ordinary people and to enhance their sense of
participation, first aroused through the January general strike.
Cubans previously cut off from the mainstream of politics,
particularly the unemployed, important segments of the rural population and the poorly educated, were now given the
opportunity to become Castro's followers and participants in
the revolution. While it is true that Castro's rhetorical questions to the crowds were invariably accepted and dutifully
applauded, it is no less certain that the Prime Minister always
made clear that the lower classes of society were the center
of his attention.[2] At almost every meeting, he tried to convince his audience that "the revolutionary process is the work
and task of every one of you."[3] So effective was this practice
of mass meetings that Castro's regime has been aptly characterized as a mobilization system.[4]

Although Castro's speeches lasted for hours and were
sometimes full of commonplaces, his delivery was forceful,
his language understandable to the common people and his
rebellious and unyielding attitude especially appealing to the
working classes. Castro was a master of emotional oratory
and theatrical effects as well as the use of language to sway
people's views and he did not care much about the ethics of
persuasion. By all accounts he was an extraordinarily able
propagandist and skillful manipulator of people.

The Prime Minister also engaged in painstaking efforts
to explain to the Cuban people the need for social change
and drastic revolution. In discharging this function, however,
he was always careful to point out, first, the evils of capitalism,
before extolling the virtues of other social systems. Every
effort was made to identify instances of workers' exploitation
and to praise the patriotism and forebearance of the working
classes. Examples of employers' abuses were usually combined with vivid references to the qualities of the working
men. This approach (which was used from January 1959 on
and remained as the leitmotif of numerous speeches
throughout 1959) played an important part in Castro's apparent desire to identify the working class with the revolutionary government. As he later recognized before the Cuban Communist Party, "time and again, an intensive mass
mobilization and political education campaign accompanied
the revolutionary process."[5]

Propaganda

Together with the direct communication approach, there
appeared the intensive use of propaganda techniques. Castro once regarded propaganda as the "spirit of every struggle" and he appeared to master from the outset the agit-
prop methodology, both with regard to "oral agitation"
and mass communication techniques. Members of the revolutionary elite availed themselves fully of the opportunities afforded by advanced mass media in Cuba and displayed an instant penchant for public relations. Radio and
television were used as educational instruments through
which the masses could be both informed and formed.[6]

Recourse was also had to other more primitive but effective methods, such as slogans, chants and posters, which were usually of a national liberation and anti-imperialist character.[7]

Many of these propagandistic efforts were geared specifically to the workers. Early in 1959 the government set up a Section on Dissemination of Information and Propaganda of the Rebel Army which undertook to publish books and pamphlets for distribution among labor unions and peasants' organizations. A semi-official news agency, *Prensa Latina*, was also set up in 1959 to disseminate information on Cuba in Latin America and to provide the Cuban people with the appropriate kind of news.[8] Government printing offices gave special attention to reproducing Castro's speeches at labor meetings. The newspaper *Revolución* devoted more space to information on labor developments than any other newspaper had before. As the government later took control of other privately owned newspapers, a similar priority was accorded to labor news coverage.

Labor organs in turn were involved full-time in propaganda efforts. When the official organ of the Ministry of Labor, *Trabajo*, appeared under Minister A. Martínez Sánchez not a single article of its 1960 and 1961 issues discussed labor problems from a technical standpoint. The review was largely devoted to reproducing speeches of Castro, the Minister of Labor, Ernesto Guevara and other revolutionary leaders; even the annual report of the Ministry's activities included propagandistic statements.[9] Other features of *Trabajo* were five articles by Nicolás Guillén, five reports intended to disseminate information on Socialist countries and six articles decrying the U.S. and multinational companies. A similar orientation was followed by *Vanguardia Obrera* and *Obra Revolucionaria* which appeared as mouth-pieces of the CTC-R and the government position within the labor movement. At the same time, the Communist (PSP) press (*Hoy*) and radio (Radio 1010), which had been operating in full swing since the early days of January 1959, were effectively engaged in other indoctrination efforts. While the primary aim of this propaganda was to support the revolution, the PSP was also intent on furthering the views of the "old guard" of the party.

Propaganda campaigns were also used for various specific purposes in connection with the eventual control of the labor movement. In the first place they were designed to portray Mujal and his colleagues as rascals and crooks without any redeeming social features. Secondly, they sought to destroy the reputation of a few non-mujalistas holdovers of the "ancien régime," like Angel Cofiño (electrical workers), during the first weeks of the revolution and Manuel Fernández (actor's guild) and Luis Penelas (construction workers) at a later stage. In the third place they were intended to promote the personality of various newcomers of Marxist leanings such as labor leaders Rogelio Iglesias and Jesús Soto, peasant leader José Ramírez and youth leader Héctor Carbonell.[10]

Broadening of Popular Support Through Income Distribution

The government's activities during the first months of 1959 were also designed to stimulate a more substantive identification of labor with the government through a series of measures aimed at improving the standard of living of the workers by means of a better income distribution.

The revolutionary chieftain could count here on wide popular support, as there was room for income readjustments and efforts to spread the fruits of economic growth to the masses of the population usually met with a favorable public opinion response.

The first government efforts towards the application of a redistributive and populist-oriented policy related to the agrarian reform problem. Some land was distributed at the outset of the revolution and an Agrarian Reform Law, enacted in the Sierra Maestra, was partially applied. It shortly became apparent, however, that it was also necessary to initiate some consumption-oriented reforms with regard to the modern sector of the economy. As early as February 1959, the government passed a law slashing rents of urban dwellings throughout Cuba by substantial percentages ranging from 30 percent to 50 percent. Telephone and electric rates were cut down at about the same time; interest rates on mortgages were reduced and installment payments were cut by half in a number of commercial transactions; the tax system was revised in order to benefit the lower income groups; the cost of medicines was diminished and even the toll of the tunnel crossing the Havana harbor was reduced. Some of these measures responded to social needs; others were of doubtful justification. But the effect of all of them was to help the lower classes materially as well as psychologically and to drive home the message that the government was taking care of the workers' aspirations.

The same ultimate purpose can be attributed to the several pieces of labor legislation enacted during the first months of the revolution.[11] The rigid system of protection against dismissal which formerly applied to industrial and commercial employees and to sugar workers was now extended to all wage earners including farm labor. Lay-offs or dismissals for economic reasons were prohibited for a period of 180 days.[12] Private industry employees who were fired from their jobs between March 1952 and December 31, 1958, without proper legal proceedings or through coercion, were authorized by law to be given their old jobs back and to receive fair monetary compensation for time lost. The level of wages in the sugar plantations was raised by presidential decrees. The minimum salary of government employees was fixed at $85.00, i.e., the same amount as that established for private industry workers. Numerous other sectors were also favored through resolutions of the Ministry of Labor ordering substantial wage increases or providing for better conditions of work and life. Havana newspapers of the first months of the revolution carried daily information on collective bargaining agreements approved by the Ministry or government decrees providing for salary increases. Lastly, social security contributions were standardized, the minimum level of pensions was raised to 40 dollars ("pesos") a month and the coverage of the system was greatly expanded.

There is no statistical basis on which to estimate the amount of income redistribution achieved as a result of these measures. Prime Minister Castro calculated in March 1960 that the purchasing power of the Cuban people increased by 200 or 300 million dollars as a result of revolutionary measures.[13] However, in December 1959 he stated before a National Federation of Sugar Workers (FNTA) meeting that the increase was of the order of 100 million and in July 1961 he asserted in the "Cuba's Socialist Destiny" speech that after the triumph of the revolution the people had more than 500 million pesos annually to spend over and above what they had had when his government took office. Other studies indicate that the standard of

living of the workers rose by approximately 20–30
percent.[14]

Whatever the amount involved, there is no doubt that
the net impact of the social policy adopted by the government between February and October 1959 put more money
in the pockets of the lower-income groups. Within the
labor sector, it was the lower strata which benefited most
from the revolutionary measures. Castro had said that the
labor demands that should first be taken care of were those
of lower paid workers, and this order elicited immediate
and warm support on the part of the poorer sectors of
society, particularly in the countryside. But urban workers
also received substantial benefits and were apparently satisfied with the increments provided by the government. A
survey prepared by the weekly *Bohemia* in June 1959 pointed
out that satisfaction with measures taken in the labor field
came only after land reform and the pacification of the
country as the main reasons for the massive support mustered by the government at the beginning of the
revolution.[15]

The redistribution policy was pursued only during the
first three quarters of 1959, when the government was
engaged in efforts to woo the trade union movement. As
will be noted later, by the end of 1959 the Prime Minister
had switched policies and was promoting a new trade-off
between economic and social objectives[16] and by March
1960 he was openly advocating a wage freeze. By that time
most trade union directorates had been purged and a pro-
Communist leadership of the CTC-R was in command.

It is also important, in discussing the labor policy of the
revolutionary government, to take account of the measures
excluded from the first "social package" of 1959. Though
Castro had promised that workers would share in the profits of enterprises, his government never approved such a

scheme.[17] Nor did Castro and his associates ever paid serious attention to a bill proposed by the Ministry of Labor
setting up a system of labor courts.[18]

One possible explanation for this relates to the government's reluctance to accept the implications of those measures, namely a recognition of employers and further institutionalization of labor-management relations. The
government was apparently prepared to effect a redistribution of income and to improve working conditions in-
sofar as these measures did not entail a basic commitment ‖
regarding the structure of a capitalist society.

Several Promises and a Warning

The first year of the revolution also witnessed the
launching of a systematic campaign of promises designed
to awaken expectations and to attract both the organized
and unorganized sectors of the labor force.

In essence, the Prime Minister was promising a new and
much better world of equality, affluence and social justice.
He promised freedom of movement for everyone, an absence of censorship, peasant ownership of land, elections
in 18 months and full respect for all civil rights. While it
is true that many of these promises were addressed to the
citizenry at large, it is no less certain that those directed to
the proletariat were particularly enticing. In one speech,
for instance, Castro held out the promise that Cuba was
going to become the most prosperous country of the
world.[19] When he took over as Prime Minister, the "maximum leader" gave assurances that in a few years' time he
would raise the standard of living of the Cubans to a level

higher than that of the U.S.[20] On other occasions, he referred to his industrialization plans and indicated that in
less than ten years Cuba would reach the level of the most
advanced European countries. When several workers' assemblies voluntarily contributed 4 percent of their wages
to the industrialization program, Castro quickly promised
to return that money with compound interest.[21]

There were also specific promises for individual groups
of workers. Rural workers, for instance, were told that in
five years' time they would be receiving a combined total
of "500 million more than they were getting in 1959."[22]
Urban workers received assurances that all Cubans should
at least enjoy a middle-class way of life.[23] There was also
a standing promise of increased employment opportunities
for jobless workers. More important in the context of the
announced industrialization campaign was the promise to
promote accelerated development without causing any of
the hardships usually involved in capital formation efforts.
To this end, the maximum leader made on February 12,
1959, the following statement:

> We have a responsibility we are all aware of and this is to
> show to the Americas the possibility of a new way of eco-
> nomic development without sacrificing a generation or more
> in the making of a decent economy.[24]

Not infrequently Castro turned loose his imagination
and made some extravagant offers. At the outset of his
regime he promised to drain the large Zapata swamp in
the south of Cuba and to provide thereby employment to
200,000 unemployed.[25] A few months later, at a meeting
of telephone workers he stated that the revolution would

give a telephone to every person who needed one.[26] By December, his Minister of Labor was promising a house to every worker.[27] The following year the Prime Minister was speaking of setting up one thousand new towns in five years.[28]

It did not bother Castro that these promises were hardly feasible and could even harm his credibility, particularly with the middle and upper levels of the population. Castro was apparently banking on the rising expectations of the lower strata of society. The important thing for him was to win over the support of labor and to do so during the critical stages of the revolution. When, later on, the economic situation deteriorated and prospects were less cheerful, the revolutionary government was already in full control and was able to lower the level of its promises and to offer more sober solutions. In March 1961, for instance, when the revolution entered a stage of increasing sacrifices, Castro more modestly indicated in one of his speeches that the humble people "will not lack essentials."[29]

Even before that date, however, other statements made by Castro during the first months of the revolution were also somewhat stern and apparently at odds with the bonanza promises. Expectations of riches were occasionally combined in effect with ominous warnings addressed to the population at large in respect of forthcoming scarcities and economic difficulties. At a time when the Cuban economy was relatively prosperous, absolutely no food problem existed and no apparent reason seemed to justify belt-tightening measures, Castro warned the Cuban people of imminent shortages and even mentioned the possibility of its having to eat "malanga," an edible tuber that was considered in Cuba as a symbol of hard times. Such shortages, which Castro emphasized would be of a short-term nature, could only be understood in the context of the drastic changes that the Cuban economy was bound to experience. They were presented as an inevitable part of the transition and did not affect the longer-term expectations.

Worker-Peasant Alliance

Emphasis was placed at the outset on the role played by peasants in the Rebel Army and the contribution of Sierra Maestra "campesinos" to the guerrilla fight. Castro himself repeatedly stressed the peasant character of the Rebel Army and paid tribute to the vanguard role of the peasant in winning and consolidating the revolution.[30] Soon the myth of a peasant uprising was being fanned as a means of dramatizing the need to implement a far-reaching land reform. Urban workers were asked to contribute to the Agrarian Reform Fund through voluntary contributions or deductions at the source of 1 percent of their salaries. Labor rallies were organized in the principal cities to demonstrate support for the agrarian program of the revolution. Courses and lectures were organized to familiarize trade union members with the problems of the rural population.

Peasants, in turn, were brought to Havana to mingle with the urban groups and get in touch with the leaders of the revolution. Three weeks after victory, one thousand campesinos were brought to Havana from different rural areas to attend a meeting organized by the CTC-R to support the execution of "war criminals." Several thousand rural workers from the sugar fields paraded during the May Day 1959 celebrations, wearing the typical native rural straw hat and carrying machetes. On July 26, half a million

rural workers were also invited to the anniversary celebrations and mingled with the people of Havana, who had
been asked to lodge them free of charge.

The worker-peasant alliance was further promoted by
the educational and military programs of the revolutionary
government. Large-scale adult educational programs with
a strong political component were introduced in mid-1959
for the benefit of humble people in the cities and the countryside. Fellowships were almost exclusively granted, from
the outset, to the children of workers and peasants.[31] Efforts were also made to step up the recruitment of workers
and peasants for the Rebel Army and to constitute the
militias mainly on the basis of these two social groups. At
the May Day, 1959, parade a platoon of infantrymen of
the Rebel Army carried a huge sign reading: "In war and
in peace the workers and the Rebel Army are the same
thing."[32] It was also rather symptomatic that the Guevara
manual on guerrilla warfare addressed its instructions for
the conduct of military operations in case of invasion to
urban workers and peasants.[33]

All these efforts were coupled with statements and exhortations designed to drive home the message that workers and peasants were regarded as the backbone of the
revolution. In his political tract *History Will Absolve Me*,
Castro had given a narrow definition of the people which
left aside the "comfortable and conservative sectors of the
nation."[34] This definition was now implemented in such
drastic terms that, for all practical purposes, the notion of
the people became coterminous with labor. As early as
February 1959 Castro declared in a televised interview that
the workers were posing some problems to the revolution
because they had not yet realized that the government in
power was "their" government.[35] In the same month of
February, at a meeting held at the CTC-R, the maximum

leader further pursued his insinuating messages to the workers by saying that it were they and not the capitalists who comfortably seated in their Wall Street offices, who were the real, principal creators of all wealth.[36]

Later, when he took leave from the Cuban people before his trip to the U.S., his farewell words were as follows: "I am saying goodbye to the working class of Cuba until we meet again on May Day."[37] The message was further emphasized at the July 26, 1959 celebrations when the Prime Minister virtually conditioned his wielding of political power on the support of workers and peasants.[38] Finally, when he wanted to impress upon people the kind of collaboration that his government appreciated most, Castro made clear that "the real revolutionary merits could only be earned as work heroes in the factories and farms of the island."[39]

Other revolutionary elements were also contributing to the promotion of proletarian unity. Ernesto Guevara, for instance, pointed out at a labor rally held in Santiago de Cuba in the month of May, 1959, that "there are two classes whom we shall never forget nor betray: the workers and the peasants. We are committed to their well-being in all our social and economic endeavours."[40]

The PSP leadership in turn published in *Hoy* a manifesto praising the July 26 celebrations which ended with the traditional battlecry: "Long live the alliance of workers and the peasants."[41]

The emphasis placed on the worker-peasant alliance served to highlight the class character of the revolution and to mobilize these two groups for the anti-capitalist struggle. The idea of the alliance was probably born in connection with the Soviet claim that the October Socialist Revolution was brought about by the workers and peasants of Russia. Because the middle class had played an essential role in the Cuban Revolution and this departed from the Soviet model, the ruling leadership felt the need to introduce some urgent adjustments in its image. True, some of the early references to the worker-peasant alliance were somewhat veiled or obscured. On one occasion Castro even lamented that he could not be more specific at that time about his intentions towards the working class.[42] But the message was always there and it became more and more explicit as the revolution advanced. A speech delivered in October 1959, for instance, listed the soldiering peasants and workers as "the best allies of the Revolution" and contained at the end the following paragraph:

> Don't they know by now that we will remain as long as the last peasant of Cuba remains? Don't they understand we will remain with the last worker?[43]

Before the end of the year he felt obliged to tell a meeting of the National Federation of Sugar Workers that "the positions are now perfectly clear, there are no in-betweens, the workers know quite well that we do not defend any other interests but the interests of labor."[44] He admitted quite bluntly that the revolution had lost some time during the first year but indicated that it was going to gain real momentum in its second year. In the meantime, Castro advised industrial workers not to worry about their demands and gave assurances to the peasants that the sugar cane would in due course be theirs.[45]

It is also important to recall that workers and peasants were not regarded as separate entities liable to develop different sectorial interests. The revolutionary elite took, on the contrary, special care to underscore the unity of the working class and the need to avoid factional approaches. The principle of the universality of labor, central to Marxist teachings, was thus consistently stressed from the outset as a cornerstone of the revolution. On one occasion, for instance, the maximum leader indicated that "there is no such thing as sugar cane work or transportation work or electrical work. All the workers have the same rights, all are equal."[46] This idea was further developed until it became the central theme of a speech delivered in early 1960 on the need to teach workers to think as a class and not as a sector.[47]

Together with the worker-peasant alliance, efforts were made from the beginning towards a gradual levelling of conditions of work and life in the urban and rural sectors. Reference was already made to the extension of certain benefits and protective measures to the rural workers. As regards living conditions, while few public works were carried out in the urban sector and cities were generally neglected, the government took steps to strengthen the infrastructure of social services in the rural areas. The objective was to eliminate differences between town and country, an objective so important to a Communist society that it is enshrined in the Constitutions of the U.S.S.R. and the People's Republic of China.

Labour Unrest and Class Conflicts

Most crucial to the successful development of any possible plans to radicalize the revolution was the fostering of a class-conflict atmosphere. The Prime Minister had recognized in the month of March that workers lacked class consciousness and that there was no class hatred in Cuba.[48] Clearly, this situation was not conducive to the furthering of the social revolution that had already been announced in some speeches; it also hampered the development of other aspects of the revolutionary strategy, particularly those related to the seizure of private property as a result of labor disputes.

A series of government measures taken between January and November 1959 entitled workers to file claims for a variety of labor-related reasons. One of the first decrees approved by the Cabinet provided that all Labor Ministry resolutions issued between April 4, 1958 and December 31, 1958 were subject to immediate revision.[49] A subsequent measure dealing with termination of employment cases authorized and regulated the procedure to be followed concerning requests for the reinstatement of employees who had been discharged or who had resigned during the Batista period for political reasons or as a result of any form of political coercion.[50] Other measures were adopted under Labor Minister Martínez Sánchez allowing aggrieved workers to file claims related to pre-1959 cases even where the statute of limitations should have prevented such claims. Finally, other decrees extended and expanded the already mentioned prohibition of lay-offs.[51]

These measures brought about a dramatic increase in the frequency of disputes. For example, the number of cases filed as a result of the two decrees relating to termination of employment exceeded the 40,000 figure.[52] True, a number of these disputes were settled through conciliation procedures, but many others remained unresolved for lengthy periods. According to official estimates, the number of outstanding files concerning individual and collective disputes reached the 100,000 mark

in October, 1959.[53] The Labor Ministry's cumbersome machinery and the lack of experience of the newly appointed
personnel helped to create confusion and to abet labor's
unrest. Settlement of a labor conflict usually dragged on
for several months, allowing ample opportunity for a fes-
tering of the original dispute. Almost invariably, these disputes were solved in the end in favor of the workers and
the onerous economic conditions imposed on the employers brought about a considerable increase in production
costs, which many enterprises found difficult to meet. This,
in turn, gave rise to bankruptcies and new disputes between labor and management, which usually led to the
seizure of the enterprise concerned by the government.

A sudden rise in collective bargaining negotiations also
contributed to the over-all increase in the frequency of
disputes. Workers everywhere appeared to be particularly
anxious to put forward lists of demands (*pliegos de reivin-
dicaciones*) accumulated during the Batista dictatorship, and
the revolutionary government apparently encouraged this
upsurge of bargaining activities. Most existing agreements
were subject to renegotiation and firms that previously had
no agreements were faced with lengthy lists of demands.
By the middle of 1959 some 10,000 conciliation meetings
had been held in the offices of the Ministry of Labor.[54]
Some conciliation procedures lasted for months and created considerable turmoil in the premises of the Ministry.

Government support for labor-management negotiations came about only during the initial months of the
revolution when Castro and his colleagues were apparently intent on arousing workers' expectations and fomenting a climate of tension. In December, 1959, collective
bargaining activities were suspended by the government
on the ground that the procedures were excessively time-
consuming and were resulting in the accumulation of a

large number of cases that only served to make settlements more difficult to achieve.[55] Although the suspension was decreed for a period of 120 days, in actual fact the traditional process of collective bargaining ceased to operate almost completely from that time onwards.

Finally, the rise in the frequency and duration of disputes was coupled with government statements seemingly designed to foster a conflict-ridden atmosphere. The Prime Minister referred on various occasions to the employers' lack of observance of labor legislation, to the inclination of wealthy men to send their money abroad and to do little for Cuba and to the unfair treatment accorded to various sectors of the working class. On one occasion he personally instigated labor agitation in the opposition newspaper *El País*.[56] In the month of May, Raúl Castro placed at the top of the list of the enemies of the revolution the large landowners "who have lived lives of parasites," the big importers "who are against Agrarian Reform" and the sugar magnates "who submit themselves to foreign orders or dictates."[57] Pro-Communist officials of the Rebel Army took their cue from those statements and joined the chorus of criticisms. For instance, William Galvez, military chief of the Matanzas Province took advantage of a labor dispute in a sugar mill owned by the well-known industrialist and financier Julio Lobo, to make some derogatory remarks about greedy sugar mill owners.[58] Other military commanders went further and arrested cane planters and other employers so as to force labor demands upon them.[59]

Several years later, in his report to the First Congress of the Cuban Communist Party, Castro referred to this period of labor unrest and social agitation in the following words:

> *The Cuban people actually acquired a socialist awareness with the*
> *development of the Revolution and the violent class struggle that*
> *was unleashed* (by the revolutionary leaders) *at the national*
> *and international levels.* The clash of interests between the
> people and their oppressors engendered the Revolution
> and the Revolution brought this clash to the highest level.
> *This struggle served to develop the conscience of the masses; they*
> *were able to realize in a few months what only a minority had*
> *previously been able to understand after decades of ruthless ex-*
> *ploitation and imperialist domination.*[60] (author's italics)

Analysis of Four Major Disputes

Castro's handling of four major disputes that erupted
between January and April 1959 sheds additional light on
the intentions of the revolutionary government. One of
these disputes concerned both the sugar industry at large
and two individual sugar mills (Chaparra and Delicias),
two others affected individual enterprises (Crusellas and
Shell) and the fourth, the casino gambling industry. These
four disputes, which attracted considerable attention at the
time, appear now in perspective as a testing ground of the
government position vis-à-vis the working class.

The first thing to be noted in connection with these
disputes is that Castro personally dealt with all of them
(though in the case of Crusellas he delegated in his brother
Raúl for the final settlement). The second observation is
that the outcome of the four disputes was in all cases favorable to the workers, regardless of the nature of the
dispute or the different types of ownership involved. The
Crusellas dispute affected a Cuban family-type firm, the

sugar industry conflict involved Cuban and foreign concerns, Shell was controlled by a British-Dutch consortium
and the casinos were run by American and Cuban interests.
Finally, it is noteworthy that Castro sought to discourage
in all cases the use of strikes as an economic weapon, despite his expressions of support for the workers' side and
his previous endorsement of political strikes. Castro thus
seems to emerge from his personal involvement in these
disputes as an advocate of centralized methods of settling
labor disputes by the government on behalf of the workers.

A closer look at each one of the above-mentioned disputes helps to uncover some revealing aspects of Castro's
approach to labor problems. In the case of the sugar industry, the dispute involved both a particular negotiation
in which an American firm, owner of the Chaparra and
Delicias mills, had refused to meet the workers' demands
and an industry-wide discussion of working conditions for
the 1959 harvest. As regards the former question, Castro
indicated in his speech before the National Federation of
Sugar Workers (FNTA) that it would have been relatively
easy for him to send a platoon of the Rebel Army to take
over the two mills concerned. But he immediately remarked: "I would like you to tell me whether it would be
appropriate at this time to take such measures"[61] He then
proceeded to impress upon his audience the significance
of the upcoming grinding season and to outline the revolutionary strategy in the following words: "What we must
do is sacrifice ourselves for the Revolution. I do not ask
you to give up your demands, which are very just. Continue
as you are even though the sugar companies get away with
the best of the deal. I tell you that this is their year, *but I
guarantee you that it will be their last.*"[62] (author's italics)

As far as the industry-wide negotiation was concerned,
Castro was confronted with a long list of salary increases

and other economic demands, coupled with the request for four six-hour shifts in the mills instead of the traditional three eight-hour shifts.[63] Most of the economic demands were *ipso facto* accepted by the government but Castro turned down the four-shift petition, which he termed "a desperate measure" that "does not solve anything." The Prime Minister had included the four-shift demand in his 1953 program and was no doubt sure that its acceptance would contribute to alleviate unemployment; however, he was not apparently prepared to impair any possible nationalization plans ahead of time with such drastic change. A few years later, he referred retrospectively to the six-hour shifts petition and indicated that it was put forward by the sugar workers to alleviate the exploitation of which they were victims and because they did not know that the sugar mills were going to belong to the people. He then explained his reluctance to meet such a demand by saying: "But we knew that in a not distant future those mills were going to belong to the nation."[64]

Castro's speech before the meeting of representatives of the sugar workers deserves some additional comments. In it, the maximum leader gave labor some advice on its future course of action and stated that "the right attitude (of the workers) is to think not of *immediate solutions* but rather of a *final solution*." He suggested that "in the long run the government will have to solve the question in favor of the great majority by acquiring the sugar mills.[65] No mention was made at the time of expropriation or nationalization without compensation. The term "acquiring" was carefully chosen to convey, on the one hand, a message of hope and patience to the workers and to assuage, on the other, the apprehensions of the still powerful *hacendados*. It was, by the way, in this same speech that Castro made it clear that the revolution would go as far as necessary but that the critical turning point would be fixed by the Revolutionary Government and not by the sugar companies.

The casino industry dispute originated in the closing down of various casinos and night clubs where gambling was permitted before Castro. The provisional government nominally led by President Urrutia and Prime Minister Miró had clamped down on the casinos for moral considerations, but their closing led to the laying-off of a considerable number of workers. The workers concerned protested, and their protests immediately found sympathetic ears in Fidel Castro who indicated that "gambling in responsible hands had a place in Cuba." Castro's position ran counter to President Urrutia's and Prime Minister Miró's previous statement and gave rise to a government crisis. At one point, Castro threw a few barbs at Urrutia and Miró saying that "it was very easy from air-conditioned rooms to take bread from the mouths of casino employees" and charged them publicly with wanting to inflict hunger on the workers.[66]

In the end the difference between Castro and Miró led to the latter's resignation from the Cabinet and to the reopening of the casinos under government control. It is interesting to note that Castro's view with regard to the reopening of gambling casinos fully coincided with the stand taken by the Restaurant and Hotel Workers' Union, whose president, Alfredo Rancaño, had even threatened a nationwide strike in protest against the government's failure to resolve the gambling issue. Whether the gambling issue was used by Castro as a pretext to force Miró out and to assume the Prime Minister's position or whether he really wanted to alleviate the lot of the 4,000 persons involved, is not easy to ascertain. But the outcome of the dispute led to the seizure of an industry by the government and contributed to enhance Castro's image as a stubborn defender of workers' interests.

The Crusellas dispute, in turn, involved a series of economic demands and a claim to reinstate a few Marxist activists. The dispute lasted for several weeks and was concluded by the acceptance of all the demands put forward by the union. Raúl Castro's appearance at the meeting organized by the Crusellas local union to ratify the new agreement signalled the government's approval of a collective agreement, the conditions of which amounted to unconditional surrender on the part of the employer. Salary increases amounting to some $300,000 had been obtained, and other benefits including the reinstatement of the three workers involved, were also included in the final settlement. The revolutionary chieftain indicated in his speech before the firm's executives and some 1,200 workers that he had not attended any labor-management meeting before and said that he was willing to make an exception in this case in view of the excellent results secured by the union. But Raúl also profited from the occasion to voice some ominous warnings about the "powerful national and foreign monopolies which were opposing the revolutionary program."[67] He also alluded to the government's determination to pursue a revolutionary course, with labor's help, up to the bitter end.[68]

Finally, the Shell labor dispute demonstrated how quickly the government was willing to abandon a Sierra Maestra war edict for the sake of a closer identification with the working class. Shell had been undergoing a boycott because the British Government had permitted the sale of planes and arms to the previous administration and as a result of the close association between Batista and Shell's President, Julio Iglesias. The boycott had injured the company economically and prevented it from meeting the workers' demands for higher salaries. Since the middle of January, however, newspaper ads and workers' demonstrations had drawn attention to the plight of Shell's workers. Castro soon intervened and asked the nation to end the boycott of the Shell Company "for the sake of the 4,500 workers whose interests are threatened."[69] Following the lifting of the boycott, he managed to work out a settlement of the dispute by which workers won a 100 percent salary increase in the lower grades and 50 percent in the higher ones. A quarter of a million dollars was, in addition, paid by the company as war compensation, to build rural farm dwellings. In addressing an assembly of oil workers at the beginning of February, Fidel Castro stated that it was the people who decided to lift the boycott and to make it possible for workers to earn, for the most part, twice as much as they earned before. "This," he added, "is a magnificent victory."[70]

It was also during the Shell controversy that Castro spelled out his objection to the use of economic strikes, already formulated at the FNTA meeting. In Castro's own words, economic strikes were "inopportune and out of order." He added that "a rash of strikes carried seeds of discontent and anarchy."[71] He made clear, however, that he was not going to suspend the right to strike as it belonged to the workers themselves to take appropriate measures thereon. "We must carry forward this Revolution with all the freedoms,"[72] he insisted. It is interesting to note that Castro's views on economic strikes were particularly well received in certain sectors close to the PSP. His call for a suspension of strikes in the sugar industry was immediately supported by the top Communist leader of the sugar workers.[73]

The pattern of settlements favorable to labor was further utilized in other labor disputes. Bank employees fired

in 1955 on account of a political strike against Batista's
dictatorship were reinstated in their jobs with back pay.[74]
Radio and television workers who claimed compensatory
pay from the CMQ network to reimburse them for the time
they had lost in underground activities received $60,000
lump sum compensation, which was subsequently donated
to the Agrarian Reform.[75] Construction workers employed
by a French firm on an Almendares river tunnel project
were paid the differential between land construction wages
and maritime construction wages; the difference amounted
to one million dollars.

For those workers whose benefits did not measure up
to their expectations, the Castro brothers made clear in
their speeches that the government had other plans in store
for their long-run interests. Speaking at a labor rally in
Havana Central Park on February 11, Raúl Castro plainly
indicated that labor's demands were justified but that
"workers must be patient and wait until the Revolution is
consolidated."[76]

Confiscation and Seizure of Enterprises

Phase one of the revolution finally included some initial
steps towards transfer of ownership from private hands to
the government. These steps were not taken openly in the
name of a national liberation movement, or because of a
nationalization program, but rather indirectly and following a piece-meal approach. The only exception was the
Agrarian Reform program which enjoyed wide popular
support, was envisaged in the 1940 Constitution, and had
its roots in the Sierra Maestra struggle. Here, the govern-

ment was able to pass in the month of May drastic legislation which effectively terminated private ownership of
the land in all estates of over four hundred hectares.

For the industrial and commercial sectors, however, there
was no previous revolutionary program nor constitutional
provision which could justify government expropriation.
The Revolutionary Government consequently resorted to
two indirect but quite effective procedures in order to step
up government intervention in the private economy.

The first procedure was the confiscation of property
belonging to officials of the previous administration who
were considered guilty of corrupt practices. A special ministry was set up for this purpose, and a massive drive intended to recuperate all ill-gotten gains and properties was
shortly launched. This campaign was aimed not only at
government officials but also at people suspected of collab-
orating with Batista and enterprises accused of obtaining
illicit profits during his administration. The word collaboration was never defined and was applied to practically
anyone who had served the previous government in any
important post.[77] Mujal's properties, for instance, including a dairy farm, were confiscated and converted into a
cooperative. Nine sugar mills were immediately seized and
later transferred to the Agrarian Reform Institute. The
four Cuban airlines were also placed under government
administration as of January 1959. So were the concerns
of contractors and middlemen suspected of paying kick-
backs or receiving unduly high profits. By the month of
April, the Ministry for the Recovery of Stolen State Property made public a list of 236 business firms which had
been seized in the Havana province alone.[78] It should be
added that the public sector of the economy was further
expanded in December, 1959, when punishment by con-

fiscation of property was provided by law for counter-revolutionary activities.

The second instrument was the seizure of industrial and commercial concerns affected by labor disputes. A legal provision dating back to 1934 authorized government occupation (*"intervención"*) of private enterprises by the Ministry of Labor in some exceptional cases of management's refusal to comply with a government decision. This provision, which had only been invoked before in a handful of cases, began to be generously applied from the beginning of the revolution. In the month of March, for instance, the government took possession of the Cuban Telephone Company, the two main urban bus companies of Havana and an important rum and distilling factory, on grounds that such action was necessary in order to avert a labor crisis. In many instances, small groups of workers submitted exaggerated lists of demands with the sole purpose of creating a conflict and provoking the seizure of the enterprise concerned. Indeed, the number of "seizures" due to labor problems rose so sharply that by August 1959 the Labor Ministry deemed it appropriate to deny that the revolutionary government was carrying out a program of deliberate "interventions."[79]

In November 1959, the legal procedure for government seizure of industrial and commercial enterprises in case of labor disputes was reaffirmed and expanded. The new Minister of Labor alleged that it was necessary to guarantee the functioning of all enterprises without undue interruptions and consequently added new grounds to those provided for the "intervention" procedure, including the existence of any serious labor dispute and the ostensible decline of normal output rates.[80] The law empowered the Minister to decide in his own discretionary judgment whether there was reasonable cause for taking possession of an enterprise, and this led to further increases in the number of government seizures. According to an official report of the Labor Ministry, the government seized 23 additional enterprises during the two months following the enactment of the new procedures.[81] Also significant was the provision authorizing interventions to last for as long as twelve months. In point of fact, however, there were almost no instances of a government intervention being called off in order to return the industry concerned to the owner. Once a seizure was ordered by government, the industry in question remained indefinitely in public hands.

NOTES

1. *Discurso del máximo lider de la revolución Cubana y Primer Ministro del Gobierno Revolucionario Dr. Fidel Castro Ruz. En la plenaria nacional azucarera del día 15 de diciembre de 1959* (Havana, 1960), p. 3.

2. On one occasion he even conditioned the adoption of a government decree aimed at increasing taxes of alcoholic beverages on its previous approval by the CTC-R National Council (see *Havana Post*, September 15, 1959), p. 1.

3. Fidel Castro, *Cuba's Socialist Destiny* (New York: Fair Play for Cuba Committee, 1961), p. 8.

4. See Richard Fagen, "Mass Mobilization in Cuba: The Symbolism of Struggle," in Rolando E. Bonachea and Nelson P. Valdés, *Cuba in Revolution* (New York: Anchor Books, 1972), p. 205.

5. Informe central al Primer Congreso del Partido Comunista de Cuba, *op. cit.*, p. 5.

6. José Antonio Portuondo, "Los intelectuales y la revolución." *Cuba Socialista* (Havana), June 1964, pp. 62–63.

7. A few samples: "We shall overcome," "Cuba SI, Yankees NO!", "Fatherland or Death!"

8. See, for example, the section "América Latina al día," which appeared in *Trabajo* as from its third issue.

9. See, for example, "Recuento de la labor revolucionaria del Ministerio del Trabajo." *Trabajo* (Havana), No. 1, May 1960, p. 84 and "Libre de viejos conflictos el Ministerio del Trabajo se prepara para la segunda etapa de la Revolución." *Trabajo*, No. 8, diciembre de 1960, p. 54.

10. Iglesias, Soto and Carbonell were later elected members of the Executive Committee of the CTC-R.

11. A fairly comprehensive list of these legal texts can be found in the following two books prepared by the Cuban Economic Research Group: *Labor Conditions in Communist Cuba* (Coral Gables: University of Miami Press, 1963), Chapter V and *A Study on Cuba, op. cit.*, Chapter 46.

12. Law No. 52 of February 17, 1959 (*Official Gazette*, February 20, 1959). This law was subsequently extended for two additional 180 day periods.

13. See "El fusil del sacrificio." Discursos de Fidel Castro. *Trabajo*, No. 1, May 1960, p. 41.

14. *Bohemia*, Year 51, No. 29, July 19, 1959, p. 56.

15. *Ibid.*, p. 9.

16. See, for instance, Fidel Castro's speeches of September 15, 1959, and December 20, 1959, which will be commented on in *infra*, pp. 145 and 209.

17. In February 1960, E. Guevara, for instance, said in a TV appearance that the government was not concerned with profit sharing but that it was interested in workers' participation in the running of enterprises. (See *El Mundo*, (Havana) February 17, 1960, p. 1).

18. The text of this bill—which was prepared by the author and two collaborators—was published later in Movimiento Revolucionario 30 de Noviembre, *Los tribunales del trabajo en Cuba* (Miami, 1963).

19. Fidel Castro, *Humanismo revolucionario, op. cit.*, p. 101.

20. Quoted by E. González Pedrero, *La revolución cubana, op. cit.*, p. 239.

21. See *Discurso del máximo líder de la revolución cubana y Primer Ministro del Gobierno Revolucionario Dr. Fidel Castro Ruz. En la Plenaria Nacional Azucarera del día 15 de diciembre de 1959, op. cit.*, p. 22.

22. See *Havana Post*, July 7, 1959, p. 1.

23. See *Havana Post*, March 19, 1959, p. 1.

24. Quoted in C. Wright Mills, *Castro's Cuba* (London: Secker and Worburg, 1960), p. 82.

25. See *Havana Post*, March 17, 1959, p. 1.

26. See *Havana Post*, March 8, 1959, p. 13.

27. See A. Martínez Sánchez's speech of December 1, 1959 in *El Mundo*, December 3, 1959, p. A8.

28. See *Trabajo*, No. 1, May 1, 1959, p. 54 and *El Mundo*, April 2, 1960, p. A1.

29. Fidel Castro, *Always Determined, Always Ready to Make Sacrifices* (Havana: Editorial en Marcha, 1961), p. 7.

30. Leo Huberman and Paul M. Sweezy, *Cuba: Anatomy of a Revolution, op. cit.,* p. 78.

31. See Fidel Castro, *Brigadas de alfabetización en Varadero. El día de las Madres* (Havana: Imprenta Nacional de Cuba, 1961), p. 24.

32. *Havana Post,* May 1, 1959, p. 1.

33. See Ernesto Guevara, *La guerra de guerrillas* (Havana: Departamento de Instrucción del MINFAR, 1960).

34. *History Will Absolve Me, op. cit.,* p. 51.

35. Fidel Castro, "La mayor batalla del gobierno: la batalla contra el desempleo." *Diario de la Marina* (Havana), February 20, 1959, p. 18.

36. *Revolución,* February 1, 1959, p. 2.

37. Quoted by Andrés Suárez, *Cuba, Castroism and Communism, op. cit.,* p. 63.

38. See *Havana Post,* July 26, 1959, p. 8.

39. *Bohemia,* Year 51, No. 39, September 27, 1959, p. 79.

40. See *Bohemia,* Year 51, No. 19, May 10, 1959, p. 103.

41. See *Hoy,* July 26, 1959, p. 1.

42. Speech of September 15, 1959, before the CTC-R National Council (see *Fidel en la CTC-R. Discurso a los trabajadores. 1er Congreso Nacional Revolucionario* (Havana: *Cooperativa Obrera de Publicidad,* 1959), p. 14.

43. *Fidel Castro Speaks, op. cit.,* p. 68.

44. Fidel Castro, *Discurso del máximo líder de la Revolución cubana y Primer Ministro del Gobierno Revolucionario Fidel Castro Ruz. En la Plenaria Nacional Azucarera del día 15 de diciembre de 1959, op. cit.,* p. 12.

45. *Ibid.,* pp. 30 and 41.

46. Quoted by Angel Fernández González, *Derrotismo y contradicciones de Fidel Castro Ruz* (México: Ediciones Ataque, 1965), p. 110.

47. Fidel Castro, "A los trabajadores hay que enseñarles a pensar como clase y no como sector." *Revolución,* May 30, 1960, pp. 1, 4, 6 and 14.

48. See *Havana Post,* March 17, 1959, p. 1.

49. Law No. 10 of January 13, 1959 (*Official Gazette* of January 11, 1959).

50. Law No. 34 of January 29, 1959 (*Official Gazette* of January 30, 1959).

51. See Law No. 490 of August 19, 1959 (*Official Gazette* of August 21, 1959) and Law No. 738 of February 19, 1959 (*Official Gazette* of February 23, 1960).

52. See "Recuento de la labor revolucionaria del Ministerio del Trabajo," *Trabajo, op. cit.,* p. 86.

53. *Ibid.*

54. See *Revolución,* May 4, 1959, p. 6.

55. See Roberto Hernández and Carmelo Mesa Lago, "Labor Organizations and Wages in Cuba" in Carmelo Mesa Lago, ed., *Revolutionary Change in Cuba, op. cit.,* pp. 216–218.

56. See *El Mundo,* March 17, 1960, p. 1.

57. See *Havana Post,* January 27, 1959, p. 7.

58. See *Revolución,* January 27, 1959, p. 7.

59. See, for instance, *Havana Post,* May 29, 1959, p. 1.

60. *Informe central al Primer Congreso del Partido Comunista Cubano, op. cit.,* p. 5.

61. *Political, Economic and Social Thought of Fidel Castro, op. cit.,* p. 204.

62. *Ibid.,* p. 205.

63. This request had been put forward by FNTA on January 15, 1959, and reiterated during the meeting with Castro.

64. Fidel Castro, *Sobre el trabajo. Cuatro discursos del Comandante Fidel Castro* (Havana: Ministerio del Trabajo, 1963), p. 13. See also *infra,* Chapter XI, p. 300.

65. *Political, Economic and Social Thought of Fidel Castro, op. cit.,* pp. 206–207.

66. Manuel Urrutia, *Fidel Castro and Company, op. cit.* pp. 35, 36 and 37. See also R. Hart Philip, *Cuban Dilemma, op. cit.,* p. 50.

67. *Havana Post,* March 31, 1959, p. 1.

68. Raúl Castro, *Y el que por creerse lo contrario intente apoderarse de Cuba en una forma u otra recogerá el polvo de su suelo anegado en*

sangre (Havana: Cooperativa Obrera de Publicidad, 1959), p. 5.

69. *Political, Economic and Social Thought of Fidel Castro, op. cit.,* p. 199.

70. *Ibid.*

71. *Ibid.,* p. 192.

72. *Ibid.,* p. 193.

73. See Ursinio Rojas, "Cómo defender las demandas de los obreros azucareros." *Hoy,* 20 February 1959, p. 1.

74. *Havana Post,* February 15, 1959, p. 1.

75. Bethel, *op. cit.,* p. 156.

76. *Havana Post,* February 12, 1959. p. 1.

77. Lowry Nelson, *The Measure of a Revolution* (Minneapolis: University of Minnesota Press, 1972), p. 19.

78. See *Havana Post,* April 4, 1959, p. 1.

79. See *Havana Post,* August 7, 1959, p. 1.

80. See Law No. 647 of November 24, 1959 (*Official Gazette* of November 30, 1959).

81. "Recuento de la labor revolucionaria del Ministerio del Trabajo," *op. cit.,* p. 88.

V

The Anti-Communist Reaction

The Dual Attitude

CASTRO'S COURTING OF LABOR WAS TAKING PLACE AT A TIME when many urban workers were showing signs of suffering from a sort of social schizophrenia; on the one hand, they considered themselves enthusiastic supporters of the revolution, while on the other hand, they were also opposed to the so-called Communist infiltration. While many rural workers and poor wage earners became unconditional followers of Castro, the majority of those belonging to the medium and upper levels of the working class remained fascinated with Castro's personality but also wanted to believe that the Prime Minister was not a Marxist and that at the proper time—after stealing more thunder from the left—he would rid himself of Communists.

Whatever their views with regard to Castro, neither rural nor urban workers were particularly predisposed towards Marxist ideas concerning class struggle, the elimination of private property, the one-party system and the establishment of a dictatorship of the proletariat. Memories of class struggle had vanished after two decades of relative prosperity. Rural workers were hardly in a position to understand collective ownership systems, as there was no tradition of communal experiences in Cuba. Urban workers who had just lived the Batista regime were instinctively hostile to any suggestion of dictatorship or totalitarianism. Their notions of what the revolution was going to be were still rather diffuse but they were unquestionably in favor of the principles thus far expounded by Castro regarding the establishment of a democratic government, the eradication of corruption, poverty and unemployment, the carrying out of an agrarian reform and the rapid industrialization of the country. To be sure, they were also counting on a windfall of benefits, but these were expected to come about in the context of a nationalistic and populist revolution.

This dual pro-Castro, anti-Communist position was made possible by Castro's continued denials of any Marxist leanings. For instance, in connection with his trip to the U.S., Castro saw fit to reiterate his liberal, non-Communist position on April 2 in Havana before the trip, on four occasions during his stay in the U.S. (before the American Society of Newspaper Editors, at the National Press Club, at Princeton University and in a Meet the Press Program) and immediately upon his return to Cuba.

The New Leadership Takes Up Its Duties

Nothing can better illustrate this dual attitude of the labor movement than the actions taken by the Provisional Executive Committee of the CTC-R. Salvador and his colleagues demonstrated from the outset an enthusiastic willingness to support Castro and all his revolutionary measures of 1959. Popular demonstrations were organized by the CTC-R to defend the execution of war criminals and to offer organized labor's support to the Prime Minister; circulars were distributed among affiliated unions to mobilize workers in favor of the government's nationalistic decrees; meetings were held to endorse government seizure of public utilities and agrarian reform measures. On May 1, the CTC-R even demanded the creation of workers' militias to defend the revolutionary laws. As mentioned earlier, on July 23 it declared a nationwide work stoppage to demand Castro's return to power, following his resignation as Prime Minister.

Special emphasis should be placed on the fact that the July 26 Movement trade union leaders also supported structural changes and went along with Castro's policies until the Communist issue came to a head. Many of them actually favored a substantial measure of collectivization in domestic affairs and non-alignment policies in foreign relations. It should be noted in this connection that a number of July 26 Movement labor leaders had previously belonged to the PSP or were of Trotskyist origin. Others who had rushed to join the Castro movement from the labor sections of the Auténtico and Orthodox parties were of hot-blooded, Jacobin temperament. Even those of reformist or moderate leanings were now imbued with a new militant spirit.

To suggest, as some authors have, that labor leaders of the July 26 Movement opposed agrarian reform and effectively placed themselves on the side of rural landlords[1] is thus a serious misinterpretation of historical facts. Not only is there abundant evidence to demonstrate that union leaders of all political orientations supported agrarian reform,[2] but it is absolutely irrational to think that leaders of a revolutionary CTC could have taken such a reactionary position at a time when the vast majority of the Cuban people, including leading business and employers' organizations, were backing a land reform program.[3]

Two indications may further serve to shed light on the position of the CTC-R leadership. The first relates to a mass meeting held in the month of March at which the ex-President of Costa Rica, José Figueres, suggested that in case of confrontation between the USSR and the U.S., Cuba should side with the U.S. David Salvador brusquely interrupted Figueres' speech at this point and shouted back that Cuba had no obligation towards the U.S. and should remain neutral.[4]

The second concerns a resolution adopted by the Tenth National Congress demanding nationalization of the public utilities, the telephone, transportation and the banking system. This resolution, submitted by the CTC-R leadership, was carried unanimously. Though critics may argue that some of the undertakings included in the four sectors mentioned in the resolution had already undergone "intervention" under various pretexts, the fact remains that the CTC-R resolution actually demanded outright nationalization of the whole of those sectors.

This is not to say, however, that July 26 Movement leaders were opposed to all forms of private enterprise. On various occasions, David Salvador declared that progressive-minded private employers had an important role to perform in the revolutionary process. Furthermore, another resolution approved by the Tenth Congress invited the Social Security Bank to grant loans to industrialists who were willing to expand their industries. Though vociferous and radical, these leaders were thus reluctant to engage in ideological squabbles or to follow a rigidly dogmatic line.

In fact, most July 26 Movement leaders wanted to keep their options open, to maintain contacts with all ideological currents and to avoid commitments with the Communist world. This explains why certain steps were taken by the provisional Executive Committee in the field of international labor relations which seemed to indicate that the Cuban labor movement was going to follow an independ-

ent course. Right after the Committee took charge of
CTC-R affairs, there was an exchange of cables between
the AFL-CIO and the CTC-R. Salvador sent his greetings
to George Meany, President of AFL-CIO, and the latter
offered cooperation "in any possible way."[5] Contacts between the Inter-American Regional Organization of Workers (ORIT) and the provisional Executive Committee were
established. For instance, the Secretary-General of ORIT
visited Havana in February and held conversations with
CTC-R officials. Some differences of opinion were expressed, but in general these talks were conducted in an
atmosphere of frankness and understanding. Though Salvador had previously formulated strong reservations about
ORIT's policies vis-à-vis Latin American dictatorships, he
did not rule out a possible CTC-R affiliation. Other visits
of ORIT's Secretary-General A. Sánchez Madariaga and
his collaborator Daniel Benedict took place in 1959. Together with two members of the CTC-R Executive Committee, Plana and González, ORIT's representatives organized a number of training courses for metalworkers,
oilworkers and others.

   In the month of April, Reynol González and José de
Jesús Plana appeared before the ORIT Administrative
Committee in Mexico and expressed interest in continuing
the CTC-R affiliation to the International Confederation
of Free Trade Unions (ICFTU) and ORIT. The following
month, at the International Labor Day celebrations, representatives of all international trade union centers
(ICFTU), International Federation of Christian Trade
Unions (CISC) and World Federation of Trade Unions
(WFTU) were invited to attend the ceremonies. All these
global confederations, as well as the international trade
secretariats and American regional organizations, were obviously seeking to influence the trend of developments in

Cuba. Later on when the International Labor Conference
met in Geneva in June 1959, the Cuban workers' delegate,
Conrado Becquer, made clear in his speech before the
conference that the Cuban Revolution was a humanistic
one and that to claim otherwise was a reactionary attempt
to mystify the world about it.[6] Finally, when three months
later Salvador attended a meeting of the Mexican Labor
Confederation National Council, he characterized the Cuban Revolution as "an insurrection of the Cuban people
in the fight for their freedom, their democracy and welfare."[7] Indeed the democratic attitude of the leadership
and the anti-Communist reaction of the rank and file
seemed so strong that by March 1959, the organ of the
ICFTU, *Free Labour World*, somewhat prematurely reported that the Communist attempt to cash in on the revolutionary situation in Cuba had been nipped in the bud.[8]

Anti-Communism Gains Momentum

Following the first instinctive reaction against the PSP
attempt to control the trade union movement, the anti-
Communist movement seemed to coalesce in more organized forms. By mid-February, a group of revolutionary
leaders within the CTC-R announced a nationwide program "to combat Communist infiltration in the labor
ranks."[9] The program included an appeal to strengthen
anti-Communist unity within the labor movement, the
holding of special assemblies in all trade unions to prop-
agate democratic principles and full support for anti-Communist leaders in their aspirations towards key executive
positions.

This initial step was followed in the month of May by the formation of a Humanist Labor Front (FOH) which was clearly conceived to carry on the ideals of the revolution and to eliminate the Communist influence within the labor movement. The Front was constituted of representatives of 20 of the 33 federations of industrial workers' unions, but a spokesman of the FOH indicated at its founding meeting that at least 9 other industrial unions intended to join it.[10]

In its first declaration of principles, the new organization stated that international Communism was trying to infiltrate the revolutionary movement through the old tactic of preaching unity. Raising the slogan "Neither Washington nor Moscow," the leaders of the FOH pledged to support the struggle against oppression "whether from the right or the left."[11] "We shall wholeheartedly support," the manifesto said, "the policy of the July 26 Movement in defense of our national sovereignty in the face of the political, economic and military oppression of any world power or imperialism, be they of the left or right, capitalist or proletariat."[12] The manifesto also upheld the right to private property but underlined its social function and the need to promote economic policies designed to make the proletariat disappear by making everyone a property owner.

There were also various minor but significant incidents which served to highlight the extent of anti-Communist feelings. The Bricklayers' and Carpenters' Union of Havana, for instance, ousted its Secretary-General on charges of playing up to the Communist vote.[13] In March, when the Cuban Telephone Company was taken over, a small group of Communists staged a demonstration and asked the Prime Minister to speak. Following Castro's speech a Communist leader climbed to the rostrum to address the audience, whereupon he was booed and forced to leave the premises of the Company.[14] Two months later, bruised feelings between Marxists and non-Marxists were peaking to the point where the Secretary of Propaganda of the National Federation of Sugar Workers (FNTA) had to deny a report published in *Hoy* that a group of organized workers planned to attack the Communist organ. The FNTA official made clear on this occasion that "*Hoy* may rest assured that no matter how much they (the Communists) twist the facts, organized Cuban workers will not respond with violence but only with statements of true facts."[15]

Finally, mention must be made of a statement made by the Young Catholic Workers (JOC) in the month of July, following some anti-Communist remarks made by President Urrutia. After pointing out its moral authority based on its attitude against the deposed tyranny and its responsible support of the revolutionary government, JOC congratulated President Urrutia for his "Cuban, democratic and revolutionary words" by which the President "refused the support of the Communists and exposed the danger of foreign imperialism which wanted to undermine the forces of the Revolution."[16] The statement concluded by emphasizing that nobody could expect democratic collaboration from an intrinsically anti-democratic group such as the Communist Party.[17] It is interesting to note that exactly two days after the JOC declaration was issued, President Urrutia was forced to resign.

Trade Union Elections

This mounting anti-Communist sentiment found reflection in the local union elections held during the months of April and May, 1959. Through the island, in every "sin-dicato" or local union, the workers cast their ballots in free and orderly elections that seemed to honor Castro's prom-ises of restoring union democracy. At the request of the Labor Minister, the chief of the Rebel Army, Camilo Cien-fuegos, detached members of the Rebel Army to guarantee order and to safeguard trade union rights at the polling places. As a result, only in a few cases was it necessary to postpone elections because of disturbances or accusations of fraud. To be sure, not all the political tendencies were allowed to put up slates of candidates, since trade union leaders who had been elected or remained in office in their unions during the dictatorship were not allowed to take part in the elections.[18]

In a number of cases, the Communist candidates sought to combine their strength with the July 26 Movement forces, but the success of this maneuver was usually determined by the attitude of the local July 26 Movement leadership. Where weak or pro-Communist leaders were in command of the union, "unity" slates were put up; where local leaders disliked the PSP or lacked Marxist inclinations, they tended to follow the recommendations of David Salvador and re-fused to collaborate with the Communists. This meant that, in reality, for the most part the elections boiled down to a contest between Communist and anti-Communist forces.

When the electoral returns were announced it became clear that the July 26 Movement had won an overwhelming victory. Herbert Mathews reported in a 1959 article that the Communists had tried hard to win the election but the July 26 Movement ended up with 90 percent of the trade union elective positions.[19] In some of the most important industries the leaders of the PSP were completely wiped out. At the Havana Provincial Union of Commercial Em-ployees, for instance, the tally showed that 3,700 members had voted for the July 26 Movement and only 29 for the PSP candidature. In other sectors, the Communists won only a few locals or some scattered positions in the executive committees. The balloting in the sugar industry, for example, showed that only eight of the 243 locals were Communist controlled.[20] In one typical case reported by the newspaper *Revolución* (the Tacajó sugar mill) the July 26 Movement obtained 1,559 votes against 102 for the PSP candidates.[21] Even traditionally pro-Communist sectors like the Sindicato de Omnibus Aliados (where Communist leader José María Pérez enjoyed broad support) or the Sindicato de Tabaqueros de la Habana (formerly the stronghold of Lázaro Peña) went decidedly against these leaders.[22] Only in the textile, aviation and hotel and restaurant workers' unions did the Communists score substantial victories.

There is no gainsaying the fact, however, that some of the victories credited to the July 26 Movement were rather dubious or ephemeral ones, as they had been secured by opportunistic or crypto-Marxist leaders whose real ideologies were not yet fully known. This happened, for instance, with the Ariguanabo textile union and the bank workers' unions where the July 26 Movement slates represented by Jesús Soto and J.M. de la Aguilera had won. This explains why some conservative estimates have fixed the real strength of the anti-Communist groups—as they emerged from the local elections—as representing 75 percent of the labor movement.[23]

The national union conventions of June, July and August followed the same anti-Marxist pattern. Of the 33 national unions or federations, 26 elected anti-Communist directorates, three went Communist and the remaining four named executive committees which were divided or non-committed in their orientations.[24] At the first revolutionary national congress of the National Federation of Sugar Workers (FNTA), attended by one thousand delegates representing roughly half a million sugar workers, not a single Communist leader was nominated for the executive committee. Further indications of anti-Marxism came when a motion to censure *Hoy* was approved and the credentials of the veteran Marxist leader, Ursinio Rojas, were rejected.

The National Congress of Construction Workers passed a strongly worded resolution rejecting any form of collaboration with the PSP leaders. Similar resolutions were adopted by the commercial and pharmaceutical workers. In a number of other congresses the PSP minority abstained from the final voting and departed in anger from the meeting rooms. As Ralph Woodward pointed out later, the open attempts of the Communists to push their way into the vacuum created by the removal of the Batista labor leaders had no doubt provoked a strong anti-Communist reaction.[25]

Small wonder that the top PSP leadership showed frustration and disillusionment at the results of the elections. In May, Communist Party Secretary-General Blas Roca, writing in *Hoy*, angrily declared that "the alleged unity at the grass-roots level is a subterfuge to sabotage and combat the unity that is necessary."[26] Lázaro Peña also wrote lengthy articles decrying the non-cooperative posture of the July 26 Movement labor officials. In one of these articles he accused right-wing leaders of promoting the non-unitarian line and sabotaging the revolution.[27] He also charged that pockets of mujalismo survived and that the Communists were about to become "a disfranchised representative minority within the labor movement."[28] By way of response,

Revolución noted that mujalismo had been eliminated from the CTC-R since January 1959 and that Cuba was enjoying for the first time full trade union freedom.[29]

The following month, *Hoy* resumed its attacks on the CTC-R. This time it was Anibal Escalante who complained about the results of the elections and indicated that they had made possible the temporary victory of a counter-revolutionary policy which failed to reflect the real interests of the workers and the revolution. The trade union situation, he added "is one of the weaknesses of the Revolution, probably the main one."[30] *Revolución* replied to these charges by stating in a front page editorial that to be counter-revolutionary meant to oppose the work and laws of the revolution, to favor Batista and the imperialists, and to conspire against the revolutionary government. Since the CTC-R does not engage in any of these activities, the editorial indicated, "it is a calumny to call the labor center counter-revolutionary."[31] The editorial reiterated that the CTC-R was not mujalista because it did not use any of the old methods of the CTC; if there still was any former follower of Mujal hidden in the CTC-R, it added, so there still remained quite a few in the PSP. Finally, *Revolución* suggested that the PSP campaign was aimed at forcing the CTC-R leadership into a high-level unity pact or else discrediting it in the eyes of the rank and file, so that the Communists could then win control of unions.[32]

It would be misleading to think, however, that the quarrel brought about by the trade union elections concerned only the PSP and *Revolución*. The whole episode also served to bring to the surface a more ominous rift involving some of the most important personalities of the revolutionary government: on the one hand, those led by Raúl Castro and Che Guevara who preached unity from above and on the other, those in favor of unity from below (which included all but one of the provincial coordinators of the July 26 Movement). Some of the echoes of this disagreement can also be found in the newspaper *Revolución* of the Spring of 1959.[33]

Castro's Attitude: The Final Stages of Phase One

What was Castro's reaction to the anti-Communist movement and the trade union elections? As mentioned above, fresh denials of Marxist leanings came out in the months of April and May, followed by other pro-democratic assurances throughout the summer. Early in April, for instance, the Prime Minister declared in a televised interview that the fears that some minority groups seemed to have that Communism was growing in Cuba did not correspond to reality.[34] A few days later at Princeton University he declared that his revolution was not based on the principle of class struggle and made clear that he had no intention of doing away with private property.[35] During the same trip to the U.S., Castro encouraged American businessmen to invest in Cuba offering them all possible guarantees. "We are interested in promoting private investments and attracting financial capital," he said at a meeting with U.S. newspaper editors.[36]

There were also references to freedom of the press and the return of other liberties as proof of non-Communism. On one occasion, Castro asked his audience: "Why should we persecute the Communists because they are Communists? It is just like persecuting a Catholic because he is a Catholic."[37] In October, the Prime Minister was still saying that the accusation of Communism was false, adding this time that he regarded such charges as slanderous and treasonous.[38] Coming on the heels of the re-establishment of military tribunals, these remarks acquired particular significance.

As Castro moved up Marxists to key positions in the government, they all proceeded first to proclaim their liberal non-Communist beliefs. Thus, when Antonio Núñez Jiménez, a well-known Marxist, was appointed Executive Director of the National Institute of Agrarian Reform (INRA) he immediately declared: "We are convinced democrats."[39] And shortly afterwards, when Guevara was sworn in as President of the National Bank, he affirmed on the TV, "We can say very loudly that we are not Communists. Our policy is Cubanization."[40]

In the month of September, Castro felt the need to dispel fears on the economic front by attending a banquet offered to him at the Havana Hilton by the representatives of 45 leading business organizations. This was Castro's first appearance in a business meeting after more than nine months of revolution. The prime Minister took advantage of the occasion to indicate that his government was not against any particular class or group and urged businessmen to accept some sacrifices "during the process of adaptation."[41]

Specific denials were also made for the benefit of trade union leaders. When Castro learned of a report presented by David Salvador which was critical of Communist attempts to infiltrate the government, he summoned the provincial secretaries of the CTC-R for consultation. The CTC-R chief in Las Villas Province, C. Rodríguez Quesada, told Castro on that occasion that he agreed with the report and was unalterably opposed to Communism. Castro replied that he was also in agreement with the report and

called the Communists "trouble-makers." Shortly afterwards, however, it was alleged that an army officer, on
Castro's orders, began to investigate Rodríguez's activities
in Las Villas.[42]

There was also an attempt to elaborate on the meaning
of humanism and to define the position of the revolutionary government vis-à-vis contemporary ideological trends.
"We have been placed," said Castro in a televised speech
on May 22, "in a position where we must choose between
capitalism which starves people and Communism which
resolves the economic problems but suppresses the liberties
so greatly cherished by men. Our Revolution is neither
capitalist nor Communist; our Revolution is not red but
olive green, the color of the Rebel Army that emerged
from the heart of the Sierra Maestra."[43]

At the same time, however, the revolution was quickly
radicalizing itself. Schools of revolutionary indoctrination
were opened in July and Raúl Castro announced at the
opening ceremony that "the civil war has not ended, it has
only changed its forms."[44] At the May Day celebrations,
the younger Castro chastised David Salvador for his unwillingness to collaborate with the PSP labor leaders. The
Minister of the Armed Forces did not mention Salvador's
name specifically, but his phraseology indicated that he
was talking about the CTC-R Secretary-General.

Vehement exhortations were constantly addressed to the
working class to remain alert against the enemies of the
revolution. At the July 26 celebrations, thousands of campesinos were asked to raise their machetes as a sign of
willingness to defend the Cuban Revolution at any cost. It
may be noted, in passing, that the whole character of the
celebration was definitely class-oriented and belligerent.
The question of Castro's resignation as Prime Minister or

his return to power was put before a predominantly worker-peasant rally and when the crowd roared its approval, Castro stated that the "greatness and strength of our Revolution lies precisely in its concern for farmers and the downtrodden."[45] But, more explicit and consequential statements were not yet made. If Marxism was gradually becoming the dominant force at work, Castroism was still its only visible manifestation.

There existed, however, a certain disparity between developments in the agricultural and urban informal sectors and developments within organized labor. While most unorganized workers and poor peasants appeared willing to support Castro unconditionally, many sectors of organized labor remained cautious and independent-minded. In giving overwhelming support to David Salvador after his refusal to collaborate with the Communists, the trade union movement appeared to deal a blow to the unity efforts sponsored by the PSP. Further, the workers had established a dangerous precedent which could be followed by other social groups. Indeed, the success attained by non-Communist forces in the labor movement encouraged other sectors of the population to voice their dissatisfaction with the gradual radicalization of the revolution. Radio broadcasters and newspaper columnists became more outspoken; business circles and professional associations formulated strong pro-democratic statements. It did not require too much perspicacity to suspect that trade union events may even have influenced the fateful anti-Communist statement made by President Urrutia as well as the hardening of the position of some military commanders, such as Hubert Matos.[46]

The leaders of the revolution saw the writing on the wall and decided, accordingly, to change their methodology. On the political front, President Urrutia was summarily dismissed in July and Castro's feigned resignation as Prime Minister withdrawn. Urrutia's reputation as an honest judge was immediately subjected to a slanderous campaign personally orchestrated by Castro. The leader of the revolution did not replace, however, President Urrutia but preferred to continue as Prime Minister and to appoint a relatively unknown lawyer, Oswaldo Dorticós, to fill the presidency.[47] Although the premiership post had little significance in the Cuban political tradition, Castro chose to hold this position instead of becoming President of the Republic. This decision brought about a shift in the center of gravity of Cuban politics from the presidency to the premiership; the former became a largely ceremonial post while the latter came to be the effective locus of power. As it turned out, this change did not signal the establishment of a system of Parliamentary democracy but rather foreshadowed drastic changes in Cuban political institutions.[48]

On the labor front, Castro probably thought that the time had come to apply more effective pressures on organized labor and to make provision for his personal intervention in internal trade union affairs. For the first time since his accession to power, he twice openly criticized organized labor leaders. On May 21, in a televised speech, he denounced extremist labor agitators and hinted that there was a collusion between business and certain "demagogic" labor leaders "who were making demands designed to sabotage the Revolution."[49] Four days later he intervened personally to end a hunger strike in the Havana water works and angrily told the strike leaders that he would not accept, under any conditions, impositions or ultimatums; he even tore up the letters of resignation of some 1,500 workers, although he later apologized for his harsh words. In September, at the closing meeting of the

CTC-R National Council, he criticized those workers who in his view were "blocking the path to progress" and told them "to erase ideas from the past from the workers' minds."[50] Other more direct exhortations and pressures were soon going to be applied in connection with the Tenth Congress of the CTC-R.

NOTES

1. See, for instance, James O'Connor, "Political Change in Cuba, 1959–1965," *Social Research* (Albany), Vol. 35, No. 2, Summer 1965, p. 322. See also, *The Origins of Socialism in Cuba, op. cit.,* p. 191.

2. In July 1959, for instance, the CTC-R and the University Students' Federation (FEU) agreed to offer their "joint and utmost support" to the agrarian reform; later at the Tenth Congress in November a motion to support the government agrarian law was unanimously approved.

3. The National Association of Sugar Mill Owners and the National Association of Tobacco Growers, for instance, went on record as supporting agrarian reform (see *Havana Post*, July 10 and July 14, 1959).

4. See *Havana Post*, March 24, 1959, p. 1.

5. *Inter-American Labor Bulletin*, Vol. X, No. 2 (February 1959, p. 1).

6. International Labor Conference: Forty-third Session, *Record of Proceedings*, 1959 (Geneva, 1959), pp. 225–229.

7. ORIT-ICFTU, *Trade Unions and People of Cuba Against Despotism* (Mexico: ORIT Press and Publications Department, 1961), p. 27.

8. *Free Labour World* (March 1959), p. 56.

9. *Havana Post*, February 19, 1959, p. 1.

10. *Havana Post*, May 24, 1959, p. 1.

11. *Ibid.*

12. *Ibid.*

13. *Havana Post*, May 23, 1959, p. 1.

14. *Havana Post*, March 19, p. 1.

15. *Havana Post*, May 25, 1959, p. 1.

16. *Havana Post*, July 19, 1959, p. 1.

17. *Ibid.*

18. See Charles Porter and Robert J. Alexander, *The Struggle for Democracy in Latin America* (New York: Macmillan, 1961), pp. 136–137.

142   *Efrén Córdova*

19. Herbert Mathews, "Cuba 1959," *Bohemia,* Year 51, No. 46, November 15, 1959, p. 8. This article reproduced a paper submitted to a Latin American Forum organized by Stanford University in 1959.

20. *Hispanic American Report,* Vol. XII (July 1959), p. 266.

21. *Revolución,* May 7, 1959, p. 1.

22. See *Revolución,* May 4, 1959, p. 1; May 6, 1959, p. 4, and May 8, 1959, p. 6.

23. See José Alvarez Díaz, et al., *Cuba: Geopolítica y pensamiento económico, op. cit.,* p. 383.

24. See *Hispanic American Report,* Vol. XII (July 1959), p. 266.

25. Ralph Woodward Jr., "Urban Labor and Communism: Cuba," *Caribbean Studies* (Rio Piedras, P.R.), Vol. 3, No. 3, October 1963, p. 34.

26. Quoted by Jay Mallin, *Fortress Cuba, op.cit.,* p. 31

27. Lázaro Peña, "Los redescrubridores de la unidad," *Hoy,* July 16, 1959, p. 1.

28. *Ibid.*

29. "Cuba y la democracia sindical," *Revolución,* July 26, 1959, p. 6.

30. See *Hoy,* August 25, 1959, p. 1.

31. "Ataques comunistas a la CTC," Zona Rebelde, *Revolución,* August 26, 1959, pp. 1 and 19.

32. *Ibid.*

33. See in particular the issues of 4–8 May 1959.

34. *Economic and Social Thought of Fidel Castro, op. cit.,* p. 125.

35. See Jorge Edwards, *Persona non Grata* (Barcelona: Barral Editores, 1973), p. 57. Mr. Edwards was present at the University when Castro delivered his speech. He later became Chile's first chargé d'affaires in Havana during the Allende government.

36. Fidel Castro, *Humanismo revolucionario* (Havana, Editorial Tierra Nueva, 1959), pp. 66 and 83.

37. *Havana Post,* April 3, 1959, p. 1.

38. *Fidel Castro Speaks, op. cit.,* p. 67.

39. *Havana Post,* June 19, 1959, p. 1.

40. *Havana Post,* September 8, 1959, p. 1.

41. *Bohemia,* Year 51, No. 36, September 6, 1959.

42. Carlos Rodríguez Quesada, *David Salvador, Castro's Prisoner* (New York: Labor Committee to Release Imprisoned Trade Unionists, 1961), p. 15.

43. *Fidel Castro Speaks, op. cit.*, p. 220. See also *Havana Post,* May 22, 1959, p. 1.

44. *Havana Post,* July 14, 1959, p. 1.

45. *Havana Post,* July 25, 1959, p. 8.

46. Hubert Matos, who was military chief of the Camagüey Province had charged that the INRA organization in his province was "heavily infiltrated with Communists." See Neil Macaulay, *A Rebel in Cuba. An American Memoir.* (Chicago: Quadrangle Books, 1970, p. 183).

47. Dorticós had previously held for a few months the post of minister without portfolio in charge of drawing up the revolutionary laws. For many years before the revolution he was apparently a bourgeois attorney well connected with the establishment of his home city, Cienfuegos. Relatively few people knew at the time that he had an earlier Communist background and close links with some of the top PSP leaders.

48. This arrangement lasted until 1976 when Castro took over the job of President. By then the presidential office had gained in importance in the Soviet Union and was filled by the Secretary-General of the Communist Party.

49. *Havana Post,* May 22, 1959, p. 1.

50. *Havana Post,* September 15, 1959, p. 1.

VI

The Tenth Congress of the CTC-R

Preparations

Castro before the CTC-R National Council

THE FIRST INKLING OF WHAT LAY AHEAD CAME IN THE MONTH of September with an appearance of Castro before the National Council of the CTC-R. The main theme of Castro's speech was once again the important role of the working class and the need to foster a closer identification between labor and the government. The speech was also significant because in it the Prime Minister announced a switch from a redistribution-oriented policy to a productionist one and launched what was later called Operation Productivity. Even more important, however, was the language used by the Prime Minister which became more explicit and revealing than ever before. As the revolution advanced and the National Congress of the CTC-R approached, the Prime Minister obviously felt the need to drive his message further home by using plain words and clearer metaphors.

Castro began his speech by contrasting the times in which workers were the victims of abuses, exploitation and repression with the situation prevailing in September 1959, when labor was already "a decisive element in the power structure."[1] But the present battle, he indicated, was not for additional pennies or dollars but for rather different objectives. In fact, he added, the "whole destiny of the working class is now at stake." Borrowing from Lenin's views about the state as an instrument of exploitation, Castro said that "the entire state apparatus existed only for the purpose of defending the privileges of those who owned Cadillacs, kept the land unproductive and were the beneficiaries of irresponsible policies." This picture, Castro emphasized, was giving way to a new situation whereby the government defended only the interests of workers and peasants and was squarely on the side of the poor. He repeatedly suggested that he could not care less about the interests of the wealthy and the fortunate and went on to say that "just as the labor movement had a Secretary-General it also had a Prime Minister."

But the workers' accession to power—Castro continued —also entailed some sacrifices as well as the need to increase productivity. Lack of suitable levels of productivity, he stated, was "explainable in the past when workers were being robbed by private employers but was not justified under present conditions in which workers would be cheating themselves." Labor was thus asked to work harder, to engage in the practice of saving and to loan money to the revolutionary government. He also underscored the need to favor, first, the unemployed and those at the bottom of the economic ladder, but stopped short of proposing a wage freeze for the other sectors of the labor force. In fact, he assured the CTC-R Council that the revolutionary government would not deprive labor of any benefit and insisted that "the future was extraordinary."

Two additional features of this speech are noteworthy. One is the introduction of a few Marxian tenets of a simple nature, such as the notion of work as the only source of wealth, the distinction between monetary wages and social wages and the different effects of productivity increases under socialist and capitalist societies. The other was the repeated references to the need to transform the workers' mentality in the light of changing conditions, "so that we can all follow the right path."[2]

Changes in the Labor Ministry

The next step in the preparations for the CTC-R Congress was the removal of Manuel Fernández García as Labor Minister and his replacement by a member of the inner circle, Augusto Martínez Sánchez. Fernández had already been used by the revolutionary leaders to the limit of his unwilling collaboration. Imbued with deep revolutionary fervor and lacking administrative experience he had helped create the atmosphere of confusion and conflict that had characterized the first stages of the revolution. By October 1959, however, he was no longer useful and even represented an obstacle for the development of subsequent phases.

Following the trade union elections, Minister Fernández had been severely criticized by the newspaper *Hoy* on grounds of being prejudiced against Communist candidatures.[3] On several occasions, he had also spoken in favor of harmonious labor-management relations and even emphasized on May Day that the new policy of the Labor Ministry was to lessen tensions between employers and workers. Though somewhat embittered and bizarre in his attitude (Castro would call him, in 1961, a mad anarchist, "anarcoloco"), he was in fact a well intentioned and honest man, a true representative of the liberal breed.

The elimination of the liberals from the Cabinet took place gradually through 1959. It started in February with the removal of Miró Cardona as Prime Minister, continued with the Cabinet shake-ups of June and October and ended in November with the sacking of the top liberal representatives Manuel Ray and Felipe Pazos.

But the change in the Labor Ministry was especially significant because of its influence in the trade union movement and because of the personality of the new Minister. Martínez Sánchez was an obscure, small-town lawyer from the Oriente Province who had been closely associated with Raúl Castro since the days of the guerrilla fighting in Sierra Cristal (the so-called Second Front).[4] His only claim to distinction related to the period when he was the top legal adviser to Raúl Castro and organized a Northern-Oriente labor congress heavily dominated by the Communists. That he was a member of the inner circle was clearly demonstrated by the fact that he was appointed Minister of Defense and, in April, acting Prime Minister during Castro's absence in the U.S. and Latin America.

After his appointment, Minister Martínez immediately endeavoured to reorganize the Ministry of Labor both in terms of structure and personnel. The new organization included various training units (Oficinas de Superación) which were actually intended to step up the indoctrination process. Crash training courses were immediately organized for the benefit of the Ministry's staff and they invariably included a strong political component. Special emphasis was also placed on the dissemination of information among workers and trade unions. The new Minister also made changes in the staff of the Labor Ministry, eliminating a number of officials who were not in sympathy with Marxist philosophy, including two of the survivors of the Granma expedition,[5] and filling key positions with Communist supporters such as Arnaldo Escalona, Candelaria Rodríguez and Juan Leonet.

Another important step taken by the Minister in preparation for the CTC-R Congress elections consisted in building up the status within the Ministry of pro-Communist leaders Jesús Soto and José María de la Aguilera and diminishing the influence of Salvador, González, Plana and other non-Communist and anti-Communist leaders. The idea was to enhance the prestige of the former as potential candidates for the Executive Committee of the CTC-R and to undermine the ability of the latter to perform their functions. While this tactic was executed tardily, i.e., a few weeks before the elections, it was unquestionably well conceived. After all, it was largely through the benefits granted by the Labor Ministry that Cuban labor leaders of Communist and non-Communist orientation had in the past been able to enhance their position vis-à-vis the rank and file.

On the PSP side, the preparations for the congress included fresh and more vigorous appeals for the achievement of "revolutionary unity" as well as intensive mobilization drives. Since the Communists were not satisfied with the results of the local union and national federation elections, they also began to press for a special balloting to choose the delegates to the national congress. This election, they insisted, should be "genuinely democratic" and open to all the affiliates from the various unions.[6] The Communists expected that their superior ability at political organizing would enable them to do well in these elections.

Opponents of the Communists were not idle either. Spurred by the success of the previous electoral contests, they threw themselves into frenzied preparations for the coming meeting. Most of them were convinced that the congress would signify the end of Communist aspirations and were eager to engage in battle with the PSP old guard and its sympathizers. Thus, when the Labor Minister announced his intentions of postponing the CTC-R congress, the non-Communist leaders threatened to resign *en masse* and forced the Minister to rescind his order.[7] Communist officials supported on the contrary the Minister of Labor and criticized those labor leaders who had objected to the proposed postponements.[8]

There was also an element of internal negotiation and personal bickering within the ranks of both non-Communist and pro-Communist leaders. At least five members of the Provisional Executive Committee harbored aspirations to become the next Secretary-General, namely, Salvador, Soto, Aguilera, Louit and Becquer. The position of CTC-R Secretary-General carried considerable power in Cuban politics and this prompted would-be candidates to engage in hectic maneuvers and alignments of forces. A few days before the event, Salvador and Louit appeared to join forces while Aguilera and Soto seemed to work in close collaboration. Becquer remained independent in hopes of gaining support as a "third force" candidate. This element of personal ambitions no doubt added to the dramatic atmosphere that permeated the preparations for the congress and the congress itself.

Composition of the Congress

The elections to designate delegates to the Tenth Congress of the Cuban Confederation of Labor were scheduled for November lst. The day before, however, the Minister of Labor postponed the elections, alleging that to hold them at the scheduled time would prevent the participation of the workers in the search for Camilo Cienfuegos, the Army Chief of Staff who had mysteriously disappeared three days earlier.[9] A new resolution issued by the Labor Ministry prescribed that the local union conventions to elect the delegates should take place within the week of November 2–8. On November 7, the semi-official organ of the Government, *Revolución,* indicated that one million organized workers went to the polls and that elections were being held in an honest, democratic and secure manner.[10] On November 8 neither *Revolución,* nor *Hoy* carried any news about the results of the election on their front pages. *Revolución* reported on page 2 that, according to hundreds of telegrams received, almost all the delegates from the July 26 Movement had been elected.[11] However, other organs of the Havana press provided more specific information on the election returns.

According to these estimates, the July 26 Movement had elected 2,784 of the 3,200 delegates, i.e., 87 percent of the total, while the Communists mustered 224 delegates, or less than 7 percent of the total, and the independent groups 192 or 6 percent.[12] Though subsequent studies offer slightly different figures of the number of Communist delegates, they all agree that the PSP candidates elected represented less than 10 percent of the total number of delegates.[13]

Of course, not all the July 26 Movement delegates were of the same political caliber. While many did appear to profess strong nationalistic and democratic convictions, a number of others lacked firm ideological commitments and were liable to follow last-minute appeals. There is no gainsaying, however, the fact that anti-Communist feelings had gained considerable momentum among both leaders and rank and file, to the point of becoming the chief rallying cry of the congress.

One additional point must be discussed here. An analysis of the list of delegates attending the congress shows that a few hundred of them had also been elected to the Ninth congress held in 1954. Does this mean that Fidel Castro was right in his subsequent allegations about the mujalista penetration and the need to uproot the last vestiges of the past? In fact, the bulk of these delegates were probably not "mujalistas" in the sense of people politically connected with the previous regime; they were simple trade unionists, workers' representatives, business agents and minor union officials who conducted the day-to-day business of the union out of militancy or sheer professionalism. Many of them just happened to enter trade union activities during the ten years of Mujal incumbency; others received training during the Mujal period as they might have received training under any other leadership. The fact that they had chosen to remain in the trade union movement instead of accepting government posts and had now received a renewed mandate from their constituents provided further indication of their political neutrality.[14]

The Congress Proceedings

The congress opened on November 18, the meetings being held at the Convention Hall of the Workers' Palace in Havana. Approximately 3,200 delegates representing 1,800 trade unions claiming to have one and a half million members attended the inaugural session. Conrado Becquer was elected chairman and a credentials committee

was appointed to check the validity of the election certif-
icates. Two days later, this committee reported that the
credentials of only 2,948 delegates were in order. This
report was approved by the assembly.[15]

Attending the congress were also fraternal delegations
from the World Federation of Trade Unions (WFTU) and
the International Confederation of Free Trade Unions
(ICFTU), as well as from ORIT and the Latin American
Confederation of Workers (CTAL). The President of the
latter, Vicente Lombardo Toledano, addressed the Congress and Walter Reuther sent his greetings on behalf of
the UAW. A cable from George Meany conveyed the sol-
idarity and support of the AFL-CIO. Workers' representatives from Communist countries, including the USSR,
Yugoslavia and Albania, were also present as observers.
The Soviet delegation was headed by P.T. Pimenov, then
Chief of the International Department of the All-Union
Central Council of Trade Unions and Member of the Supreme Soviet and later Secretary of the All-Union Central
Council and Member of the Central Committee of the
Communist Party. The Yugoslav representative was Asser
Deleon, Secretary-General of the Confederation of Yu-
goslav Trade Unions.

At the inaugural meeting of the congress, the top level
government figures addressed the convention and made
several suggestions concerning its work. The Minister of
Labor, Augusto Martínez Sánchez emphatically stated that
"the key word on this occasion must be unification."[16] In
his characteristically blunt style, Raúl Castro advised the
delegates that they should "shake the tree" and eliminate
all those that were lukewarm and counter revolutionary;
he added that the proletariat and the Rebel Army were
the same thing.[17] Finally, Fidel Castro delivered one of his
usual long speeches in which, after praising the cohesion

and discipline of the Cuban working class, he stressed that "the congress must be an example of harmony, of revolutionary spirit, of elimination of evils through the tacit agreement of everybody." "Our weakness," he said, "would be to split ourselves." He asked whether there was one single worker who was not in agreement with the revolutionary measures and who was not willing to defend the revolution. He next alluded to the latest political developments, and emphasized that the role of the working class was decisive to the country and that the revolution was in its hands. Castro also suggested that nothing would please the enemies of the revolution more than the spectacle of division and rift within the congress. "Workers and peasants," he pointed out towards the end of his speech, "must be organized in battalions to defend the Revolution and a battalion should not fight against other battalions. In the Army of the Workers there must be discipline, brotherhood and unity."[18]

Shortly after Castro's speech, a unity slate of candidates, including the Communists, was informally submitted to the delegates by a few members of the Provisional Executive Committee of the CTC-R. Both the Minister of Labor and Raúl Castro strove earnestly to get the congress to accept it. A letter written by Octavio Louit to the Chief of Police during Batista's time, in which he pleaded to be left alone, "since he had sufficiently cooperated," was shown to the delegates supporting him so as to discredit him. A photograph showing the Secretary-General of the Artists' Union, Manuel Fernández, in the company of a police captain of the Batista regime, was also widely circulated. To complement these devices, Lázaro Peña rented premises in a hotel near the Workers' Palace and from there developed the strategy to be applied.[19] But no matter how intense the efforts made, the fact is that anti-Communist feelings kept running high. On November 20, for instance, the Labor Section of the Auténtico Party announced its rejection of the unity slate "because such candidature would imply the participation of Communists and other totalitarian groups."[20] Similar categoric statements were made public by the leaders of the commercial, hospital and pharmaceutical employees.[21]

At the first all-night session a riot broke out when the delegates learned that three well-known Communists were to be nominated among the candidates to the Executive Committee. At the same time, representatives of 22 of the 33 national federations met and decided not to accept any Communist leader in the said Committee. This decision was supported by three more federations,[22] and Castro was notified of it through David Salvador. It should be noted that the resolution adopted by this group included the decision to withdraw from the CTC-R if the Communists were included in the proposed slate.[23] This was evidently something more than a bureaucratic competition for leadership; it was a clear indication of a basic trade union reaction to an attempt to manipulate the labor movement for political purposes. Anti-Communist feelings were indeed so strong that on one occasion the assembly hall remained for more than ten hours occupied by July 26 Movement delegates who displayed anti-Communist banners and vociferously expressed their rejection of Marxism. Copies of a pamphlet documenting the old Communist alliance with Batista were also circulated.[24]

The unity slogan appealed, of course, to a considerable number of delegates, who wanted a strong and broadly representative labor movement. Most of them resented, however, the imposition of such unity through bloc arrangements in which the PSP group was treated on equal footing with the July 26 Movement. While many other delegates were not opposed to the idea of unity, they soon realized that the question of the independence of the trade union movement vis-à-vis the government was also at stake and this became an even more important issue.

According to the report of a Uruguayan labor leader present, the only foreign delegate who was hissed and whose statements provoked protests was the workers' delegate of the USSR.[25] The Soviet delegate, P.T. Pimenov, drew the delegates disapproval by making two mistakes. One was his interminable listing of clinics, rest homes, etc., run by the official unions in his country. The other was his irritating attack on the ORIT representative, Daniel Benedict, who had just spoken. The latter defended the right of all countries to self-determination—including Yugoslavia, then being menaced by the USSR—and after thanking the Cuban metalworkers and the CTC-R congress for their telegrams of support to long-striking U.S. steelworkers, expressed his assurance that both Cuban and U.S. metalworkers would back their Soviet counterparts so that they could obtain the right to strike. For some reason, this infuriated Pimenov, who lost his temper and antagonized his audience.

The open rejection of the Communists forced the revolutionary leaders to change their plans. Instead of proposing unity with the "old guard" of the PSP, Castro and his associates sought to promote the nomination of new leaders liable to give unconditional support to the revolution. Raúl Castro, in particular, tried to push the candidacy of José María de la Aguilera as Secretary-General of the CTC-R. However, this maneuver met immediately with the same heavy opposition within the congress that the previous one had encountered. Fidel Castro's remark that his revolution was not red but olive green inspired a typical Cuban rejoinder: "The Revolution is really like a melon," people said, "green outside, red inside." So as part of the demonstrations, many delegates brought to the convention watermelons which they held aloft while chanting: "Melones!" "Melones!" in defiance of the pro-Communists.[26]

Castro's Second Intervention

When all other procedures had failed, the Government resorted to the authority and charismatic attraction of Fidel Castro. After the closing session of the congress had been postponed on three occasions the Prime Minister again appeared before it near midnight of the 22nd. He spoke in the midst of an extraordinary and gripping tension made even more dramatic by the security measures taken. Castro began by recognizing that he had been advised not to go to the congress due to the conditions prevailing in it. He characterized the convention as a "shameful spectacle" and a "lunatic asylum"[27] and lamented that workers' delegates had reacted so vigorously against those who had done so much for them.[28] Moreover, he admitted that the Revolutionary Government was running the risk of a severe moral blow.[29]

The Prime Minister went on to accuse those who shouted and insulted the government of being counter revolutionaries, at the same time that he expressed his conviction that he was able to understand, and be understood by, the "true" worker of Cuba.[30] Then he elaborated on the meaning of the July 26 Movement, indicating that he was more capable of comprehending its objectives than any other person. If, in the name of that movement, he added, a blow were to strike the revolution, then July 26 would no longer be a glorious date but would become a symbol of treason. Furthermore, he pointed out that the mere fact that the principal leaders of the labor movement had been worried about the presence of the Prime Minister in the congress was in itself a disgrace. Later on, he confessed that at the beginning of his speech he was afraid that he would not be able to keep on talking to the congress and that this was a hard and unpleasant feeling. "I cannot help but feel unhappy when I see that the working class is denying itself the chance to defend and lead the Revolution," he added. A few paragraphs later he insisted that the working class should turn into an army to defend the revolution and that an army has no room for factions. Yet he made it clear that while he recommended harmony, he did not propose the making of any specific pact; what counted, he stressed, was the election of "true revolutionary leaders" and the elimination of dead-wood. For the working class, he insisted, had a political role to perform and the leaders should be able to understand it.

At the end of his speech Castro asked whether the working class was willing to respond to the revolutionary appeal. In one dramatic paragraph he mentioned King Solomon's judgment about the division of the disputed child and said that if he could not count on the support of the entire working class, he was not interested in receiving a portion of it. He mentioned the power of the enemy and suggested that it was possible that reactionary circles were using the Tenth Labor Congress as a dagger to stab at the heart of the Cuban Revolution. He then proposed that the assembly confer an ample vote of confidence on a qualified person who should be responsible "before the workers and before us," i.e., before the working class and the government. Acknowledging the repeated clamor of the delegates in support of David Salvador, Castro finally submitted his name to the assembly. Castro's words were met with louder and more enthusiastic expressions of support for Salvador, but the Prime Minister insisted on knowing whether his nomination was made unanimously by the congress or by a majority. The assembly finally unanimously approved the vote of confidence in David Salvador to select the Executive Committee.[31]

It was apparent that Castro's second intervention represented a determined attempt to preserve Communist influence by imposing unity from the top. Once again, the Prime Minister had staged a superb performance of deceit, anger and persuasion. He had spoken under the most difficult circumstances and before the most hostile crowd he had ever faced. His speech was frequently interrupted by angry catcalls and yells from the delegates. He was visibly furious at the beginning and at one point even suggested that opponents of revolutionary unity were "the echo of counter-revolutionary voices originating perhaps from the chorus of war criminals."[32] But he later managed to regain composure and to develop the full strength of his arguments. The delegates, mostly hostile at the beginning, were finally swayed by the Prime Minister's words and prepared to accept some compromise solutions.

A lengthy recess followed Castro's intervention, during which Salvador, the Prime Minister and the Minister of Labor gathered in the office of the *Revolución* editor, Carlos Franqui. Thus far, only six federations had shown indications of accepting a coalition with the Communists (aviation, banks, textile, wood cutting, cattle raising and hotel and restaurant) and twenty-six were firmly opposed to any such arrangement, while the Executive Committee of the National Federation of Sugar Workers (FNTA) had adopted a cautious stand, intimating its intention of accepting "any decision" taken by the Provisional Executive Committee of the CTC-R.[33] In the light of those circumstances, David Salvador and his companions apparently decided to present a slate in which neither the well known Communists nor the well known anti-Communists were included. The Catholic leaders González and Plana were therefore dropped and so were the Communist leaders of the "old guard." David Salvador was retained as Secretary-General and four of the previous members (Pellón, Louit, Soto and Aguilera) were also put up for renomination. The rest of the twenty-two members of the Executive Committee were unknown and second rate labor leaders. Suffice it to indicate that the second and third slots were given to two virtual non-entities called Noelio Morell and Armando Cordero.

When the final list was presented to the plenary, the Communists announced their intention of abstaining from voting. Speaking through one of its spokesmen, Faustino Calcines, the PSP disclaimed any responsibility for the new Executive Body and conditioned eventual Communist support for the new leadership on the way in which it implemented the resolutions adopted by the congress. Calcines made it clear that the PSP was in full agreement with Castro's speech, but indicated that the new Committee did not reflect Castro's recommendations. It may be noted that, according to the weekly *Bohemia,* Calcines encountered some difficulties in reading the document because of continuous heckling from the audience. At one point during his speech the Chairman had to remind the delegates that Calcines was a duly elected representative and was entitled to speak from the floor.[34]

At 5 a.m. on November 23, after 18 hours of continuous plenary session, the congress finally approved the proposed slate. The delegates were physically exhausted and were willing to accept, or did not pay attention to, the fact that three of the key positions in the Executive Committee were in "pro-Communist" hands, i.e., those of Secretary of Organization, Secretary of Press and Propaganda and Secretary of International Relations. The first position involved the internal control of union affairs, the second one was in charge of press releases and of the official publications of the CTC-R, and the third would facilitate closer relations between the Cuban labor movement and the pro-Soviet international labor organizations. Soto, Aguilera and Alvarez de la Campa were respectively appointed to these posts.

Resolutions

Almost forgotten in the turmoil of the elections were the resolutions adopted by the congress. While they were rather different in character, most tended to reflect the national liberation stage of the revolution. To begin with, the congress had approved a resolution disaffiliating the CTC-R from ORIT and ICFTU, and proposing the establishment of a new trade union international organization composed exclusively of Latin American workers. The disaffiliation from ORIT was proposed by delegate Conrado Rodríguez and recommended by one of the congress' committees on grounds of ORIT's "identification with imperialism" and the criticisms it had addressed to the revolution. Upon learning about this resolution, ORIT's representative Daniel Benedict indicated that "even if Cuba is no longer a member of ORIT, ORIT will continue to support the positive aspects of the Revolution."[35]

Cuba's withdrawal from ORIT, though included in Salvador's report to the congress, had been anticipated by the President of the Republic, Oswaldo Dorticós, who 24 hours before the opening of the congress, made a public statement against the ICFTU regional branch, accusing it of being an instrument of Yankee imperialism and of having supported Latin American dictatorships.[36] At the same time, government supporters within the labor movement launched a plan for organizing a Latin American confederation of labor under revolutionary leadership to supplant and absorb existing regional organizations.[37] Other manifestations of anti-U.S. feelings were to be found in many of the resolutions passed by the delegates, including a protest against the U.S. Government for the alleged arming of planes on American territory for attacks on Cuba and discrimination against Cuban workers in the wages paid to laborers of the Guantánamo Naval Base.[38] There was also an expression of the congress' support for American steel workers then engaged in a long strike. All these resolutions were in keeping with the radical attitude of Salvador and his followers and reflected the tense atmosphere that prevailed in the congress. It is interesting to note in this respect that many militant anti-Communists were not entirely happy with Salvador's behavior during the congress and at one moment they even sponsored the candidacy of Octavio Louit for Secretary-General.[39] Ironically, within a few months Salvador would be heading a combative anti-Castro group and Octavio Louit would be regarded as one of the principal figures of the Communist labor hierarchy.

There were also some "revolutionary" resolutions dealing with domestic affairs. One of them recommended to the government to postpone the holding of general elections "until the country was on the road to honesty, economic security and social well-being." Others requested organized labor to invest 4 percent of wages in government industrialization bonds. As mentioned earlier, the congress also approved resolutions concerning the nationalization of certain enterprises. The Prime Minister expressed satisfaction with these resolutions and with the workers' determination to back and finance his government plans.[40] He further announced his intention to float a savings bonds issue with a view to capitalizing $200 million in five years.[41]

A few other resolutions retained the traditional businesslike nature of the Cuban labor movement. Included in this group were the resolutions relating to a Christmas bonus for commercial employees, a raise in minimum pensions, a one-year ban on strikes and the construction of a housing project for railway workers. There was even a resolution aimed at reintroducing the check-off system but this was never implemented despite the voluntary character of the proposed scheme. Not approved by the congress was a proposal to increase the monthly minimum wage to $100.00, which was rejected on grounds of its incompatibility with the government economic policies.

Of crucial importance to subsequent developments was a congress resolution aimed at ridding the labor movement of spurious elements. This resolution had not been officially submitted by any delegate but suggested by the Castro brothers and the Minister of Labor. Fidel Castro, in particular, had pointed out in the course of his second speech the need "to use a broom to sweep away the mujalista elements" and this suggestion met with thunderous applause.[42] Its spontaneous approval by the congress was later construed as a mandate to the Executive Committee to carry out a house cleaning operation within the labor movement.

At first glance, the approval of this resolution was rather puzzling. It was generally assumed in November 1959 that the leadership of the whole Cuban Workers' Confederation (CTC-R), down to the level of local unions, had by that time been purged of Batista's appointees and collaborators.[43] The newspaper *Revolución,* for instance, had explicitly pointed out a few months earlier that mujalismo had been eliminated from the CTC since January 1959.[44] Moreover, the credentials committee of the Tenth Congress had raised no objections with respect to the background or trade union record of nearly 3,000 delegates. As will be seen in the next chapter, the purification resolution was actually meant to be an instrument to secure quick government control of the labor movement.

Balance

In appraising the significance of the congress, one thing remains absolutely clear, namely, that the anti-Communists would have scored an overwhelming victory over the Marxist groups had Fidel Castro not appeared before the congress to block a free election and demand a vote of confidence. That the Tenth Congress should be regarded, in any case, as a defeat for Communism and a setback for Castro was recognized at that time by the foreign and national press. *The New York Times* indicated, that through the confused atmosphere of the congress, one could see how the Communists were thwarted in their attempts to secure positions in the Executive Committee of the CTC-R.[45] Another New York Newspaper, *The Daily Mirror* observed that while Castro was successful in agitating the masses, he did not have similar effectiveness with the leaders.[46] The weekly *América* (New York) reported that the Tenth Congress was ostensibly a defeat for Communism and perhaps also for Castro.[47] The *Havana Post* said that the majority of the delegates disregarded Castro's appeal for unity.[48] The Cuban papers — *Presna Libre, Información* and *Diario de la Marina*—dealt at length with the topic, pointing out that a great majority of the 33 national federations courageously endeavored to reject the Communist elements that were seeking to control the labor movement.[49] *Diario de la Marina* further indicated that the congress had been a democratic one until the moment of Castro's intervention; thereupon, it added, the congress took place under government pressure.[50]

A closer examination of the congress proceedings show, however, that Castro managed to score some important points. First, he succeeded in avoiding a vote within the congress which would have inevitably led to the election of an anti-Communist leadership of the CTC-R. Secondly, he was able to place some unconditional supporters in key positions of the labor movement. Thirdly, and most important, he had effectively silenced the July 26 Movement wing, as none of its more energetic and outspoken leaders (save Salvador) had been included in the CTC-R directorate. All the rising young leaders who had expressed opposition to Marxism, such as Humberto Escandón (commercial workers), Gabriel Hernández (pharmaceutical workers) and Luis Moreno (tobacco workers) had in effect been dropped altogether. So had the articulate Catholic leaders Plana and González. Instead, the Committee had been padded with a number of obscure, second-rate leaders whom Castro and his colleagues certainly expected would prove more amenable to going along with government policies. Fourthly, Castro and his associates had successfully introduced the "purification" resolution, which was soon to be fateful for the future of the Cuban labor movement. Finally, the frantic maneuvers within the congress and its bedlam-like atmosphere brought to light the real thinking and position of many leaders and delegates. The government had taken note of this and was now in a position to launch a series of organized and planned purges with a view to eliminating anti-Communist elements from the labor movement.

NOTES

1. *Fidel en la CTC. Discurso a los trabajadores, op. cit.*, p. 10.
2. *Ibid.*, p. 26.
3. For a typical PSP attack on Minister Fernández, see the article "Con cien ojos." *Hoy,* 19 June 1959, p. 1.
4. Guerrilla activities in Oriente Province broke out first in the Sierra Maestra and later extended to the Sierra Cristal on the north coast.
5. Fernando Sánchez Amaya and César Gómez (Chief of Labor Inspection and Under-Secretary of Labor, respectively). Also dismissed was the other Under-Secretary, Carlos Varona, a competent and prestigious non-Communist official who had actively participated in the underground movement against Batista.
6. See Carlos Fernández, "Un Congreso que sea democrático," *Hoy,* September 6, 1959, p. 3. This appeal was warmly greeted a few days later by José M. de la Aguilera (see *Hoy,* September 12, 1959, p. 1).
7. See Paul D. Bethel, *Cuba and U.S. Policy* (Washington: Citizens' Committee for a Free Cuba, 1966), pp. 27 and 28; see also Jay Mallin, *Fortress Cuba, op. cit.*, p. 32.
8. See, for instance, Carlos Fernández, "¿Independencia de qué?" *Hoy,* 5 November 1959, p. 3.
9. *Revolución,* November 2, 1959, p. 1. Cienfuegos was returning by plane from Camagüey where he had come in connection with the detention of Hubert Matos who had asked Castro for permission to leave military service on grounds that he disagreed with the Communist orientation of the government. In his letter of resignation Matos made the following statement: "Everyone who has spoken frankly to you about the Communist problem has had to leave or be dismissed." Whether Cienfuegos failed to convince Matos to stop his criticisms of the Marxist penetration or was persuaded by the latter of the growing seriousness of the situation, remains a mystery. While Cienfuegos' disappearance was officially attributed to an accident, some sus-

168   *Efrèn Córdova*

picions of foul play have since been formulated. (See, for instance, G. Cabrera Infante, *Vista del amanecer en el trópico* (Barcelona: Seix Barral, 1974, p. 195). It should also be noted that two days after Cienfuegos' disappearance Havana newspapers carried the news of the accidental shooting and death of his close collaborator and aide-de-camp Captain Cristino Naranjo.

10. *Ibid.,* November 7, 1959, p. 6.

11. *Ibid.,* November 9, 1959, p. 2.

12. See *Havana Post,* November 10, 1959, p. 1.

13. Rodríguez Quesada, Monahan and Gilmore calculated that the number of Communist delegates did not exceed 150 (see Rodríguez Quesada, *op. cit.,* p. 18 and Monahan and Gilmore *op. cit,* p. 71). The 170 figure is offered by Karol (*op. cit.,* p. 101) and Suárez (*op. cit.,* p. 65). Carlos Franqui estimated that the number of Communist delegates was 200 (*Retrato de familia con Fidel,* Barcelona: Seix Barral, 1981, p. 121). Boris Goldenberg put the Communist strength at 206 delegates (*The Cuban Revolution* and *Latin America, op. cit.,* p. 190). Hugh Thomas indicated that Communist delegates numbered 260 (*op. cit.,* p. 1,250) and M. Zeitlin and R. Scheer put the figure at 265 (*Cuba: Tragedy in Our Hemisphere,* New York: Grove Press, Inc., 1963, p. 121).

14. There was also the possibility of equating "mujalismo" to business unionism but in this count 90 percent of Cuban workers were to be considered guilty.

15. *Revolución,* November 20, 1959, pp. 1 and 15.

16. *Revolución,* November 19, 1959, pp. 1 and 2.

17. *Ibid.*

18. *Dos discursos del Comandante Fidel Castro, op. cit.,* pp. 7–14; *Revolución,* November 19, 1959, pp. 1 and 2.

19. Cuban Economic Research Project (CERP), *Labor Conditions in Communist Cuba, op. cit.,* p. 115.

20. *Diario de la Marina,* November 20, 1959, p. 14.

21. "Bajo la bandera del 26 de julio el nuevo ejecutivo de la CTC." *Bohemia,* No. 48, November 29, 1959, p. 62.

22. *Havana Post,* November 21, 1959, p. 1.

23. Acuña, *op. cit.,* p. 29.

24. Mallin, *op. cit.*, p. 33.

25. Acuña, *op. cit.*, p. 33.

26. See Monahan and Gilmore, *op. cit.*, p. 72; Wittemore, *op. cit.*, p. 25; Mallin, *op. cit.*, p. 33. See also "Bajo la bandera del 26 de julio el nuevo ejecutivo de la CTC," *op. cit.*, p. 62.

27. *Dos discursos*, *op. cit.*, p. 43.

28. Franqui, *Retrato de familia con Fidel*, *op. cit.*, p. 493.

29. *Dos discursos*, *op. cit.*, p. 44.

30. *Ibid.*, p. 45.

31. *Ibid.*, p. 60.

32. See Bethel, *Cuba and U.S. Policies*, *op. cit.*, p. 26.

33. *Diario de la Marina*, November 22, 1959, p. A2.

34. "Bajo la bandera del 26 de julio el nuevo ejecutivo de la CTC." *Bohemia*, *op. cit.*, p. 78.

35. *Ibid.*, p. 62.

36. *Revolución*, November 18, 1959, p. 1; ORIT-ICFTU, *Trade Unions and People of Cuba*, *op. cit.*, p. 14.

37. See William Benton, *The Voice of Latin America* (New York: Harper Brothers, 1961), p. 89.

38. *Revolución*, November 20, 1959, pp. 1 and 15.

39. *Diario de la Marina*, November 21, 1959, pp. 1–2.

40. *Dos discursos*, *op. cit.*, p. 12.

41. *Havana Post*, November 20, 1959, pp. 1 and 6.

42. *Revolución*, November 22, 1959, pp. 1, 7 and 8.

43. Maurice Halperin, *The Rise and Decline of Fidel Castro: An Essay in Contemporary History* (Berkeley, Los Angeles, London: University of California Press, 1972), p. 31.

44. "Cuba y la democracia sindical," *Revolución*, July 26, 1959, p. 6.

45. *New York Times*, November 23, 1959, p. 22.

46. *Daily Mirror*, November 23, 1959, p. 15.

47. *América*, Vol. 102, No. 304 (December 5, 1959), p. 3.

48. *Havana Post*, November 24, 1959, p. 1.

49. See, for instance, *Diario de la Marina*, November 21, 1959, p. 12.

50. *Ibid.*, November 25, 1959, pp. 1 and 2.

VII

Castro Turns to the Use of Direct Methods

Purges

Role of the Revolutionary Elite

FROM THE RESULTS OF THE TENTH CONGRESS, CASTRO MUST have drawn the conclusion that a more direct form of intervention was necessary in order to secure a firm control over the labor movement. Up to this point, the Prime Minister had had to work almost in stealth on developing his strategy concerning the Cuban labor movement. He had preached trade union unity, and counted on the success of his unconditional supporters while consolidating his personal appeal to the working classes. But the unmistakable signs of independence, outspokenness and growing opposition to Marxism that he had witnessed during the congress must have convinced him that he could not wait any longer to assume the control of the trade union movement. His revolution was moving fast in all other areas and particularly on the agrarian front (where the Institute for Agrarian Reform (INRA) was rapidly becoming an all-powerful agency) and in the dramatic expansion of the public sector. How could he afford to leave unguarded the most crucial flank of the revolution, that concerning the control of organized labor?

Other circumstances appeared to warrant a change in Castro's strategy. In the first place, those who were in favor of a government domination of the labor movement could now count on the "house cleaning" resolution adopted by the congress with a view to eliminating the mujalista elements. Though the meaning of this resolution was open to different interpretations, it undoubtedly provided an effective instrument for the launching of a campaign of purges. In the second place, the anti-Communist leaders had acted during the congress in a somewhat visible and over-confident fashion, thus becoming easy targets for possible reprisals. Finally, Castro now felt more secure and confident than before, as he had already placed some of his most trusted collaborators in the commanding positions of the government. He felt so secure, indeed, that at the end of November he indicated that his revolution was then much stronger than in January and he even regarded it as invincible.[1]

That the switch to more drastic tactics was actively sponsored by the government appears to be beyond any doubt. As mentioned in the previous chapters, Castro himself initiated the process when, in his second speech before the congress, he proposed the total eradication of the last vestiges of, "mujalismo" and "immorality" within the labor movement. His words intimated that "cleaning" was not a one-day task and that a complete uprooting of mujalismo required "surgical work to be performed with a surgical knife."[2] It should be added that the Prime Minister reiterated his exhortations to wipe out mujalistas, counter-revolutionaries and the like, on December 15 before the sugar workers and on December 20 before the commercial employees. On the former occasion, the Prime Minister

lashed out at the newspapers' criticism of the reorganization of the labor movement. The newspaper *Avance* had
published an editorial entitled "Democracy Made in Moscow" in which editor Jorge Zayas decried the way union
leaders were being deprived of their elected positions. The
editorial infuriated Fidel Castro, who called it libelous and
questioned the moral authority of those who dared to criticize his regime and kept silent over the sins of mujalismo:

> What right do they have to attack the Revolution when the
> CTC is just complying with the order of its National Con-
> gress—which is in turn the reflection of the will of all Cuban
> workers—to eradicate counterrevolutionaries from the la-
> bor movement, now that the fatherland is in danger and
> needs loyal men instead of those whose history makes them
> unreliable.[3]

In the December 20 speech, delivered at the Blanquita
theater,[4] the Prime Minister referred to the growing counterrevolutionary activity and advised his audience to be
watchful and to denounce any suspicious movement. He
also made clear that:

> For each servitor of the wealthy people who attacks the
> Revolution there is a working man who must defend it and
> be willing to look after its progress and see to it that no
> one blocks its path towards the general well-being.[5]

Castro's recommendations were followed up by the Minister of Labor's actions. At the inauguration of the new

CTC-R leadership on December 1st, Martínez Sánchez attacked the trade union leaders who tried to divide the trade union movement and reminded the Executive Committee of the need to eradicate the mujalistas and "batistianos" still hiding in the local and national unions.[6] Two weeks later, at the December 15 meeting of the sugar workers, Minister Martínez Sánchez expressed his belief that not a single mujalista would be left as a result of the coming shake-up.[7]

Implementation of the Tenth Congress Resolution

Small wonder that the "purification" process was immediately set in motion. Only a week after its inauguration, the Executive Committee of the CTC-R decided to suspend the trade union rights of the Secretary-General of the Federation of Artists (Show Business) (ACAT), Manolo Fernández, who was accused of having participated in social gatherings with police officers of the dictatorship. Fernández, who during the congress had actively opposed the unity slate with the Communists, had come under fire since the end of November when a press campaign was launched against him.[8] Though his suspension was subject to ratification by the general assembly of the Federation, the CTC-R leadership made it clear that if the ratification should fail to materialize, the Federation would be expelled from the CTC-R.[9] Finally, on December 15, the general assembly of the Federation expelled Fernández from the post for which he had been elected in June and disqualified him as a labor leader for ten years.

Various developments should be highlighted in connection with the latter meeting. Though the majority of the members attending the December 15 meeting appeared to be against the ousting of Fernández,[10] the accused leader chose to resign, bowing to the advice of some of his supporters who wanted to avoid a split within the union. Following the withdrawal of Fernández and his supporters, the remaining participants decided to expel the whole Executive Committee of the ACAT. This was indeed a bizarre decision, inasmuch as the evidence produced against the union Secretary-General was of a personal character and related specifically to his individual acquaintances. It is also interesting to indicate that the deposed leaders were replaced by Violeta Casals, Paco Salas and other Communists of long standing. Finally, note should also be taken of the fact that once the relevant resolutions were approved, the meeting decided, on Jesús Soto's proposal, to send a telegram to the Prime Minister advising him of the successful beginning of the "purification" process.[11]

The example of Fernández's expulsion was promptly imitated. During the following weeks, various national federations and local unions held special assemblies to pass judgment on the revolutionary fitness and past history of their leaders. The steps taken were usually the same. As a point of departure, there was a campaign of innuendos and criticisms which sometimes amounted to character assassination. So aggressive indeed was this campaign that in the cases of the Secretary-General of the Hardware and Glass Factories Workers' Union and the Federation of Hospital and Pharmaceutical Workers, the whole Executive Committee resigned in protest against the public smearing of their leaders.[12] Following the smear campaign, special stress was laid on equating opposition to the purges with counterrevolutionary activity. This was hinted at by the Minister of Labor, for instance, in two speeches delivered before trade union meetings.[13] Every effort was also made to broaden the initial reasons for the purges with a view to including anti-Communist leaders not connected with the pre-1959 mujalista leadership. In the case of the tobacco workers' leader Antonio Morejón, for instance, the reason invoked by his critics was that the accused leader had addressed a petition to the Ministry of Labor in 1955 asking protection for certain rights of his constituents;[14] in another case the Secretary-General of the National Federation of Musicians was expelled for "conduct contrary to the interests of the sector concerned."[15] Finally, special care was taken to proceed with the purges on an individual basis, so as to avoid over-all reactions within the labor movement.

There is reason to believe that David Salvador went along at the beginning with the "purification" process but later withheld his cooperation when he perceived the magnitude of the changes the government had in mind. The CTC-R chief had personally participated in the sacking of Manolo Fernández and had expressed support for the elimination of the mujalista officials in various labor meetings. However, he probably realized afterwards that the resolution approved by the congress was being used by Jesús Soto and the Minister of Labor to sweep away all forms of opposition within organized labor. By the month of January he was already engaged in a polemic with Soto about the scope and significance of the congress resolution. Soto had pointed out the urgency of proceeding inflexibly to implement the resolution at all levels of the trade union movement. Quoting from Castro's speech, Soto also insisted on the need for a complete uprooting of counterrevolutionary and mujalista elements.[16] Salvador replied that remnants of mujalismo existed only in a few organizations and that it was also necessary to carry on with the other important tasks that the labor movement was supposed to perform in support of the revolutionary government.[17]

It was largely as a result of this polemic that the new Executive Committee of the CTC-R met on January 7, 1960, to discuss the "purification" problem. The Committee adopted a resolution proposed by Jesús Soto empowering the CTC-R leadership to purge any official or member of any affiliated organization whom they considered mujalista or counterrevolutionary. A "Committee for the Purification of Trade Unions," made up of Salvador, Soto, Aguilera, Alvarez de la Campa, Pellón and Louit, was appointed to hear the accusations, gather relevant evidence and transmit this information to the unions and federations concerned, where workers were to meet in general assemblies to decide whether or not to expel their leaders. The Committee was supposed to meet twice a week and the accused persons were entitled to make presentations only when the evidence appeared to be flimsy or insufficient.[18] It was thus clear from the outset that respect for due process was not going to be a prime concern of the Committee.

It is important to recall that the January 7 meeting of the Executive Committee was attended by the President of the Republic and the Minister of Labor. Also instrumental in facilitating the passage of the "clean-up" resolution was the atmosphere of collective hysteria provoked by growing counterrevolutionary action as well as the confused state of affairs still prevailing with respect to Castro's ultimate aims. Many members of the Executive Committee were still sincerely convinced that Castro's denunciations of the mujalista threat were part of his efforts to protect the country against counterrevolutionary and anti-patriotic activities. As it turned out however, the power granted to remove counterrevolutionaries was mainly used to eliminate all those leaders who had shown anti-Communist feelings. As mentioned before, the events of the Tenth Congress served in the long run to further the government objectives. By identifying themselves as outspoken opponents of the Marxist line, the liberal and democratic leaders had, in effect, signed their death warrants as trade unionists. They had come to the attention of their opponents at an early stage and this enabled the regime to decapitate the opposition before it could take a definite form. Moreover, the selection of an Executive Committee filled with unknown and second rate leaders had debilitated at the top the resistance power of organized labor.

During the first period, the purges were aimed primarily at the most prominent leaders of the federations. Two months after the beginning of the purges, the CTC-R Executive Committee announced the holding of special assemblies to elect the replacements of the secretary generals of six federations (Construction Workers, Tobacco Workers, Musicians, Medical Workers, Barbers and Show Business).[19] By April, more than twenty-five top leaders of the July 26 Movement, *auténtico, orthodox, independent or Christian* affiliation had been expelled and subsequently forced to leave the country or put under arrest.[20] At a later stage, however, the purges reached down to the level of local leaders and simple unionists, as was the case with the Tiles and Quarry Workers' Union, where a CTC-R press release in late March contained a long list of trade-unionists which were about to be expelled from the union.[21] Robert Alexander estimates that the secretaries general of approximately 1,400 of the country's 2,490 unions and at least half of the nation's 34 national industrial federations were removed by the "purges" committee.[22] According to the testimony of Carlos Franqui, who as Editor of the newspaper

Revolución was involved in the turmoil of the early months of 1960, 90 percent of the union leaders democratically elected a few months before were ruthlessly removed from their offices during the purges.[23] Franqui's estimate may not be entirely accurate, but it gives a clear idea of the magnitude of the purges and the firmness of the government's determination to rid the CTC-R of individuals held to be opposed to Castro's intentions.

The procedures utilized were for the most part irregular. In the National Agricultural Federation, a secret meeting of 24 Marxist delegates was held without notifying the remaining 350 delegates. Subsequently it was announced by the press that the Secretary-General had been expelled by majority vote.[24] In the Federation of Tobacco Workers (FNTT), the ousting of its two principal leaders was so anomalous that it gave rise to strong public protests. The Executive Committee of that Federation issued a statement claiming that Jesús Soto had never consulted with them nor informed them of any irregularity. Soto had unilaterally called a meeting of the FNTT, presided over it and with only a minority of members present, decided on the expulsion of the legally elected officials. The Acting Secretary-General of the CTC-R, Noelio Morell, became so enraged with the procedure utilized that he felt obliged to declare the assembly illegal and refused to accept the new members.[25] Mr. Morell's fit of rage did not affect the government recognition of the new leadership, but was probably a significant factor in his subsequent decline as an important labor leader.

Another tactic used to depose union officials without taking into account the will of the membership was changing the announced meeting place at the last moment. This device provided the opportunity to confuse the workers

concerned and to pack the meeting with Communist sympathizers even though they did not belong to the trade
union in question. It was effectively used in the Oil and
Petroleum Federation.[26] Fraudulent changes often affected also the time of the meeting with the result that "the
democrats arrived half an hour after the Communists to
find that all decisions had been taken". This technique had
been followed by Communist Parties with equal success in
Eastern Europe and was the main contribution by the (PSP)
Cuban Communists to the destruction of the old unions.[27]

On other occasions, the attendance was large and the
meeting was held at the union hall and at the right time,
but its holding was preceded by an active recruitment of
union members by the promoters of the purge. The latter
could also count on the cooperation of officials from the
Labor Ministry who attended the assemblies and checked
the balloting.[28]

Such irregularities gave rise to a number of protests and
objections within the unions concerned. In the Construction Workers' Federation, charges and counter-charges
were filed by Jesús Soto and the anti-Communist leaders
Luis Penelas and Nemesio Torres; at the peak of the dispute Soto advised his opponents to look for diplomatic
asylum or else face a possible jail sentence.[29] The anti-
Communist leaders were finally ousted by the Executive
Committee of the CTC-R and the Federation's congress
had to be postponed three times. In the Musicians' Federation, also, the dispute was so acute that the CTC-R appointed a special committee to deal with those intra-union
problems.[30] Finally, in the Tobacco Workers' Federation,
resentment against Soto's expeditious ways was so intense
that the members concerned published a press statement
containing the following question:

> Is it right for one of the members of the CTC-R Executive
> Committee to ignore the rights of the Federation and to
> interfere in its affairs in a dictatorial manner which seems
> a carbon copy of Eusebio Mujal's methods?[31]

Whatever the system followed, however, the result was always the same. The expelled leaders were replaced by pro-Communist officials with the approval of the government. On various occasions, PSP leaders such as Juan Taquechel, Fausto Calcines and Ursinio Rojas turned up at the meetings in order to help with the expulsion of anti-Communist officials. For the most part, however, the unpleasant "surgical work" was performed by Jesús Soto and Augusto Martínez Sánchez. This is not to say that the Prime Minister stayed on the side line. On the contrary, he participated in several CTC-R meetings, including the one convened to discuss the situation in the Construction Workers' Federation, and kept a close eye on the development of the purges.

While the purge of the hierarchy was completed in a relatively short space of time, it would be erroneous to believe that purges in general ended in the Spring of 1960. Removal of local union leaders and members continued throughout the following months and years; in fact, news about the expulsion of trade unionists accused of being mujalistas can still be found in the 1965 newspapers.[32] The practice must have gone on at a lively pace, for in 1961 the new Trade Union Organization Law gave legal support to the policy of purges followed after the Tenth Congress. Article 5 granted the workers "the right to revoke or invalidate the election of any or all of its officials, regardless of the level of union organization."[33] Furthermore, it prescribed that the constitution and by-laws of all unions should establish a summary procedure to that effect so that "purification" could be efficiently and quickly accomplished.

The Intervention of the Labor Ministry

However drastic the clean-up process might seem, the government was apparently not convinced that the purges alone could change the direction of the labor movement toward a position of full cooperation. Therefore, in order to buttress and complement that approach, the Castro regime decided to authorize the Minister of Labor to seize unions and eliminate summarily unreliable leaders. Already in November 1959, measures were adopted empowering the Minister of Labor to dismiss elected union officials and to replace them with ministerial appointees. The new statute also provided that the Minister of Labor could order any measures leading to intervention in any trade union or federation whenever he saw fit to take such action.[34] Subsequently, the first Law respecting the Organization of the Ministry of Labor conferred authority on the Minister "to seize organizations of workers when circumstances so require."[35] This text was later revised and a second Law respecting the Organization of the Ministry empowered the Minister of Labor to take control of privately-owned undertakings and employers' or workers' organizations, when circumstances made such action necessary in order to maintain production or to guarantee the exercise of trade union and social rights, provided that valid reasons existed for such measures and that they were carried out in accordance with the law by government appointed controllers.[36] Minister Martínez Sánchez made frequent use of these exceptional powers. Between November 1959 and June 1960, some 75 labor organizations were taken over by the Department of Labor[37] and numerous internal changes were imposed upon them.

The fact that these statutes, which violated elementary principles of freedom of association, were enacted immediately after the Tenth Congress is indicative of the government's early determination to suppress all signs of trade union opposition. The stiff measures also revealed that the revolutionary elite was now prepared to do away with all previous pretenses of tolerance and to set aside legal obstacles and moral inhibitions.

On several occasions, the Minister went beyond his official duties and saw to it that the removal of anti-Communists was speeded up. This happened, for instance, in the case of the Havana Construction Workers' Union, on the occasion of a meeting convened to replace seven delegates to the congress of the Federation. After a brawl had taken place and the outcome of the assembly was in doubt, the Minister of Labor went personally to the meeting, bringing with him an inspector of the Department, various members of the Rebel Army and 80 Communist party members. He proceeded then with absolute safety to bring about and formalize the change of Directors.[38]

The Use of Police and Military Forces

Whenever the above-mentioned methods failed to accomplish the desired results, there was always the possibility of resorting to sheer coercion, i.e., the use of the armed forces. Sometimes it was the militia which was used to back up the imposed decisions and intimidate the rank and file. On other occasions, the same result was accomplished by using members of the Rebel Army. In some critical moments both instruments were employed. This happened, for instance, when the majority of the Executive Committee of the CTC-R refused to recognize the new officers elected at the above-mentioned meeting of the Havana Construction Workers' Union. Upon receiving word of that decision, on April 5, 1960, the Minister of the Armed Forces, Raúl Castro, sent troops and militiamen to the Workers' Palace and ordered its military occupation in order to enforce the will of the Minister of Labor.[39]

The display of military forces was also used in national trade union assemblies that were divided in their loyalties to the government. It happened, for instance, at the National Plenary of Sugar Workers held in Havana in December 1959 and which was attended by the Chief of Police and the military commanders of the six provinces. The purpose was to show the identification of the armed forces and the workers and to exert psychological pressure on the hesitant and the indifferent.

Police persecution was not limited, on the other hand, to those trade union leaders who opposed the Communists in the Tenth Congress of the CTC-R.[40] Labor organizations or trade unionists who subsequently ventured to take a similar stand, or dared to criticize the government, were also subjected to repression. This was the case, in particular, of the *Auténtico*, Catholic and Anarchist groups.

On February 12, 1960, the National Labor Commission (CON) of the Cuban Revolutionary Party (PRC) issued a manifesto in which the *Auténtico* leaders challenged the statement made by the President of the PSP Juan Marinello, that " Whoever raises the anti-Communist flag is a traitor to the Revolution."[41] Actually, this was the third manifesto issued by the CON against Marxist penetration, since during the holding of the Tenth Congress it had produced two strong pronouncements condemning the "unity slate" strategy and rejecting any pact with the PSP delegates.[42] Such aggressive statements could hardly be tolerated by the government; within a week of the issuance of the last one, two of the most prominent members of that organization, César Lancís and Rodrigo Lominchar, were being subjected to harassment and sporadic detention which lasted until they were forced to abandon their trade union responsibilities and escape to the United States. Pressure to emigrate was applied to other *auténtico* and *orthodox* activists in both direct and indirect fashion.

A similar fate befell the anarcho-syndicalist group. In June, 1960, the "Agrupación Sindicalista Libertaria de Cuba (ASL)" published a declaration of principles in which it advocated direct administration by the workers of the nationalized industries and decried "the military pressure to subjugate the people and force them to accept political systems entirely foreign to their national idiosyncrasy or social ideology, as has happened in Europe and Asia".[43] This statement was immediately refuted by the PSP leadership which branded the anarcho-syndicalists as agents of the U.S. State Department. The ASL replied one month later by reaffirming its critical stand in an article published in its official organ *El Libertario*. This time a member of the G2, the political police, called on the newspaper offices and warned its editors that the government could not permit further statements of that sort. *El Libertario* soon ceased publication and its editor-in-chief, the anarchist leader Abelardo Iglesias, joined the ranks of the exiles.[44] Another anarchosyndicalist figure of old standing, the transport workers' leader Lauro Blanco, was arrested some time later and condemned to a long prison term.

At the other extreme of the ideological spectrum, the Young Catholic Workers (JOC) encountered the same type of harassment and persecution. In March 1959, a group of promising young leaders of that affiliation including Reynol González, José de Jesús Plana, Eduardo García and Rodolfo Riego set out to promote a Christian Democrat group (the Union of Christian Workers, UTC) in the hopes of establishing a larger trade union organization. By the fall of that same year, however, they had been deprived of any authority within the labor movement and in June 1960 they had gone underground and were trying desperately to elude the police. González was eventually able to flee the country but he was captured while trying to re-enter Cuba and was sentenced to twenty years' imprisonment. Plana managed to escape to Venezuela.

A Background Note on the Success of the Purges

It follows from the foregoing discussion that the government resorted in many cases to heavy-handed, arbitrary and irregular methods in order to secure control of the labor movement. Given the attitude shown a few weeks before by the delegates attending the Tenth Congress, it might be assumed that Castro's open interference in internal trade union affairs would have aroused considerable shock and resentment within organized labor. The fact is, however, that the reorganization process came about with relative smoothness. True, there were objections and protests from the leaders and unions concerned, but the rank and file remained for the most part quiet and subdued. No mass demonstrations were staged; few important protest strikes were declared. The Cuban labor movement, which had clearly rejected the Communist position in three recent elections, was now apparently incapable of resisting the government onslaught or willing to cast aside its most conspicuous anti-Communist leaders.

Any explanation for the above must begin with an analysis of the relationship between Castro, the trade unions and the workers. By the beginning of 1960, there was little doubt that Castro had undermined the position of trade union leaders by appealing directly to the masses. Throughout the first year of the revolution, the Prime Minister had been striving to identify his government with the working class and this policy was now paying off. Castro's following was indeed so strong among the rank and file, who remembered his promises and the social and economic benefits of the first months of the revolution, that no labor leader could have hoped to challenge him. Further, many workers were now so thoroughly imbued with revolutionary doctrines that they were prepared to go all the way with him.

It is important to indicate in this respect that the populist measures of 1959 were reinforced during the period of the purges by a new set of decrees specifically intended to please the working people. All private clubs and recreational societies which had been expropriated since the beginning of 1960 were turned over to local unions, for the enjoyment of their members. The first beneficiary of this policy was the Hotel and Restaurant Workers' Union, which was designated to operate the Havana Biltmore Yacht and Country Club. Other workers' social centers began to appear and by mid-1960 there were 24 in full swing. Luxurious hotels now run by the government, like the Havana Hilton, offered free parties every week for the workers. Private beaches were opened to the public, and new resorts made accessible to urban and rural workers were quickly built. Other more substantial improvements for the workers came in the form of cheaper health services, expanded educational opportunities and additional child care centers for the children of working mothers.

Castro could also count on a relatively strong political base in the countryside. Former squatters and sharecroppers who were authorized to keep the land they worked up to a maximum of 65 ha. were in favor of the revolution. Together with other small private farmers they set up a national association called ANAP which grouped some 180,000 members and represented about 20 percent of the arable land. Castro was never enthusiastic about this area of private property which was to coexist with a Communist society and the numerical importance of the Association would eventually diminish.[45] He managed, however, to tone down at the beginning his initial feelings so as to preserve the support of this group. While other agricultural workers (wage earners) employed by state farms and cooperatives did not fare well in terms of remuneration and were deprived in 1961 of the right to organize, they were not longing for a return to pre-revolutionary times either. Most were also aware of the fact that for nearly two decades Cuban governments had failed to implement the prohibition of latifundia included in the 1940 Constitution.

The cumulative effect of all these measures contributed no doubt to strengthen the government's position in its confrontation with anti-Communist leaders. Even more important were the expectations aroused by Castro's promises which were still too recent to be regarded as a chimera. Moreover, Castro's plans were also aided by the fact that anti-Communist feelings ran higher among leaders than among the rank and file. Individual perceptions of Castro's objectives varied according to the level of knowledge and analytical ability of the people involved, and these were no doubt higher among union leaders and officials than among the average workers. Not to be underestimated either were the sentiments of apathy and fear that so frequently influence the attitudes of people in large mass organizations. Finally, the social and economic upheaval already brought about by the revolution had stunned many workers into paralysis.

For the labor leaders involved, the new situation was also particularly difficult and embarrassing. Up to this moment, they had been fighting the PSP leadership while supporting Castro's policies and objectives. Now their characters were being assassinated by an enemy they could hardly dare to identify—and could not combat. In desperation they were venting their frustrations on Jesús Soto, but the textile leader was only an instrument of larger and more powerful forces.

The plight of the anti-Communist leaders was further aggravated by the prevailing political circumstances. Various incidents that took place in Cuba during the critical period of the purges (December 1, 1959–May 31, 1960), contributed to exacerbate nationalistic feelings and to prolong the heroic tempo of the revolution. There was, first, a growing anti-Castro activity on the part of right-wing elements which prompted certain sectors of labor to move closer to the more radical elements in the revolution. There were also the incursions of Florida-based planes and the ensuing aggravation of U.S. Cuba relations, which added new fuel to the government's jingoistic exhortations for unity. Moreover, the attempts to sabotage the sugar harvest by setting fire to the sugar fields created an adverse reaction on the part of many workers directly concerned, who rallied in support of the government when they saw their means of earning a living at stake. Other attacks of anti-Castro forces concentrated on economic targets, particularly the harvest of such export crops as tobacco on which Cuba also depended for foreign exchange. While these attacks served to aggravate certain operational difficulties, they were not sufficient to disrupt seriously the economy, did not succeed in frightening workers away from the fields and gave Castro the opportunity to step up his demagogic and propagandistic efforts. At a time when labor was staging the most serious threat to the Castro government, some exile groups in Florida were thus unwittingly undermining the position of anti-Communist leaders in Cuba. Castro shrewdly capitalized on all these incidents, seeking to inflame the anti-U.S. nationalistic feelings and to inculcate further in the workers a sense of mission.[46]

Nothing can better illustrate this general atmosphere than the explosion in Havana in the month of March of the French ship La Coubre. Though the explosion was probably caused by the careless unloading of arms and ammunitions brought to Cuba by the government,[47] Castro quickly jumped on the occasion to underscore the fact that most of the victims were Cuban and French workers and to denounce the explosion as sabotage engineered by the U.S. agencies. Special laws No. 755 and No. 756 were enacted to declare a day of national mourning and to provide a one million dollar indemnity for the families of the victims. The preamble of Law No. 755 pointed out the magnitude of the tragedy by indicating that it affected the armed forces of the revolution and the working class. Law No. 756 granted pensions to the victims or their families and stipulated that the Cuban Government would assume responsibility for the education of the children of the victims. The CTC-R organized a demonstration in which the coffins of the victims were carried through the streets of

Havana from the Civic Plaza to the Colón Cemetery. Fidel Castro participated in the preparation of the parade and personally headed it with other members of the Cabinet. Labor meetings were quickly organized throughout the island to stage protests against the explosion and to launch fund raising drives aimed at purchasing additional arms and military equipment. Finally, there were the inevitable speeches delivered by Castro in which the revolutionary leader emphasized the fact that proletarian blood of Cuban and French workers had been spilled, underscored the international brotherhood of labor and praised the heroism of port workers during the rescue operations.[48]

Another important reason for Castro's success with the purges can be found in the timing of the house-cleaning process. By carrying out the "purification" immediately after the holding of the Tenth Congress, the revolutionary elite was able to decapitate the opposition before it could further coalesce at the grass-roots level. Castro's determined and brutal moves had caught most trade union leaders off guard.

The fact that there was only one relatively centralized structure of organized labor also helped to bring about the change of leadership. Those who masterminded the take-over operation did not have to deal with a multiplicity of rival labor organizations. All necessary efforts were concentrated on a single target.

The composition of the CTC-R Executive Committee provides another reason for the relative smoothness of the clean-up operation. As mentioned earlier, Castro and his colleagues took special care to veto the election of strong personalities and to fill the Committee with unknown and second rate leaders. This obviously debilitated at the top the resistance power of organized labor. As Hugh Thomas put it, the end result of Castro's efforts concerning the

election of the CTC-R Executive Committee was to exclude
the strong characters among the anti-Communists and to
include a number of easily subornable bureaucrats.[49] Outside the Executive Committee, many leaders also lacked
the courage and determination necessary to express solidarity with their deposed colleagues. First to be singled
out in this respect was Conrado Becquer who had repeatedly stated in the past his willingness to oppose Communism but now remained silent regarding the purges and
was even instrumental in swaying many sugar workers to
the government side.

Finally, there was the problem of the rising cost of opposing the government plans. Cubans who disagreed with
the aims of the revolution were depicted as enemies of
the Cuban people and servants of U.S. interests.[50] As the
personality cult reached unprecedented dimensions, opposition to the Prime Minister's views was immediately regarded as unpatriotic, anti-Cuban and even subversive. By
the spring and summer of 1960, the situation had become
even more tense and anyone who expressed criticism of
the Communists was considered to be an opponent of the
revolution and therefore a counterrevolutionary subject
to harsh penalties, including the confiscation of his properties.[51] Communist sympathizers and informers belonging to the Committees for the Defense of the Revolution
were already active in transmitting to the political police
G2 any indication concerning possible counterrevolutionary activities. Anti-Communist labor leaders were thus impotent to mount any effective opposition in the face of an
increasingly repressive and ruthless government action.

NOTES

1. See Fidel Castro's speech at a labor rally held in Santiago de Cuba on November 30, 1959, in *El Mundo,* December 1, 1959, p. 1. Castro also said in this speech that his government would remain in power "as long as the people want."

2. *Dos discursos, op. cit.,* p. 60.

3. *Discurso del Máximo Líder de la Revolución Cubana y Primer Ministro del Gobierno Revolucionario, Dr. Fidel Castro Ruz. En la Plenaria Nacional Azucarera del día 15 de diciembre de 1959, op. cit.,* p. 20.

4. This theater, which was the largest in Havana, changed its name to Chaplin in 1959 and to Carlos Marx some years later.

5. *Havana Post,* December 22, 1959.

6. *El Mundo,* December 3, 1959.

7. See *El Mundo,* December 15, 1959, p. A8.

8. See, for instance, *Revolución,* November 28, 1959, p. 1.

9. See *El Mundo,* December 13, 1959, p. A4.

10. See *Diario de la Marina,* December 15, 1959, pp. 1A and 12A.

11. *Ibid.,* p. 12A.

12. See *Havana Post,* December 11, 1959, p. 1 and *El Mundo,* January 14, 1960, p. B6.

13. On the 15th and the 27th of December 1959.

14. See *El Mundo,* December 9, 1959.

15. See *El Mundo,* February 2, 1960, p. A9.

16. See *Hoy,* January 5, 1960, p. 3.

17. *Ibid.,* p. 3.

18. See *El Mundo,* January 10, 1960, p. A1.

19. See *El Mundo,* February 7, 1960, pp. A1 and A10.

20. Victor Alba, *Politics and the Labor Movement in Latin America* (Stanford, Calif.; Stanford University Press, 1966), p. 297 and CERP, *Labor Conditions in Communist Cuba, op. cit.,* pp. 115–116.

21. *El Mundo,* March 24, p. A10.

22. Robert Alexander, *Organized Labor in Latin America* (New York: The Free Press, 1965), p. 170.

23. Carlos Franqui, *Retrato de familia con Fidel, op. cit.,* p. 204.

24. CERP, *Labor Conditions in Communist Cuba, op. cit.,* p. 116.

25. International Commission of Jurists, *Cuba and the Rule of Law* (Geneva: H. Studer, 1962), p. 232.

26. *Ibid.,* p. 233.

27. Hugh Thomas, *op. cit.,* p. 1,259.

28. *Ibid.*

29. See *Bohemia,* Year 52, No. 17, April 24, 1960, p. 67.

30. See *El Mundo,* February 20, 1960.

31. *Havana Post,* December 17, 1959, pp. 1 and 8.

32. See *infra,* Chapter X and *Vanguardia Obrera,* No. 143, September, 15, 1965, p. 11.

33. Law No. 962, August 1, 1961 (*Extraordinary Official Gazette,* August 3, 1961).

34. Law No. 647 of November 24, 1959. See ORIT-ICFTU, *op. cit.,* p. 15.

35. Article 5, Law No. 696, January 22, 1960 (*Extraordinary Official Gazette,* rectified copy, February 22, 1960).

36. Article 5, Act No. 907 of 31 December, 1960.

37. *Bohemia,* No. 30 (August 1960), p. 52.

38. International Commission of Jurists, *op. cit.,* p. 232.

39. Interview with Manuel Fernández García. See also CERP, *Labor Conditions in Communist Cuba,* p. 116.

40. *Hispanic American Report,* Vol. XIII, No. 1 (January 1960), p. 26.

41. *El Mundo,* February 11, 1960, p. A6.

42. *Diario de la Marina,* November 24, 1959, p. 3.

43. Abelardo Iglesias, *Revolución y dictadura en Cuba* (Buenos Aires: Editorial Reconstruir, 1963), p. 38.

44. Woodward, *op. cit.,* p. 43.

45. ANAP has now approximately half of the original number of members.

46. An indication of the feverish, chauvinistic atmosphere then prevailing in Cuba can be seen in the fact that when the press announced the possible reduction of the Cuban sugar quota by the U.S. Government, sugar mills in Las Villas Province blew their whistles and churches tolled their bells as a sign of protest.

Some of these demonstrations were led by C. Rodríguez Quesada, who a few months later was going to become an active opponent of Castro. (See *El Mundo,* March 11, 1960, p. A1).

47. Another explanation given by the Havana press a month after the explosion related to the activities of opponents of Algerian independence. According to a report published in *El Mundo* (April 5, 1960, p. A1), the explosion had been caused by a booby trap set in the ship by members of the Organisation de l'Armée Secrète (OAS), who thought that the shipment was destined to Algerian rebels.

48. For an account of the La Coubre incident see *El Mundo,* March 5, 6 and 7, 1960. See also Fidel Castro, *Sabotage! Palabras en las honras fúnebres de las víctimas de la explosión del barco "La Coubre."* (Havana: Confederación de Trabajadores de Cuba, 1960).

49. Hugh Thomas, *op. cit.,* p. 1,251.

50. Byron Williams, *Cuba: The Continuing Revolution, op. cit.,* p. 170.

51. Lowry Nelson, *op. cit.,* p. 27.

VIII
Government Control Over Labor

The Workers' Militias

Rise and Growth of Militias

IN ORDER TO SECURE FURTHER GOVERNMENT CONTROL OVER the trade union movement, the Castro regime adopted in 1960 a series of measures designed to militarize large segments of the labor force and to subject the whole of it to a stricter, more disciplinarian regime. The former objective was achieved through the establishment of the revolutionary national militias; the latter, through a number of compulsory or semi-compulsory measures which included government control of job opportunities and the adoption of a tough "productionist" policy. Attention will be focused first on the militia and later on the other restrictive measures; a separate section will also be devoted to examining the impact of the workers' contributions campaign on the strategy to control the labor movement.

Provisional militias existed from the beginning of the revolution, but they were initially made up of people from all walks of life. Castro referred, in January 1959, to the creation of a people's militia as a means of replacing the conventional army ("all citizens will receive military instructions" [1]). The organization was at that time voluntary and the militia units performed various para-military and civil defense functions. While it is true that, over the following months, the Rebel Army was strengthened and the government's attention focused on other issues, the idea of promoting revolutionary militias was never completely forgotten.

In October 1959, the organization of militias gained new impetus with Castro's speech in front of the Presidential Palace protesting against the alleged bombing of Havana.[2] "It is time," said the Prime Minister on that occasion, "to show to the world that the Cuban people are ready to defend themselves."[3] He therefore explained to the crowd his revolutionary plans for defending the country "with the people, with all the forces, with all the arms of the people, as opposed to the notion of a professional army."[4] The CTC-R had previously requested the creation of workers' militia to defend the revolutionary laws and a number of unions had already started military training. Castro now took advantage of these circumstances to build the militia on the basis of trade union support and to emphasize its proletarian character. Efforts were also made to spread the organization of militias among peasants and students. As it happened, these efforts coincided with the period in which purges and reorganizations were taking place, within both the labor movement and the university students' associations.

The rather frantic fashion in which the government approached the organization of militias may be seen through the following indications. Circulars concerning the organization of militias were issued at the end of 1959 and a special national department was immediately set up within the government structure.[5] Though the militias were still open in principle to everybody, the instructions were largely addressed to trade unions, peasants' organizations and students. Many of the unemployed and underemployed, including newspaper boys, parking attendants and street vendors, were also incorporated into the militia. In January 1960, the CTC-R officially agreed to establish workers' militias in all shops and concerns,[6] and this sparked off a rush of paramilitary preparations. Everywhere throughout the island, in playgrounds, in vacant lots and in quiet side streets, one could hear the sounds of military commands and see groups of men in fatigues marching in platoon formation with rifles and pistols. Later in 1960, when special military training centers were set up in each municipality (nine such centers were established in Greater Havana) the scope of militia enlistment expanded significantly.

By March 1960, more than 50,000 militiamen paraded in military uniform at the Columbia Camp and Castro boasted on that occasion that he could easily mobilize half a million men.[7] For the 1960 sugar harvest, the government could already count on 55,000 men organized in the so-called Sugar Brigades. This military strength was probably the result of the exhortations addressed by Castro to sugar workers to transform each sugar mill into a fortress.[8] On the first of May 1960, the International Labor Day celebration was much less a labor rally than a huge military parade and the marchers in the day-long demonstration consisted mainly of the Army, the Police and the workers' and peasants' militias. By June, the Labor Ministry reported that in the Province of Havana alone, 70,000 workers were adequately trained in military duties; for the whole country, the corresponding figure was 500,000.[9] In six months' time the government had organized, trained and disciplined one quarter of the labor force.[10] Over the following months, the strength of the militias was increased

even more and by early 1961 they were exclusively composed of workers and peasants. "Our military units, including the militia," Castro said in a patriotic celebration,
"are made up of workers and peasants." "These humble
people," he added, "are actually defending the workers of
America and of the world with a profound sense of human
solidarity."[11]

This dramatic increase in the size and proficiency of the
militia was due to a combination of spontaneous enthusiasm, inducement and compulsion. The "flag waving" policy consistently pursued by the government since January
1959 and the constant radio and television appeals to protect the national wealth and particularly the sugar fields
from the air raids organized by Cuban exiles (the so-called
"pirate planes") helped no doubt to swell the ranks of the
militia. Patriotic feelings were also reinforced by some material incentives: militiamen were detached from their jobs
on a staggered basis and guaranteed full pay while they
were undergoing military training up to a period of three
months.[12] A subsequent regulation also provided that the
time spent by workers in military duties should be taken
into account in computing their paid holidays. By 1961,
the Trade Union Organization Law provided that all temporary activities relating to defense that workers carried
out through the militia or other auxiliary corps would be
regarded as full-time work.[13]

But there was also a certain element of coercion, as those
who refused to join the militia were regarded as counterrevolutionaries and sometimes subjected to harassment or
loss of seniority rights. Neutrality or a position of indif-
ference was hardly permitted.[14] The fact that recruitment
was performed in the workshop also contributed to push
workers into the militia and gradually to transform militia
membership into a condition of employment.

A number of non-Communist and even anti-Communist trade unionists joined the militia at the outset on the theory that it was necessary "to save the revolution from within." However, they hardly had any chance to articulate any effective opposition to government as a result of the operational characteristics bestowed on the militia by the revolutionary elite. Recruitment took place at the level of workshops, undertakings and industrial sectors, but training and military operations were conducted on an intersectorial basis. This meant in practice that workers were unacquainted with the ideological position of other workers in the same militia unit and were apprehensive about approaching them. Informers were also planted in the militia and together with the voluntary cooperation of the Committees for the Defense of the Revolution (CDR) and sympathetic workers, who were urged to keep a watchful eye for counterrevolutionary activities, created a climate of psychological terror. Moreover, since militia membership entailed special responsibilities akin to military duty, any denunciation of counterrevolutionary activity was bound to entail a court-martial type of trial which involved possible severe punishments.

Role of the Militia

In May 1961, when he inaugurated a new school for revolutionary instruction, Castro declared that at the beginning of the revolution many people thought that the militia was a sort of pastime or entertainment and others took it lightly, or even refused to participate in military drills. He indicated, however, that the revolution meant business from the outset and attached particular significance to the military preparation of the militia.[15] In fact, the role assigned to the militia corps in the revolutionary process was a multidimensional one. Militia units were first conceived as indoctrination centers where allegiance to the revolution, nationalistic feelings and Marxist principles could be instilled among workers, peasants and youth. It may be noted in this regard that the responsibility for civic indoctrination was given in January 1960, to a Marxist militant, Carlos Aldana, and that other Marxist officers of the Rebel Army, such as Dermidio Escalona, William Gálvez, Armando Acosta and Manuel Piñeyro took an active part in the training of the militias. Guevara's manual on guerrilla warfare was used as one of the indoctrination texts.

A second objective of the militia was to provide an occupation to young Cubans who would otherwise drift into the ranks of the unemployed or underemployed. Because the proposed industrialization plans required time and unemployment had meanwhile increased in the construction, petrol and dock industries, the militia served to keep the young workers busy through a sort of national youth service.

It goes without saying that the militia was also a paramilitary organization, indeed an important auxiliary body of the Rebel Army, liable to be employed to crush counterrevolutionary activities. It was in this capacity that the militia successfully contributed later to repulse the Bay of Pigs invasion and to put down the "foyers" of guerrilla activities that flared up in the mountains in 1960 and 1961. But even before that, the government frequently used the militia for real or faked defense reasons. The shortage of sugar workers in 1961, for instance, was attributed by some authors to the constant mobilization of the militia.[16]

Last but not least, the militia was a means of keeping

the Cuban people in a constant stage of mobilization and of further enhancing the sense of participation of the working class. Poor peasants, under-utilized urban workers and members of the poorer sectors of the working class, who were given uniforms, rifles and sub-machine guns, suddenly felt that they were "making history" or at least performing important functions for the revolution. Their egos were flattered and their revolutionary spirit became more determined.

As far as the capture of the labor movement was concerned, the establishment of workers' militias performed another significant function. By creating in each workshop a new structure with strong quasi-military bonds, the authority of union leaders began to weaken and was superseded in reality by that of militia chiefs. Questions of trade union discipline were overshadowed by matters relating to the fulfillment of militia duties. Authority no longer accrued to the leader by reason of his position in the union hierarchy, but to militia officers or to those militiamen who were most vocal in their support of the revolution. This meant in practice that local union leaders were relegated to a secondary position and gradually began to lose their hold on their membership. It should be noted in this respect that in a survey conducted in 1960 by a University of Havana professor, workers ranked their participation in the militia above trade union activities as the most significant form of social participation.[17]

With the growing radicalization of the revolution, the militia took on an additional duty. The very nature of militia life served to identify possible sources of opposition and to facilitate the ousting of uncooperative leaders. To some extent, each militia unit performed within the labor sector the same role that the Committees for the Defense of the Revolution (CDR)[18] played in the larger society. The

CDR supervized the country's life at the city block and rural village level, while the workers' militias took care of the labor sector's activities.

The CDR appeared in the summer of 1960 and shortly developed into a mammoth network of community-level organizations composed of full-fledged supporters of the revolution. Although some revolutionary leaders claimed later that these organizations were an original creation of the Cuban Revolution, the CDR found their origin in the local level committees set up by the CHEKA during the Communist War period in the Soviet Union and more recently in the neighborhood and factory *danweis* of Communist China. In due course however, the CDRs were to serve as an improved model for the establishment of the Nicaraguan block committees.

Together with the revolutionary tribunals, which were re-established in October 1959 in order to deal with counterrevolutionary activities, the militias and the CDRs became organs of internal control which effectively throttled any sign of agitation. They also went a long way to operate the complete reorganization of society that the Prime Minister had in mind from the beginning. As he put it a few months later:

> This is a nation which has an incomparably higher degree of organization than before and above all it is an organized nation, organized through its labor organizations, its defense committees, its militia battalions, its young rebels' association and its women's federations.[19]

Labor Census and Control of Job Opportunities

Beyond the trade union movement, the government set out in the early 1960s to establish the basis of a complete over-all control of the labor force. This ambitious scheme was to be carried out under the guise of a labor census and the reorganization of the Labor Ministry, through the establishment within it of some all-powerful employment units.

The idea of a labor census was first suggested by the Minister of Labor in December 1959, and immediately accepted by the Cabinet. The purpose was to make an inventory of all human resources available, with a view to providing the necessary data for the much vaunted industrialization program. At long last, government officials insisted, the country would be able to know the exact number of unemployed and underemployed, as well as the jobs and skills available. This, they added, would pave the way for the economic development of the country.[20]

Not mentioned by the government spokesmen, but also instrumental in the decision to carry out a census, was the need to uncover basic human resources data for the inception of a centrally planned economy. A National Planning Board (JEP) was set up in the month of March 1960, with a wide range of powers regarding the growing public sector of the economy and some directive functions concerning the rest of the economy. This initial nucleus of planning responsibilities expanded considerably after the full-scale nationalization carried out in August and September 1960. By the end of the year a full-fledged central planning board (JUCEPLAN) replaced JEP and took care of virtually the whole of the economic life of the country. Quite naturally, the government was interested in gathering and collating some basic, over-all information before such bodies became operative.

Of more immediate concern was the fact that the Labor Census Law granted full powers to the Minister of Labor to control nearly all employment movements.[21] According to the law, a national register of the unemployed was to be prepared and all future vacancies were to be filled through a lottery system among those classified in the same group. The listing of candidates, that is, the order of priority for inclusion in a given group, was determined by the number of dependents, or the needs of each worker rather than by seniority or ability.[22] Workers already occupying a job would not be allowed to be transferred, promoted or demoted without the specific authorization of the Labor Ministry. As regards the possibility of holding more than one job, further instructions indicated that this would be generally prohibited in the future and permitted only where appropriate with respect to workers already holding various jobs.

The far-reaching effects of these provisions soon became apparent. One was gradually to centralize the hiring process in the hands of the Labor Ministry so as to enable it to oversee effectively the whole labor force. Contract hiring by merit, at the discretion of the employer or by virtue of union membership was in effect to be banned. Another closely related purpose was to control industrial and geographic mobility and to influence the composition of the labor force in given areas. Finally, the new hiring arrangements served to downgrade further the employers' position by depriving them of one of the more important managerial prerogatives.

To implement the census provisions concerning employment, an Office of Labor Control was established in the Labor Ministry at the end of 1959. Provision for this office had been made in the law respecting the organization of the department and staffing arrangements were immediately undertaken. The time fixed for conducting the census was rather short, but the Labor Ministry claimed that it was so well organized that there could be no doubt that it would be carried through successfully.

In actual fact, however, the census was a complete failure. As far as the human resources data were concerned, the country had to wait until 1962 to learn how many people were employed, underemployed or unemployed.[23] The Minister of Labor had promised to reveal those figures at the 1960 Labor Day Celebration (May 1) but he subsequently decided to remain silent on this point. No information was ever made available with regard to the national register which was supposed to supersede sectoral and enterprise listings, or the lottery system. Both ideas probably proved to be impracticable and were accordingly abandoned, though they served nevertheless to emphasize once again the government's concern for the principles of equality and universality of labor.

But the government's power over the hiring process remained intact and was even reinforced. Towards the end of the year, the Office of Labor Control was elevated to the category of a Division and given authority to distribute job opportunities, to regulate promotions and to deal with regional and occupational mobility. Since the lottery procedure had already been abandoned, such authority represented in effect a discretionary power granted to the Labor Ministry to control all employment movements throughout the country. Only the dismissal aspect was still subject to other regulations, though these were also going to experience substantial changes.[24]

Other aspects of the census episode also contributed to further the government plans. Much emphasis was placed, for instance, on the indications contained in census forms with regard to the hours of work of domestic employees. Since the relevant declarations were made by the employee and the employer concerned, there appeared ample room for conflicting information on working hours and rest periods; charges of exploitation combined with threats of dismissals to create a certain amount of uneasiness.[25] Some use was also made of the provision contained in the law which declared illegal or clandestine those employers who refused to register or who provided inaccurate information concerning their personnel. Finally, stress was laid on the fact that the new powers attached to the Labor Ministry would enable it to do away with racial discrimination, nepotism and favoritism in the filling of job opportunities.

While only a few of these objectives were effectively put into practice within the next few months, the new powers of the Revolutionary Government also served to disseminate political education by making job security a function of correct political attitudes. Workers at all levels of society, from universities to sugar fields, quickly learned that any expression of disagreement with government policies spelled harassment and possible loss of employment, whereas adherence to and support of the revolution entailed stability and possible promotions.[26]

The Inception of a Production-Oriented Policy

As mentioned in Chapter IV, most of 1959 was devoted to redistributing income with a view to securing workers' support. It was rather meaningful, however, that at the culminating point of this stage Castro was already giving notice of the need to introduce a more stringent economic policy. In his May 21 television speech, the Prime Minister indicated, in effect, that the government was planning to introduce a wage control policy, in order to combat what he called a shortage of essential consumers' articles and possible inflation.[27]

No immediate implementation was given to this announcement but when Castro appeared in September before the National Council of the CTC-R he made it clear that the time to request salary increases was over.[28] He also took advantage of the occasion to praise the attitude of airport workers, who were working ten hours and receiving compensation for only eight, thus initiating the so-called voluntary work movement. As mentioned earlier, however, he did not yet propose a clear guideline for an incomes policy.

After the Tenth Congress these preparatory statements gave way to more specific enunciations of the government's policies. Two speeches delivered in December 1959 highlighted the need to secure labor support for the purpose of increasing government revenues and financing revolutionary projects. At the FNTA meeting of December 15, Castro urged sugar workers to realize that the question at issue was not how to distribute more dollars but rather how to produce more goods and services.[29] A similar exhortation was made a few days later at the Blanquita meeting of the commercial workers. "The standard of living of a country," Castro stated, "cannot be raised by simply increasing salaries; a higher standard of living depends on increased production and technical organization."[30]

The next move came on February 24, 1960, when the Prime Minister accepted the trade union offer of a 4 percent contribution to the industrialization program. Making

the most of this collaboration, the Prime Minister contrasted the time "in which workers were fighting for bread
crumbs" with the new situation "in which the national interest was at stake." "For a long time," he said, "you were
fighting for immediate income increases, because governments were not following a policy intended to defend the
people's interest; now it is different," he added, "because
we have chosen the right path."[31] He then proceeded to
link the effective improvement of the workers' standard
of living to a centrally planned development of the economy and to explain the need for accelerated capital formation and increased national savings.

The point was further elaborated the following month
in a speech delivered at another meeting of the Sugar
Workers' Federation. Here Castro referred to the rationale
of the wage freeze, pointing out the difference between
the workers' position in a capitalist system "where they
were forced to demand wage increases" and their position
in a political system where the workers' interests were identified with the national interest and with government objectives.[32] He made clear once again that the "fundamental
aim of the Revolution was to promote the workers' interest
and to free the people from exploitation."[33] While the realization of this objective required, according to the Prime
Minister, some immediate sacrifices (as wage increases
would dissipate funds necessary for investment purposes),
he made it clear that the compensations would be amply
rewarding. In a rather significant sentence (uttered 13
months before the proclamation of the Socialist republic),
the Prime Minister stated emphatically:

> Cuban workers were previously trade unionists and busi-
> ness-oriented because they could only count on the trade

union to protect them. Workers should now behave as "statesmen" because the state is theirs.[34]

It was against this background that a number of trade union assemblies decided to defer economic demands and to accept wage freezes. Typically, the government refrained from issuing any specific regulation on wage control, but rather spurred the unions to adopt their own self-controlling policies. The movement was initiated at the end of 1959 with the austerity resolutions adopted at the meetings of the sugar workers and commercial employees, both attended by Castro. In January 1960, the CTC-R Executive Committee decided to support production efforts to the maximum, but stopped short of advocating a wage freeze. As indicated earlier, however, the formal launching of the "freezing" campaign was once again made by Conrado Becquer and the FNTA Executive Committee. This initiative, adopted on March 27, 1960 (also in the presence of Castro) gained momentum and many unions decided one after the other to freeze wages and to ask their members to work harder and to be ready to accept further sacrifices.[35] On several occasions the wage freezing resolutions were adopted by the workers with the assistance of lower ranking government authorities and INRA officials. This happened, for instance, at the Amazonas and Tacajó sugar mills.[36] At the 1960 Labor Day celebrations, traditional economic demands were totally left aside and all the slogans and posters were devoted to denouncing U.S. "provocations" and to urging workers to make more sacrifices.

This snowballing of the wage freezing movement served various socialist-related objectives: first, it established the basis of government control of wages, which was essential for the central planning of the economy; secondly, it represented a first step towards a reduction of wage differentials and, thirdly, it gave the impression that the whole movement had been initiated by the workers themselves, thus accentuating the identification of the government with the working class.

From the control of wages, the "productionist" campaign moved gradually to the readjustment of other social benefits. In June, Guevara suggested in a TV speech addressed to the workers that "in due course we shall all have to give up some of our privileges."[37] Though he gave assurances that development would not entail an exaggerated toll on the people, he warned the working class that "either it understands its duties and we win the battle or it does not understand them and 'industrialization' will be a failure."[38] The message was understood by a few unions, who agreed to dispense with overtime payments, but it was not until 1961 that a massive relinquishment of other social benefits was to take place. Thus began to fizzle away the benefits granted by Castro in 1959, together with others of older vintage.

It goes without saying that the inception of a productionist policy also entailed the elimination of the strike weapon. The revolutionary leaders insisted that the abandonment of pressure tactics was not the result of government measures but a decision taken by the workers themselves, of their own free will. It will be recalled that the Tenth Congress had approved a one-year ban on strikes and that this resolution was ratified and expanded by the CTC-R Executive Committee. However, the new legal system drawn up by Martínez Sánchez went farther and virtually prohibited all strikes and lock-outs. The Law of Labor Procedures, for instance, made compulsory the submission of all disputes to the Labor Ministry and the Tribunal of Constitutional and Social Guarantees, and it also stipulated that the decisions of those bodies were final and binding for all the parties concerned. Small wonder that labor law specialists observed at the time that it was "practically impossible" to declare a strike in Cuba.[39] It should also be noted that at the FNTA meeting of December 15, 1959, Castro attached particular importance to the disturbances caused by strikes and exhorted sugar workers to avoid all possible interruptions of the production process. The reason invoked on that occasion by the revolutionary leader was that workers need not resort to strikes because the revolutionary government was entirely devoted to their interests.[40]

One final point must be made in connection with the establishment of a productionist policy. As mentioned earlier, it was the Federation of Sugar Workers which repeatedly took the initiative in promoting an austerity line. Does this mean that Castro and Guevara were correct in their repeated assertions that sugar workers were the most revolutionary of all Cuban workers? In fact, all the FNTA initiatives concerning wage freezes and workers' contributions were the result of Conrado Becquer's initial proposals. The evidence available shows no indication of previous suggestions emanating from local unions or from other individual delegates. Becquer himself acknowledged on one occasion that, in making those suggestions, he was merely interpreting the teachings of the revolutionary leaders.[41]

Workers' Contributions

Signs of a new linkage between the government's plans

to radicalize the revolution and developments in the labor field were discernible in the workers' contribution campaign. Though this campaign was launched by Fidel Castro in his September 15, 1959 speech before the CTC-R council, there were prior indications of the government's interest in securing various forms of financial support from the workers. The contributions made in the first months of the revolution for the acquisition of cattle and agricultural equipment were prime examples of this. After the September 15 speech, however, the fund-raising campaign gained momentum and was related primarily to the industrialization program and the purchase of airplanes and military equipment. As mentioned earlier, there was also a resolution approved by the Tenth Congress aimed at inviting workers to invest 4 percent of wages in government industrialization bonds. Other pledges and contributions were made in subsequent months by a number of unions and federations, which seemed to compete among themselves in demonstrating revolutionary fervor and in order to elicit government approval.

In the USSR pledges and contributions have frequently accompanied government appeals for workers' cooperation and mutual assistance particularly during the period of War Communism and the inception of plans and more recently during the economic reform. For the Cuban revolutionary leadership, the undertaking of pledges constituted a form of enlisting workers' support and of stimulating feelings of comradeship. Pledges also foreshadowed socialist emulation and prepared the way for the further involvement of workers in the handling of economic matters. It may also be noted that these practices were conceived as another step towards the full identification of the government with the working class which had been consistently pursued since the beginning of the revolution.

The contribution in particular, was regarded as a testimony of mutual support and trust and as a way of linking the material well-being of the workers to the success of the revolution.

In order to emphasize this identification, Castro alluded in various speeches to the unprecedented difficulties involved in the national liberation approach followed by the revolution. Particularly in his February 24, 1960 speech, the Prime Minister declared that his government had decided to shun the "neo-colonial approach" and to request the workers' financial contribution instead of counting on the support of Cuban and foreign investors. The maximum leader proceeded accordingly to emphasize the "feeling of pride and satisfaction" that workers would derive from the 4 percent contribution which he termed "decisive" for the economic future of Cuba.[42] He also took special care to indicate that the new factories that he planned to set up with the industrialization fund would belong to a new corporation called "Pueblo Company S.A."[43]

These declarations were accompanied by renewed promises of prosperity for the working class. On three occasions (September 15, 1959, November 20, before the Tenth Congress, and February 24, 1960), Castro reiterated his pledge to return the contributions with compound interest and gave assurances that the present generation of workers would be able to enjoy the fruits of economic progress.[44] A few months later, Guevara indicated that in ten years' time the industrialization projects prepared by the government and financed by the workers would bring about a 100 percent increase in the per capita income of the Cuban people.[45] According to Guevara, such a picture of affluence contrasted with the results of the free enterprise system "where workers are sold like commodities."[46]

But the contributions also represented a substantial economic reinforcement which helped the government to accelerate the process of capital formation. Since Castro was already openly disregarding foreign investments, which he said would only come to Cuba for profits and with strings attached,[47] some alternative form of financing became indispensable. The 4 percent savings scheme, together with the wage freeze, provided an internal loan and had the additional advantage of being owed to the workers. According to Castro's own calculations, the 4 percent contribution would represent $40 million per year and would allow the government to carry out an ambitious program which he spelled out in his February 24 speech.

Savings schemes have been used in several countries, including the USSR where a special industrialization loan issued in 1927 was also floated on a subscription basis by the workers. This type of loan was very popular during the industrialization drive of the Soviet Union, so much so that, between 1926 and 1927, fifteen internal state loans of various amounts were issued.[48]

In the case of Cuba, the government's appeal to the workers to shoulder economic development met with some interest within the trade union movement. Following the example set by the Sugar Workers' Federation in December 1959, other unions and federations approved resolutions designed to accept the 4 percent deduction and to offer other forms of economic cooperation. President Dorticós and the Prime Minister went out of their way to praise those signs of patriotism and to goad labor unions to engage in further emulation efforts. By February 1960, the CTC-R announced that 144 unions had pledged to contribute to the industrialization drive and fixed a deadline for the other unions wanting to join the savings scheme.[49] Once approved by the union, the contributions of individual workers were supposed to be made, at their request, through appropriate deductions in the payroll.

Apparently, however, the government was not entirely satisfied with the amount of voluntary subscriptions, for in March 1960 a special law was enacted to enlarge the scope of the contribution. Law No. 762 ratified the voluntary character of the payroll deduction, but introduced a significant twist in the nature of the procedures. A presumption that all workers were willing to contribute was included in the law, together with a 30-day period to allow for the expression of individual refusals to pay the contribution; if no express declaration was made during that period, the 4 percent contribution was automatically deducted from wages and salaries; if a written refusal was filed, the worker concerned would be obliged to ratify personally his refusal before an official of the Labor Ministry.[50] Some workers sought to take advantage of the escape provision and notified in writing their refusal to make contributions. But Havana newspapers of April and May, 1960, began to carry letters of repentant workers who claimed that they had been misguided but were now willing to contribute. Thus, with the inclusion of this apparently minor provision the government had ensured two things: one, that the contribution was going to be really massive and two, that the reluctant workers, like the dissident labor leaders earlier, would have to come out and identify themselves with all its attendant risks.

The CTC-R Executive Committee and Its Pro-Government Activities

While the government was adopting the foregoing series of measures, pro-Marxist members of the Executive Committee were striving hard to radicalize further the revolution. As mentioned earlier, Jesús Soto, assisted by J.M. de la Aguilera and Octavio Louit, participated actively in the purges and actually became a sort of hatchet-men ready to accuse and chase out any dissident trade union leaders. The Marxist-oriented leaders of the CTC-R displayed considerable dynamism and developed peripatetic qualities; no sooner had they participated in a purging meeting in Havana than they were boarding a plane to Santiago to perform similar functions. The purification battle, Soto admitted in 1961, was a tough and protracted one.[51]

Other members of the Committee were also playing their parts effectively. Iglesias Patiño, for instance, took advantage of his position as Vice-Secretary in charge of foreign affairs to send out numerous communiqués denouncing *urbi et orbi* any possible instance of "U.S. imperialistic aggression." In one of these communiqués, issued immediately after the passage by the U.S. Congress of the bill authorizing the President to cut down the Cuban sugar quota, Iglesias indicated that the Soviet Union was ready to make up for that loss and to purchase the balance of the Cuban production.[52] Furthermore, he predicted that in case of military aggression, the Soviet military weaponry was capable of reaching American territory.[53] A similar militancy was displayed by O. Alvarez de la Campa, who undertook to transmit copies of the most radical government measures to all Latin American labor confederations and encouraged them to urge the adoption of measures of a similar nature. Needless to say, any alleged act of aggression against Cuba elicited virulent reactions from the Foreign Relations Secretariat of the CTC-R. When the La Coubre exploded, for instance, the Secretariat sent a circular to "all the workers of the world" denouncing "the savage attack of the imperialist beasts" and raising in passing the number of victims from fifty-four to one hundred.[54]

These men were also intent on promoting close links with the socialist countries. It was on their proposal that members of the CTC-R Executive Committee travelled in February–April 1960 to Moscow, Peking, Prague and other socialist capitals. When Anastas Mikoyan visited Havana in February to sign a commercial agreement, Soto and Aguilera invited him to attend a meeting of textile workers relating to the purchase of arms and airplanes. Expressions of Soviet-Cuban cooperation were repeatedly heard in the course of this meeting in which Mikoyan contrasted the greed of exploiters with the generosity of the workers and assured his audience that the heart and soul of the Soviet people were on the side of Cuba.[55] Soto and his colleagues were also instrumental in bringing to Havana an impressive Soviet delegation to the 1960 International Labor Day celebrations. Finally, at the First National Congress of Young Trade Unionists held in Havana under the auspices of the CTC-R in July 1960, special messages were addressed to the Chilean Workers' Confederation (CUTCH), the WFTU, the West Longshore Workers of the U.S., the World Democratic Youth Organization and the International Union of Students.[56] Expressions of recognition were also sent to the USSR and Czechoslovakia for their support to the Cuban Revolution.

As regards the formation of a Latin American Confederation of Labor a meeting was held in San Salvador at the end of April 1960 with a view to organizing, first, a Central

American federation. The meeting was sponsored by the CTC-R and attended by several known Communist leaders from various countries in the region. However, unions affiliated to ORIT refused to participate and the meeting was deemed a failure.[57]

NOTES

1. *Revolución,* January 8, 1959, p. 1.
2. On October 21, 1959, an airplane piloted by the former chief of the Rebel Air Force, P. Díaz Lanz, dropped leaflets in Havana. No convincing proof was ever submitted that the plane also dropped incendiary bombs.
3. Fidel Castro, *The Revolution is Here to Stay.* Translation of Address by the Prime Minister of Cuba, Dr. Fidel Castro, to the People of Cuba at Loyalty Rally, October 26, 1959 (Havana, 1959), p. 27.
4. *Ibid.*
5. See *El Mundo,* January 21, 1960.
6. See *El Mundo,* January 7, 1960, p. 1.
7. *El Mundo,* March 28, 1960, p. 1.
8. Fidel Castro, "El fusil del sacrificio." *Trabajo,* No. 1, May 1960, p. 63.
9. "Las milicias de un pueblo libre." *Trabajo,* No. 2, June 1960, pp. 76–77.
10. See Jaime Gravalosa, "Las milicias arriban a su mayoría de edad", *Trabajo,* No. 8, December 1960, p. 151.
11. Fidel Castro, *Cualquier sacrificio siempre será poco* (Havana: Instrucción MINFAR, 1961), pp. 13 and 14.
12. See *Revolución,* November 9, 1960, p. 6.
13. See article 14.
14. CERP, *Labor Conditions in Communist Cuba, op. cit.,* p. 104.
15. Fidel Castro, *Cualquier sacrificio siempre será poco, op. cit.,* pp. 3 and 9.
16. Wyatt MacGaffey and Clifford R. Barnett, *Twentieth Century Cuba, Background of the Revolution* (New York: Doubleday, 1965), p. 141.
17. See Anibal C. Rodríguez, "La participación social y la revolución." *Revista Universidad de la Habana,* Volumen XXV, Nos. 148–150, January–June 1961, p. 17.
18. *Cuba's Socialist Destiny, op. cit.,* p. 14.

19. See, for instance, *El Mundo,* January 23, March 20 and April 18, 1960.

20. See *El Mundo,* January 26, 1960, p. 1. It is noteworthy that a similar system of labor conscription was established in the USSR during the War Communist period.

21. See "El Primer Censo Laboral," *Trabajo,* No. 1, May 1960, p. 93.

22. *Havana Post,* April 19, 1960, p. 1.

23. See Ministerio del Trabajo, *Censo Laboral 1960* (Havana: Ministerio del Trabajo del Gobierno Revolucionario, 1962).

24. See *infra,* p. 269.

25. See, for instance, *Diario de la Marina,* April 25, 1960.

26. In July 1960, for instance, approximately half of the faculty body at the University of Havana was summarily dismissed because it refused to go along with government plans to do away with the autonomous status of the University. Several thousand public employees and white-collar workers in the private sector lost their jobs for political reasons between 1960 and 1961. (See *La Universidad hacia una nueva etapa* (Havana, 1960).

27. *Havana Post,* May 21, 1959, p. 1.

28. *Fidel en la CTC: Discurso a los trabajadores, op. cit.,* pp. 20 and 21.

29. Discurso del máximo líder de la revolución cubana en la plenaria azucarera del día 15 de diciembre de 1959, *op. cit.,* p. 23.

30. *Havana Post,* December 22, 1959, p. 1.

31. Fidel Castro, *El camino verdadero* (Havana: INRA, 1960), pp. 8 and 17.

32. Fidel Castro, "El fusil del sacrificio," *Trabajo, op. cit.,* p. 30.

33. *Ibid.*

34. *Ibid.,* p. 60.

35. See Boris Goldenberg, *Cuban Revolution and Latin America, op. cit.,* pp. 206–207.

36. *El Mundo,* April 1, 1960, p. A6.

37. Ernesto Guevara, "Discurso dirigido a la clase obrera," *Obra Revolucionaria* (Havana), No. 11, June 1960, p. 7.

38. *Ibid.*

39. See C. Mesa Lago, "La huelga y el lock-out dentro del nuevo procedimiento laboral." *El Mundo,* April 10, 1960, p. A11. See also Efrén Córdova, *Legislación Obrera* (Primer Curso) (Havana: University of Havana, Faculty of Law, 1960), p. 121.

40. Discurso del máximo líder de la revolución, *op. cit.,* pp. 14–16.

41. See *El Mundo,* December 15, 1959, pp. A1 and A8.

42. Fidel Castro, *El camino verdadero, op. cit.,* p. 20.

43. *Ibid.,* p. 21.

44. *Ibid.*

45. Ernesto Guevara, "Discurso dirigido a la clase obrera," *op. cit.,* p. 14.

46. *Ibid.,* p. 9.

47. *El camino verdadero, op. cit.,* pp. 15–16.

48. V. Lelchuk et al., *A Short History of the Soviet Society* (Moscow: Progress Publishers, 1971), pp. 131–132.

49. *El Mundo,* February 2, 1960.

50. Art. 5 of Law 762 of March 19, 1960 (*Official Gazette* of March 19, 1960).

51. See, Jesús Soto, "Informe al XI Congreso de la CTC-R." *Revolución,* November 28, 1961, p. 2.

52. Undated circular signed by Noelio Morell and Rogelio Iglesias Patiño, p. 2 (mimeographed copy in the author's file).

53. *Ibid.*

54. See *El Mundo,* March 11, 1960.

55. *Bohemia,* Year 52, No. 7, February 14, 1960, p. Sup. 10.

56. *Resoluciones del 1er Congreso Nacional de Juventudes Sindicalistas* (Havana: Imprenta CTC-Revolucionaria, 1960), p. 29.

57. See William Benton, *The Voice of Latin America, op. cit.,* pp. 89–90.

IX

Changes in the Labor-Management Relationship

The End of Tripartism

AS WE HAVE SEEN IN PREVIOUS CHAPTERS, THE EMPLOYERS' PO-
sition had been consistently eroded since the beginning of
the revolution. Though by the end of 1959 they were still
entitled to discuss labor conditions and to sit in various bodies, their position was becoming increasingly precarious. This
decline in the employers' status coincided with the government objective of centralizing certain aspects of personnel
management and the whole of labor administration matters
in the hands of government authorities. Both these developments led, in turn, to the introduction of substantial changes
in the labor-management relationship, thus affecting first,
the machinery for consultation and bargaining between the
two parties and, secondly, the position and rights of the
parties themselves.

The practice of tripartite cooperation in Cuba dated back
to the early 1920s, when the first maritime committees (*juntas
de inteligencia*) were set up in the principal ports to deal with
labor disputes. From this initial experience tripartism had
expanded in the following decade to include the fields of
minimum wages, social security and labor dispute settlement
in general (*comisiones de cooperación social*).

All these instances of tripartism disappeared during the
first fifteen months of the revolution. The first to fall were

the tripartite directorates in charge of administering the various existing social security funds, which gave way to a government-administered system organized in June 1959, under the Social Security Bank (BANSESCU). Neither the board of directors nor the other authorities of BANSESCU included any representative selected by employers or employees.[1] This centralized approach was continued after 1960, when the Ministry of Labor took over all the responsibilities pertaining to social security.[2]

The other tripartite bodies, i.e., the minimum wage boards, the social cooperation committees and the maritime committees, fell in a single stroke of the pen as a result of the provisions contained in the first Law of Labor Procedures enacted in March 1960.[3] The reason given by the government related to the lack of efficiency of the bodies concerned and the need to expedite labor procedures. But other, deeper reasons were no doubt at work, including the lack of compatibility between the existence of tripartite bodies and the apparent desire to do away with all forms of institutional cooperation that presupposed the existence of private employers. Indeed, the government was so interested in eliminating all signs of labor-management cooperation that it even proceeded to amend two sections of the 1940 Constitution which recognized the existence of joint or tripartite institutions, so as to prevent any possible reappearance of those bodies.

To fill the vacuum created by the disappearance of the tripartite bodies, measures were taken to provide for a more centralized form of government intervention. A system of compulsory conciliation and arbitration, where Labor Ministry officials played an almost exclusive part, was set up to deal with all kinds of collective and economic disputes. To justify the system, the Ministry of Labor invoked reasons

concerning the need to meet an old workers' demand dealing
with the establishment of labor courts;[4] but the law actually
assigned a very limited role to the judiciary, and this only in
connection with individual disputes. As regards minimum
wages and other conditions of employment, other measures
adopted in January 1960 had already given the Minister of
Labor the authority to regulate wages and salaries, work
schedules, rest periods and other conditions of employment
in all branches of the economy. This authority complemented
the above-mentioned power to fill vacancies, establish seniority rules and provide for the transfer of workers.

The elimination of tripartite bodies was not the only measure affecting the employers. Various provisions of the Law
of Labor Procedures sought to place them in a position of
inferiority in order to diminish further their prestige and
weaken their resistance. For example, they were required to
post a bond in case of appeals, they were held criminally
responsible in case of illegal discharges and they were forced
to keep on their rosters all redundant and dismissed employees until a final administrative decision had been made.
To cap it all, the Law respecting the Organization of the
Labor Ministry provided that the Ministry should not consider itself in future as a neutral body in respect of disputes
between workers and employers.

These measures created considerable restiveness among
the employers. A newspaper columnist reported at the end
of March that conciliation procedures had become so heated
that some of them ended in fist fights.[5] The Minister of Labor
immediately rejected such reports and stated that all administrative procedures were conducted in a civilized and proper
fashion.[6] But even before this incident a newspaper editorial
pointed out in December that the revolutionary process was
clearly indicating that workers and peasants were the "chosen" people and that all other social groups were regarded

as outcasts or counterrevolutionaries.[7] Not long afterwards, MacGaffey and Barnett detected a certain hostility and distrust of the regime towards members of the liberal professions, who were regarded as belonging to the upper classes.[8]

It may be noted that a deliberate government policy of throwing its weight behind the trade unions, undermining the employers' position and altering the power relationship between them, has also been observed in other socialist countries during the transitional period from a capitalist to a socialist society.[9] At a subsequent stage, employers' organizations are formally dissolved or simply die away. Both things occurred in Cuba. Forty-four sectoral employers' and business organizations were first seized and then dissolved by the Revolutionary Government during the transitional period.[10] The process began with the official announcement, in October 1960, that the Asociación Nacional de Hacendados (composed of sugar mill owners) was *de facto* dissolved and this was followed by a similar measure in respect of the Asociación de Colonos de Cuba (sugar cane planters), which grouped more than 70,000 people. Other organizations became weaker as a result of the expropriation of the land or business of their members and gradually ceased to exist.

The Emasculation of Collective Bargaining

Also excluded from the government plans was the process of collective bargaining as developed in market-oriented economies. Not only does collective bargaining presuppose the existence of private employers, as a party to negotiations, but the resulting agreements may also run counter to the requirements of a centrally planned economy. The whole thrust of productionist policies, capital formation efforts and investment plans, which were already taking shape, was bound to be affected if free collective bargaining were allowed to continue. Hence the need to take immediate steps with regard to the conduct and content of collective bargaining negotiations.

Unlike tripartite cooperation, however, the government did not proceed to decree an outright elimination of collective bargaining. On the advice of Minister Martínez Sánchez, the revolutionary leaders rather opted for a gradual emasculation of collective bargaining so as to make it eventually reconcilable with the new economic policies. A modified version of collective bargaining procedures, consistent with economic plans, exists in socialist countries and the Castro government was probably envisaging its eventual adaptation to Cuban conditions. The nature of the institution was going to be drastically changed and even the name experienced a meaningful alteration (engagements or *"compromisos"* instead of agreements), but some mechanism for the conclusion of collective agreements was eventually going to survive, in keeping with the Soviet model. This mechanism would serve to highlight the mutual obligations of the parties with respect to the fulfillment of production targets, provision of social services, production standards, payments of wages and compliance with labor legislation.

As mentioned in Chapter lV, the first measure adopted in this regard, in December 1959, was the suspension for 120 days of collective bargaining activities.[11] The government alleged on that occasion that existing procedures were excessively time-consuming and were resulting in the accumulation of a large number of disputes that only served to make settlement more difficult to achieve. Authority was accordingly given to the Minister of Labor to fix time limits for the discussion of collective agreements. In March 1960, additional power was granted to the Minister of Labor to revise the content of collective bargaining agreements, even when they had been legally agreed to by the parties. The latter were required to follow the various procedures specified in the law and to submit a copy of the agreement to the Ministry for examination and approval. Since the Minister retained the right to approve, reject or modify the agreement, there was no doubt that the new regulations entailed an effective form of control over the contents of the agreement.

As far as the public sector of the economy was concerned, the government's authority to overrule the contents of collective agreements negotiated by the parties was even more clearly spelled out. A decree issued by the Ministry of Labor in the summer of 1960, fixing conditions of employment in state and mixed enterprises, indicated that the determination of wages, either through agreements or unilateral decisions of the government-appointed administrators, was always contingent on the approval of the Labor Ministry.[12]

This initial form of control was ratified and expanded in December 1960. A special Department of Organizations, Agreements and Disputes was created in the Labor Ministry with a view to keeping a close watch on the conduct of negotiations. This Department had to be informed of all matters concerning the negotiation, modification or termination of agreements and was entitled to make appropriate recommendations to the Minister with respect to the approval or rejection of all collective agreements. The Minister, in turn, retained full authority "to resolve all matters related to collective labor agreements."[13]

Two months later the second Law of Labor Procedures gave still greater scope to the authority of the Department of Organization, Agreements and Disputes by conferring upon it the right "to make decisions approving or changing the original provisions, introducing new ones or cancelling collective agreements."[14] Any party who objected to the decision of the Department could lodge an appeal to the Minister of Labor but the decision of the latter was final and could not be appealed against either through administrative or judicial channels. It was further stipulated that no agreements could become binding until officially approved by the Ministry.[15]

In estimating the importance of the above-mentioned provisions, note should be taken of the fact that the authority of the Labor Minister was not limited to checking the conformity of the agreement with existing statutes or to verifying whether formal requirements had been complied with. The power conferred on the Minister of Labor amounted, on the contrary, to a discretionary right to veto the contents of the agreement or to modify its clauses in accordance with government policies. Such a power was clearly intended to discourage the parties from engaging in independent negotiations and to pave the way for the adoption of over-all guidelines which the workers and the management of the enterprises concerned would have to consider as the basis for their individual negotiations. While the establishment of a model collective agreement did not come about until 1962, the component elements of such pseudo negotiating procedure were already present in 1960.

Apart from the effects of these legal provisions, collective bargaining underwent, in 1960, a process of severe general atrophy. The government was clearly reluctant to engage in negotiations regarding the public sector, alleging that the power conferred on the Labor Ministry to fix all working conditions obviated the need for labor-management discussions. Moreover, the government-appointed administrators lacked experience in personnel matters and were afraid to increase costs by agreeing to additional benefits and charges. A few collective bargaining negotiations took place in the private sector before the 1960 nationalization decrees, but they were affected by increasing government intervention and a pervading sense of futility due, *inter alia*, to the trend towards a wage freeze and a growing perception that private enterprises were destined to disappear.

Finally, there was the question of the absence of strikes and lockouts. As indicated in the previous chapter, the government authorities frowned upon the use of industrial action and made virtually impossible the declaration of a legal strike. All existing provisions intended to recognize the right to strike and lockout were deleted and all references relating to the declaration and exercise of work stoppages left in a limbo of semi-legality. Once again Castro here followed the Soviet model, according to which strikes are not officially prohibited or permitted, although they simply are not supposed to take place and they do not occur in practice.

Large-Scale Nationalization

Expansion of Indirect Measures

The disappearance of tripartite cooperation and the emasculation of collective bargaining were followed by the demise of one of the actors of the industrial relations system. A series of government decrees signed by Fidel Castro and/or Martínez Sánchez continued to siphon off individual properties from the private to the public sector and this was followed by a large-scale nationalization of large and medium-sized enterprises. Though this nationalization took place in various stages throughout 1960, some interconnections seemed to be discernible between the different stages.

As a point of departure, mention should be made of the fact that the 1959 approach for expanding the public sector, i.e., recovery of "stolen" properties and "interventions" due to labor problems, peaked significantly during the first months of 1960. The official interpretation of what "ill gotten gains" exactly meant continued to expand as the revolution kept moving ahead. Thus, the nine sugar mills originally confiscated by the relevant Ministry grew to 25 by March 1960;[16] other important concerns, such as the Amadeo Barletta conglomerate (including the newspaper *El Mundo*) and the Burke Hedges textile enterprises, were seized as a "precautionary" measure despite the rather flimsy circumstantial evidence gathered by the Ministry for the Recovery of Stolen Property.

As regards the "interventions" ordered by the Labor Ministry, a glance at Havana newspapers during the first quarter of 1960 shows a dramatic increase in the pace of intervention.[17] The review *Trabajo* indicated in June that 107 enterprises of all sizes and types of activities had been seized by the Labor Ministry since the enactment of the revolutionary "intervention" law.[18] A special department was established in the Labor Ministry to handle seizure matters and a law was passed in June authorizing the Minister to prolong indefinitely the takeover of any enterprise. A number of resolutions issued by Martínez Sánchez also included a new provision whereby government administrators were authorized to obtain credits from INRA with a view to maintaining firms in operation. While this injection of government funds served to prop up business, it also gave the government the option of becoming either the chief creditor of such enterprises or a privileged stockholder.[19]

Another device developed during this period was the direct occupation of the business concerned by the workers, following a real or fabricated dispute, as a pretext to provoke the government intervention. This procedure proved especially useful in connection with certain newspapers and radio and television networks which had criticized government actions. It is interesting to note that the first two newspapers occupied by the workers as a demonstration of protest and placed immediately afterwards under government control, namely, *Avance* and *El País*, had become involved in labor disputes following confrontations between their editors and Prime Minister Castro. *Avance*, which had criticized the government role in the trade union purges, was occupied by a group of workers and forced to fold up in January 1960. *El País* followed suit after editor G. Martínez Márquez twice appeared on television to refute Castro's allegations against him. The latter newspaper was immediately converted into a government printing agency for the purpose of publishing literary and social works which, according to Castro's announcement at the confiscation ceremony, "would open the doors of knowledge to workers and peasants."[20]

The practice of forcing out management by the workers was extended in the month of May to other news media including *Diario de la Marina* and *Prensa Libre*. The pattern for the takeover was for the workers to send a committee to discuss with management a tough series of demands threatening a strike unless all of them were met. Usually

included among the demands, as in the case of those presented to *Diario de la Marina,* was an outright call for the
management's resignation. When the demands were turned
down, the group of workers involved proceeded to occupy
the enterprise concerned. Street demonstrations usually
followed the occupation; in the case of *Diario de la Marina,*
which was the second oldest newspaper in Latin America,
a mock funeral was staged and 15,000 people paraded
through the streets of Havana. It should be added that
members of the *Prensa Libre* staff union announced their
intention to continue publishing the newspaper on a self-
management basis, but this failed to materialize as all relevant assets and equipment were transferred to the
government.

On the basis of the property placed in government hands
through the agrarian reform, the recovery of stolen properties and the labor-instigated interventions, the revolutionary leaders quickly undertook to organize a vast, cen-
trally-controlled public sector of the economy. Almost all
enterprises were administered by INRA, through an Industrialization Department set up in November 1959, and
by its various agricultural units. Enterprises subjected to
intervention because of labor disputes were temporarily
run by the Labor Ministry, usually through members of
the Rebel Army of proletarian origin or trusted officials
of the department, until they were transferred to INRA.
In addition to industrial and agricultural undertakings,
INRA established in late 1959 and early 1960 nearly 1,400
non-profit "people's stores" (*tiendas del pueblo*), which, according to a French expert,[21] were not at all consumers'
cooperatives, as the revolutionary leaders claimed for some
time, but government operated stores.

Outright Nationalization

Whatever doubts may have existed about the nature of the government plans were soon to be dissipated with the five massive nationalization drives carried out during the summer and fall of 1960. The first step was taken in June when all the oil refineries were nationalized on grounds that they refused to process the Russian oil. The second step came about the following month when a law was passed authorizing the government to nationalize any enterprise belonging to American citizens or financed with American capital. According to the official explanation, this measure had been prompted by the threatened cancellation of the Cuban sugar quota in the United States and the need to make up for the damage thereby inflicted on the Cuban economy.[22]

Under the authority granted by this law, three government decrees were promulgated in quick succession. The first one, issued in August, nationalized 26 American corporations, including the telephone and electricity corporations, the oil companies and 21 sugar mills. The second one, in September, expropriated all American-owned banks. The third, dated October 24, 1960, covered 163 American companies in various economic sectors.

The reasons invoked by the Cuban Government for these expropriations did not appear to be consistent with the fact that the third nationalization of American property was preceded by the expropriation of several hundred Cuban enterprises on October 14. No nationalistic retaliatory measure or existing labor dispute or connection with the previous regime was now invoked for this new wave of nationalizations which affected large and medium scale enterprises in thirteen different fields of economic activity.

The main reasons now provided by the government related to the need to control basic national resources in order to implement effective economic planning.[23] There was also a reference to the attitude assumed by many corporations in opposition to the interests of the revolution and the incompatibility between government control of exports and the subsistence of large importing concerns. A final argument contained in the preamble of the government decree stated in more candid terms, that:

> It is the duty of the Revolutionary Government to take whatever measures may be considered appropriate to liquidate definitely the economic power of the privileged who conspired against the people, and to proceed accordingly to nationalize the large industrial and commercial enterprises which have failed to adapt themselves to the realities of the Revolution and which will never be able to adjust to the Revolution.[24]

It was also rather significant that the nationalization decree contained a provision authorizing the National Planning Board to nationalize further any enterprise not included in the expropriation lists but which had been previously seized by the government. No specific reason was given for this, though it was presumably covered by the same general explanation of the law. While this provision gave support to many government critics who had claimed all along that most seizures were an excuse to expand government property, it also served to formalize in perpetuity the government operation of a large number of agricultural, commercial and industrial undertakings.

With these nationalization laws, the government brought

to culmination the drastic transformation of the Cuban economy that had been begun in January 1959. By the end of 1960, roughly 80 percent of Cuba's industrial capacity had become state-owned. The state held the most strategic industries: sugar, petroleum, telephone and electricity, cement and all modern manufacturing plants. The state also held the banking system, the railroads, the airlines, the ports, the department stores and an assortment of hotels, casinos, cafeterias and various movie houses. State plants produced 90 percent of Cuba's exports.[25] In terms of the labor force employed, 80 percent of all Cuban workers were already working for the state on October 15, i.e., before the final expropriation of American properties.[26] As Edward Boorstein put it, Cuba had already become a socialist country, although such a conversion would not be announced until April 1961.[27]

A few comparisons with the Russian and Chinese revolutions may be appropriate at this point. In the USSR, the over-all nationalization of large enterprises took place in June 1918, i.e., eight months after the October Revolution and fourteen months after the February Revolution. In China, Mao Tse-Tung took seven years to achieve a complete change in ownership. Both revolutions had proclaimed from the outset that nationalization was one of their primary objectives. In Cuba, the basic expropriation program was completed in less than twenty-two months, and this despite the initial assurances that the government had no socialistic aims in mind. As recently as December 1959, Castro had said that "only a lunatic would think of nationalizing Cuban enterprises."[28] In April 1960, the Minister of Foreign Affairs Raúl Roa still defined the ideology of the revolution as "reformist" and "sui generis."[29]

The massive transfer of wealth to the public sector did not take government agencies by surprise. Neither serious

production breakdowns nor administrative entanglements
were visible. In the very month of October during which
the bulk of the nationalizations took place, 14 industrial
conglomerates (*consolidados*), grouping hundreds of enterprises and operating in accordance with socialist planning
were already in full operation.[30] Not a single enterprise or
consolidado was given to the workers for self-management
purposes. Though certain revolutionary leaders had previously expressed an interest in workers' participation in
management, at the moment of nationalization the government adhered to the orthodox Soviet approach of placing a single state administrator in charge of each enterprise. Self-management was in fact never seriously
considered by the Castro Government.

Changes on the Worker's Side

Substantial changes were also taking place on the workers' side both at the level of the individual and of the labor
organizations. Castro knew quite well that the emergence
of a socialist society required profound changes in the hab-
its and thinking of workers as well as in the nature of social
organizations. Socialism, he was going to observe in 1961,
is a complex process which cannot be reached in months
or even in two years.[31] He accordingly set out in mid-1960
to mold workers' thinking and to readjust the structure
and functions of unions to the new realities of the emerging Marxist regime.

As far as individual workers were concerned, priority
was given to the adoption of measures intended to inculcate among workers notions of dedication to work, self-

discipline and closer identification with the management of state enterprises. The first two notions were supposed to replace the profit-oriented and "economist" motivation of capitalist society and also to stimulate economic development. The third aimed at substituting collaboration for the previous inclination to contest private management decisions. All three, which were supposed to provide the psychological infrastructure of the new socioeconomic system, came gradually into being through: (1) the promotion of voluntary work; (2) the setting of norms of work or standards of performance; and (3) the establishment of new labor relations institutions.

Voluntary Work

The promotion of voluntary work was actually initiated in the summer of 1959 when various transport unions with government support embarked on a campaign to relinquish overtime pay. This movement was shortly expanded to include work on Sundays and other holidays and the setting up of the shock brigade movement.[32] These practices appeared first in an informal and haphazard fashion but were later reinforced and institutionalized with the establishment in September 1959 of the Organization of Voluntary Workers (OTV). The apparent purpose of OTV was to supply workers for emergency tasks in agriculture and transportation, but other objectives were also involved, including stimulating collective purposes in life, reducing differences between manual and intellectual work and convincing people that the creation of wealth and economic development depended on the population's own efforts.

Not surprisingly, voluntary work is regarded in Marxian theory as the element that most actively develops the workers' conscience preparing the road to a new society.[33]

While voluntary work profited at the beginning from the revolutionary fervor of many workers, it also meant for many others a disguised form of forced labor. Workers who refused to perform voluntary work were subjected to a barrage of political and social pressures. They were frequently regarded as social parasites and were in danger of being labelled as counterrevolutionary elements. They could also lose the right to obtain the coupons or bonuses that would have entitled them to purchase certain goods, e.g., refrigerators, washing machines, radios, lamps and other electric appliances that are an integral part of modern life. Refusal to carry out voluntary work, especially in the agricultural, construction and sugar industries, appeared in the workers' record as a serious and negative factor liable to affect their whole working life.

When work was carried out outside normal duties, workers enlisted under the voluntary program were called upon to perform different kinds of work for which they usually lacked appropriate skills and training. Working conditions were sometimes dangerous (e.g., in the construction industry and cane cutting) and inadequate attention was given to preventive and security measures. All this inevitably led to an increase in the frequency and gravity of occupational accidents. Small wonder that in actual practice the so called "voluntary work" disrupted in many cases normal production activities, affected the long-term needs for rest, study, training and leisure of the workers, had adverse repercussions on labor productivity and proved to be socially criticizable and economically counterproductive. Yet Castro and his hard core of Marxist advisers showed from the beginning a strong ideological attachment to the principle of voluntary work. The fact that 25 years later the Fifteenth Congress of the CTC regarded voluntary work as the cornerstone of a Communist and revolutionary conscience throws further light on the early and consistent way in which Castro had adhered to the principle of voluntary work.[34]

Standards of Production

To set forth norms of work or standards of production the government issued in mid-1960 the aforementioned resolution concerning conditions of employment in state and mixed enterprises.[35] This resolution laid down the rules for the determination of minimum output standards to be performed during the working day and with regard to the system of bonuses or additional payments which would be granted to those who exceeded the minimum.

Less than 20 months after the beginning of the revolution, the government was thus heading away from the traditional systems of remuneration into the complex area of job evaluation and individual work requirements, which are so deeply rooted in the socialist mode of production. Time rate systems were also beginning to give way to payment by results schemes; the latter constitute the prevailing form of remuneration in the Soviet Union and their first regulation dates back to two decrees signed by Lenin in 1920 and 1921.

Some elements of socialist emulation and planning of collective production at the enterprise level were also contained in the 1960 resolution. This explains why sporadic

competitions of an emulative character were already
launched in the second half of 1960, first in the cutting of
sugar cane and other agricultural work and later in the
industrial sector.[36] However, a clear authority to regulate
the practice of emulation did not come about until the
second Law respecting the Organization of the Labor Ministry, which empowered the Department for the Development of Human Resources to establish emulation systems with a view to increasing production and labor
productivity.[37] Detailed instructions were subsequently issued by JUCEPLAN on the basis of which emulation commissions were set up in 1961. A basic principle of the socialist system was thus subtly introduced by the government
at an early stage of the revolution.

New Labor Relations Institutions and Practices

Finally, to change the workers' view of management, the
same August resolution provided for the setting up of
technical advisory councils in which "vanguard-workers"
advised management on production and welfare problems.
The councils concerned themselves with questions of discipline, safety and health, improvement of working conditions, production and investment plans, conservation of
raw materials and voluntary work. Later, in February 1961,
grievance commissions, in which workers and representatives of management sat together, were created to deal
with individual disputes. Though these bodies remained
practically inoperative for a long time,[38] the government's
intentions to replace negotiations across the bargaining

table by joint collaborative efforts were clearly formulated as early as the summer of 1960.

This emphasis on cooperation at the level of the undertaking does not mean that the revolutionary leaders were neglecting the social aspects of the workers' role in the larger society. On the contrary, every effort was simultaneously made to create a more militant proletarian image which helped to consolidate working-class support for the revolution. While some of these efforts were simply a continuation of the mass mobilization policy pursued from the outset, there were also others aimed at fostering a feeling of comradely cooperation and class solidarity. Numerous articles appeared in the press pointing out the potentialities of the working class and its intrinsic opposition to other social groups. Since the government could now avail itself of all the news media (except the newspaper *Información* which was not nationalized until October 1960), the effects of this campaign were of far-reaching proportions.

Castro's speeches were also instrumental in instilling class militancy. "The true democracy," he said at the 1960 May Day celebration, "consists in giving arms to the workers, the peasants, the students, the blacks and to every citizen willing to defend the Revolution."[39] "Our duty," he remarked fifteen days later at the meeting of the construction workers, "is to forge a revolutionary conscience in every worker; wherever there are misguided workers, our duty is to orient them." "It should not be difficult," he added, "to foster a revolutionary conscience in workers and peasants, humble people, who instead of exploiting others have always been victims of exploitation."[40] His brother Raúl was also doing his best to step up workers' indoctrination. In a speech delivered on November 30, 1960, he had already alluded in undisguised terms to the beginning of the transition to socialism and the vanguard responsibilities therein attributed to the "powerful working class."[41] A few months before (in July), Guevara had indicated in a speech delivered at a youth congress that the government was already implementing Marxism ("*haciendo eso que se llama marxismo*") though he made clear that the application of Communist theory had been a spontaneous development of the Cuban Revolution.[42]

Far-reaching changes were also affecting specific sectors of labor. Domestic service, for instance, was rapidly fading out as a result of lack of job opportunities and because of government plans. In mid-1960 the Government set up night schools to provide former cooks, servants and gardeners with some training as typists, stenographers and drivers. These courses also included the teaching of Marxism-Leninism and many of their graduates were later transferred to the schools for revolutionary indoctrination.[43]

It may be noted, on the other hand, that not a single worker had yet been appointed to an important government position. Cabinet responsibilities were first given to distinguished personalities of liberal orientation, capable of inspiring confidence in the people, together with a few Marxist representatives. The proportion was gradually changed in favor of the latter but preference was still given, in 1960, to white middle class professionals with Marxist credentials. Either Castro thought that the ranks of Communist workers were still too thin to fill both government and trade union posts or he did not want to move too fast in his timetable for socialism. He carefully chose, however, people of proletarian origin to high-level positions in the Rebel Army and other military or para-military bodies.[44] The first signs of institutionalizing the workers' accession to power seemed to appear at the end of 1960. On December 14, in effect, a Board of Coordination and Inspection was established in the Oriente province and this modest event was characterized as a manifestation of the power that workers and poor peasants might assume in local government.[45]

Changes in Trade Union Structure and Functions

The government efforts to change the workers' mentality were coupled with sharp modifications in the trade union set up. Government spokesmen took pains to emphasize from the first part of 1960 (i.e., a year before the formal acknowledgment that Cuba was a socialist republic), that the traditional functions of trade unions were no longer appropriate to the new revolutionary situation. Castro, for instance, declared in May 1960 that the new trade union leaders were no longer supposed to put forward demands and that they were instead assigned the tougher job of urging workers to step up production efforts.[46] Once the "maximum" leader had set out the new approach, the words "demands" and "bargaining" were virtually eliminated from the trade union vocabulary. Time and again, the editorials in *Trabajo* pointed out that the two new duties of the labor movement were to defend the country and to increase production.[47] There were also repeated references in the government press to the need to save raw materials, improve the quality of products and take good care of equipment. Guevara even launched, in June 1960, a new trade union slogan consisting of the words: production, savings and organization.[48]

The new policy made instant headway among trade unions. During 1960 it became more and more apparent that the political functions of the labor unions were overshadowing their role as representatives of their members' economic interests.[49] It became customary, for instance, to discuss Fidel Castro's speeches at national congresses and to stimulate labor organizations to engage in revolutionary discussions. Trade unions were asked to discuss the bellicose Declaration of Havana approved on September 2, 1960 by "the general assembly of the Cuban people" convened by the "revolutionary trade union organizations."[50] The Declaration was a veiled but ardent appeal to armed insurrection in Latin America[51] and contained references to the "iniquitous exploitation of human work by bastards and privileged interests," the rights of peasants to the land, the rights of workers to the fruits of their work and the right of workers to nationalize "imperialist monopolies." Texts of the Declaration were put to a vote in each union and following its approval workers were invited to sign it.

The new leadership also displayed an instant willingness to understand the functioning of production-oriented policies. For instance, Conrado Becquer, speaking at a FNTA meeting in August acknowledged that the task of the unions could no longer be the old one; trade unions, he declared, must now work together with government officials in order to plan and promote production.[52] Similar views were expressed by Francisco López of the typographical workers and Antonio Torres of the railwaymen. Moreover, at a joint meeting of seven national unions held in November 1960 two secretaries-general dwelt at length on the need to save raw material, raise productivity and make more profitable the running of each specific undertaking.[53]

But other sectors of the labor movement apparently did not show the same degree of understanding. Most vocal in their expressions of disagreement were workers in the construction industry, the food industry, the bus drivers' union and the electric power industry. Castro soon singled out some of these groups (particularly the construction industry and public utilities workers) for public criticism. The government followed suit by embarking on a massive ideological offensive designed to eliminate bargaining-oriented leaders as well as all signs of business unionism within the rank and file.

Preliminary steps were also taken in 1960 to change the trade union structure in accordance with the socialist principle "in every industry a union, in every undertaking a trade union branch." Actually, the move to merge existing unions and to do away with enterprise and craft labor organizations had already been started at the end of 1959 by the Hotel and Restaurant Workers' union. Once the whole labor movement was placed in sympathetic hands, a nation-wide drive to end fractionalism and to amalgamate existing unions was set in motion. For example, the first item on the agenda of the construction workers' congress held in May 1960 was the restructuring of labor unions.[54] In August, a unified maritime-port workers' union was formed in the city of Nuevitas and Puerto Tarafa.[55] The following month, hotel and restaurant workers in the Havana Province merged nine unions into one.[56] Further efforts to unify all similar unions were made in the airline, mining, metal and petroleum industries during the fall of 1960. With characteristic foresight, the revolutionary government was thus introducing the subject of trade union restructuration one year before the enactment of the Law of Trade Union Organization of August 1961. In this respect, the government was able to count on the support of traditionally pro-Marxist unions which led the move towards amalgamation.

Obviously, the new tasks called for qualities of discipline and knowledge of Marxist doctrines that only the old-guard members of the PSP would be able to possess. The Prime Minister had recognized, in May, that under the new "revolutionary" conditions, the position of trade union leader was an unpleasant and tough one, though he anticipated that it should become more agreeable as the revolutionary conscience of the people developed.[57] Such words probably anticipated the need to resort to Lázaro Peña and his colleagues, some of whom, including Juan Taquechel and Ursinio Rojas, had already assumed important trade union functions in 1960. PSP's cadres and unionists were older, more experienced and better attuned to the new political realities than those who belonged to other groups. There was no need to hurry, however, as the new breed of aggressive and radical leaders who had taken command of the CTC-R Executive Committee were discharging their responsibilities with flying colors. On the domestic front, Jesús Soto and Octavio Louit were pushing hard for the new production-oriented line, while substantial progress was also being accomplished by the same leaders in the public relations field. At the Eighth National Congress of the PSP in August 1960, Blas Roca reported with satisfaction that the Cuban Revolution was using radical methods and was advancing without interruption. In September, USSR Ambassador S.M. Kudryatsev paid a call on the CTC-R and was welcomed by Jesús Soto who asked him to feel at home and to work for closer links between Cuba and the USSR.[58] Next month, J.M. de la Aguilera spoke at the reception offered by the CTC-R to commemorate the anniversary of the Russian Revolution and had the following words to say:

It is time to state without fears, with untrembling voices, with unshaking knees and with our heads held high, that we are marching inexorably towards socialism.[59]

NOTES

1. See Cuban Economic Research Project, *Social Security in Cuba* (Coral Gables, Fla.: University of Miami Press, 1963), p. 43.

2. However, certain responsibilities over social security claims were later assigned to grievance, appeals and revision commissions, composed of representatives of the state enterprise, the union and the Labor Ministry.

3. Law No. 759 of March 11, 1960 (*Official Gazette* of March 22, 1960). This law was superseded by the second Law of Labor Procedure enacted in February 1961.

4. See *El Mundo,* March 15, 1960, p. 64.

5. See Benjamín de la Vega, "Bisturí," *El Mundo,* March 30, 1960, p. 4.

6. *El Mundo,* March 31, 1960, p. A10.

7. *Diario de la Marina,* December 6, 1959, p. 1.

8. MacGaffey and Barnett, *op. cit.,* p. 42.

9. See for instance Julius Rezler, "The Industrial Relations Systems in Hungary after the Economic Reform," *Annuaire de l'URSS et des pays socialistes européens, 1972–1983* (Université de Strasbourg, France, 1983), p. 3.

10. The list of these organisations can be found in Corporaciones Económicas de Cuba—Exilio. *Cuba y la OIT. Denuncia e impugnación,* (Miami: Talleres Tipográficos de 104 SW 22nd Road, 1968), pp. 24–27 and 40.

11. Law No. 678 of December 23, 1959 (*Official Gazette,* December 24, 1959).

12. Resolution No. 16,782 of August 23, 1960 (*Official Gazette,* August 25, 1960).

13. Article 5, Law No. 907, December 30, 1960.

14. Article 36; see CERP, *Labor Conditions, op. cit.,* p. 147.

15. See "La nueva Ley de Procedimiento Laboral," *Trabajo,* No. 3, March 1961, p. 11.

16. See *El Mundo,* March 20, 1960.

17. See, for instance, the editorial carried by *Diario de la Marina* on April 27, 1960 and the *Havana Post* of the following day.

18. "La ley de intervención," *Trabajo*, No. 2, June 1960, p. 64.

19. See Article 8 of Law 647 of November 24, 1959.

20. *El Mundo*, March 17, 1960, p. A6.

21. René Dumont, *Cuba: Socialism and Development* (New York: Grove Press, Inc., 1970), p. 37.

22. Law No. 851 of July 6, 1960 (*Official Gazette* of July 7, 1960).

23. Law No. 980 of October 3, 1960 (*Extraordinary Official Gazette* of October 15, 1960).

24. *Ibid.*

25. Edward Boorstein, *The Economic Transformation of Cuba* (New York: Monthly Review Press, 1968), p. 33.

26. See Otto Vilches, "Dos días históricos," *Trabajo,* No. 7, November 1960, p. 67.

27. E. Boorstein, *op. cit.*, p. 33.

28. *Bohemia Libre* (Miami), Year 52, No. 9, December 4, 1960.

29. *El Mundo*, April 1, 1960, p. A4.

30. O. Vilches, *op. cit.*, p. 67.

31. *Cuba's Socialist Destiny, op. cit.*, p. 9.

32. Work on Sundays and holidays closely resembled the "subbotnicks" (Communist Saturdays) practice of the first years of the Russian Revolution.

33. See Carmelo Mesa Lago, "Economic Significance of Unpaid Labor in Socialist Cuba," *Industrial and Labor Relations Review* (Ithaca, N.Y.), Vol. 22, No. 3, April 1969, p. 344.

34. XV Congreso de la CTC. Informe central presentado por el compañero Roberto Veiga (Havana, 1984), p. 8.

35. Resolution No. 782 of August 23, 1960.

36. See "Un nuevo paso para el desarrollo de la emulación socialista." *Cuba Socialista,* Year 4, No. 36, August 1964, pp. 108–111. See also Carmelo Mesa Lago, *The Labor Sector and Socialist Distribution in Cuba* (New York: Praeger, 1968), p. 131.

37. Article 23 of the second Law respecting the Organization of the Labor Ministry (Law No. 907 of December 31, 1960 in *Official Gazette* of the same date).

38. See Augusto Martínez Sánchez, *La política laboral de la revolución socialista* (Havana; Editorial CTC-R, 1962), p. 15.

39. "La verdadera democracia," *Trabajo,* No. 2, June 1960, p. 25.

40. "Los trabajadores son aliados naturales de la revolución," *Trabajo,* No. 2, June 1960, p. 96.

41. *Revolución,* December 1, 1960, p. 1.

42. Ernesto Che Guevara, "Somos una antorcha encendida," in *Cuba: Una Revolución en marcha,* Suplemento 1967 de *Cuadernos de Ruedo Ibérico* (Colombes, France: Imprimerie Cary, 1967), p. 126.

43. See Fidel Castro's speech on the concept of the revolution addressed to government instructors and published in *Autocrítica de la Revolución Cubana* (Montevideo: Ediciones Uruguay, 1962), pp. 64–69.

44. The Chief of the Rebel Army, later Vice-President of Cuba, was Juan Almeida, a former *carpenter.* Almeida was also a Communist militant.

45. See A. Suárez, *Cuba, Castroism and Communism, op. cit.,* pp. 117 and 118.

46. "Los trabajadores son aliados naturales de la revolución." *Trabajo,* No. 1, May 1960, p. 96.

47. See, for instance, *Trabajo,* No. 2, June 1960, pp. 2 and 3, and No. 6, October 1960, p. 3.

48. Ernesto Guevara, "Discurso dirigido a la clase obrera." *Obra Revolucionaria* (Havana), No. 11, June 16, 1960, p. 13. In the Soviet Union, slogans designed to strengthen workers' discipline, improve production management and combat waste and inefficiency are frequently coined by the party and official leadership.

49. MacGaffey and Barnet, *op. cit.,* p. 150.

50. See the CTC's circular of September 6, 1960 signed by O. Alvarez de la Campa, with which the Declaration was transmitted to most trade union centers in the world. According to the circular, the Declaration of Havana was conceived as a reply to the "infamous" Declaration of San José adopted by the OAS in

August of the same year. The latter condemned extra continental intervention in Latin American affairs.

51. A more explicit announcement of Cuba's intention to promote "anti-capitalist revolutions" in Latin America was made by Castro five months later (in February 1961).

52. *Bohemia,* Year 52, No. 33, August 21, 1960.

53. *Revolución,* November 9, 1960, p. 6.

54. See "El congreso de la construcción," *Trabajo,* No. 2, June 1960, p. 94.

55. See *El Mundo,* August 23, 1960, p. D3.

56. *El Mundo,* August 27, 1960, p. A13.

57. "Los trabajadores son aliados naturales de la revolución," *op. cit.,* p. 96.

58. "Un mes de acontecimientos laborales," *Trabajo,* No. 6, October 1960.

59. See *Revolución,* November 7, 1960, p. 1 and *Bohemia libre* (Miami), Year 52, No. 9, December 4, 1960, p. 7.

X

The Last Vestiges of Opposition

Exit David Salvador

THE DRASTIC TRANSFORMATION OF THE LABOR MOVEMENT carried out during 1960 shows that the government plans left little room for dissenters or opponents. Once the revolutionary strategy entered into its final stages, labor leaders faced a critical choice: either to adhere to the new revolutionary credo or to face the risk of being treated as enemies of the regime. While other sectors of Cuban society, particularly the middle class, were initially given the choice of joining the revolution or assuming a neutral attitude, members of the working class had few alternatives other than to participate in the revolutionary process.

For the rank and file, the revolutionary tests were their attitude towards the militia, workers' contributions, voluntary work, and the increase of productivity. Failure to meet these tests entailed a possible loss of job opportunities and eventually a sort of social ostracism. For the leaders, there was much more to risk, as any sign of non-compliance with the government line could be construed as a deviationist attitude liable to be equated with counterrevolutionary activity. Should the dissenting position reach the point of open challenge to the government's plans, the dangers involved were, of course, even greater. What was considered in February 1960, as a sudden outburst of the PSP President Juan Marinello, namely that anti-Communism was in itself a counterrevolutionary position, became a few months later the official government policy.

It was against this background that a number of previously non-Communist or anti-Communist leaders decided in the spring and summer of 1960 to join the revolutionary process. Overwhelmed by the irresistible pressure of the revolution from above and below, from government and the lower strata of labor, they cast off their independence or their anti-Communism and accepted the unity with the Marxists that they had tried to prevent.[1] The government resorted for the most part to coercive tactics but did not hesitate to entice vacillating union leaders, such as Antonio Torres and José Pellón with special favors. However, not all of these newly converted leaders were considered reliable, for, along with the continued purges of mujalistas, several trade unions held assemblies in the summer of 1960 designed to eliminate lukewarm or vacillating leaders (so called "piernas flojas"). At the same time, other less malleable but somewhat weak labor leaders decided, on their own accord, to give up leadership positions and to fade away gradually from the labor movement. Finally, a number of leaders who were still faithful to their convictions as to what an independent labor movement should be, tried firmly to stem the revolutionary tide, even if the odds were heavily against them. One outstanding member of this group was the Secretary General of the CTC-R, David Salvador.

As indicated in previous chapters, Salvador did his best to follow the revolutionary current. He had been personally involved in all the major disputes that erupted in 1959, accompanying Raúl Castro to critical meetings and voicing support for the Prime Minister in numerous workers' assemblies. The top labor leader proposed some of the most radical resolutions at the Tenth Congress and was even willing to preside over the first phase of the purge committee set up

by the CTC-R. As late as January 1960, he referred enthusiastically in a "Meet the Press" program to the organization of workers' militias and the formation of a new hem-
ispheric labor organization.[2] Two months later, he signed a
"solidarity pact" with the Venezuelan Labor Confederation
(CTV) which contained ardent calls for continental solidarity
"in the fight for the redemption of the proletariat."[3] It seems
likely, however, that the CTC-R Secretary General had already fallen into disgrace with Castro even before the holding of the Tenth Congress. Not only had he refused to form
a united front with PSP leaders, but he had approved the
attempts made in October to establish contacts with the AFL-
CIO[4] and had repeatedly referred to the future role of private employers in Cuba. It may be noted in this connection
that in his second speech before the Tenth Congress, Castro
intimated that Salvador had made many mistakes in the past
and that he expected that the labor leader would be able to
rectify them.[5]

Salvador's fall may also be explained, in part, by the Prime
Minister's fears about his popularity. Castro never permitted
any trade unionist to emerge as an independent political
power. Those who did move up in the trade union hierarchy
limited themselves to acting as the Prime Minister's deputies;
their success depended largely on their ability to read Castro's
mind and to foresee his next moves. Salvador was an exception to this rule. Both because of his previous stature in the
underground movement and his personal appeal, he enjoyed
a measure of public support that was inevitably bound to
arouse Castro's suspicions.

Further events contributed to embitter the relationship
between the CTC-R leader and the government. Salvador
resented the overt intervention of the Labor Minister in internal trade union affairs through the "purification" procedures, as well as the rude methods used by Raúl Castro and

Jesús Soto. Because he was not prepared to cooperate in the promotion of Marxist-oriented competitors, he also grew disillusioned when he saw that the purges were being used to dump all the leaders who objected to the growing Communist influence within the labor movement. By the end of January, Salvador complained to Castro about what was happening. Castro appeared to agree and even rebuked his brother Raúl for his interference in trade union affairs. According to the report of a first-hand witness, Fidel told him that if it were not for the difficulties he was having with the U.S. he would kick the trouble-making Communists out of the labor movement. He promised Salvador that "as soon as the Yankees left him alone," he would do that. This, Rodríguez Quesada observed, was shrewdly calculated to quiet down Salvador who had always been strongly anti-American.[6]

The purges, however, continued and Salvador's position became increasingly embarrassing. He stayed away from some CTC-R events, including the Mikoyan visit to the Workers' Palace and continued to complain of the expanding scope of the purges. His opponents also grew impatient and decided to get him out of the way. By March 1960, the Prime Minister sent him on a mission to France to hand over a $10,000 indemnity to each one of the families of the French workers killed in the La Coubre explosion.[7] While Salvador was absent, the purges reached a climax; when he got back three weeks later, leaders of 22 of the 28 non-Communist federations had already been deposed or had resigned.[8] Salvador flew into a rage and had a bitter confrontation with the Labor Minister in the Presidential Palace. He sharply criticized the labor policies being applied in Cuba, but this time he realized that his disagreement was not only with Martínez Sánchez and Raúl Castro but with Fidel himself.

The last straw was probably the election of a new leadership in the construction industry which Salvador refused to

recognize, thereby prompting a sharp attack from the newspaper *Hoy*. By the end of April, he resigned as head of the
CTC-R and resisted all the pressures aimed at making him
change his mind. Though he was conspicuously absent from
the May Day parade, not a word was published in the government press about his resignation.

Not long afterwards, Salvador went into hiding and set
up the underground November 30 Revolutionary Movement, which took its name from an uprising against Batista
that took place in Santiago before the Granma landing. A
number of trade union leaders, including Luis Moreno (tobacco workers), Gabriel Hernández Custodio (pharmaceutical workers) and Jesús Fernández (electrical workers), joined
Salvador in setting up clandestine cells as the basis of the
new organization.

Conditions were not propitious, however, for a large-scale
operation of underground movements. A fully-fledged apparatus of control and repression was already in operation
and the contours of a totalitarian regime of Stalinist orientation were beginning to take shape. Not only were the militia
and the committees for the defense of the revolution prepared to avert the effective functioning of clandestine operations but also the political police (G2) and the armed
forces made it extremely difficult to carry out any form of
domestic anti-government action. On November 1, 1960,
Salvador tried to leave Cuba with some friends in a small
boat and was arrested. Next day, the Executive Committee
of the CTC-R expelled him dishonorably from the labor
movement and asked the revolutionary tribunals to impose
a harsh penalty on him. Numerous trade unions demanded
his execution, and even Salvador's own local union in the
Stewart sugar mill denounced him as a lackey of imperialism.
A revolutionary tribunal finally sentenced the former Secretary General to 30 years in prison.

The Electrical Workers' Demonstration

Aside from Salvador and his revolutionary movement, there were other pockets of resistance within organized labor. In the Electrical Workers' Federation (FSPE), for instance, July 26 Movement leaders had managed to survive several Communist attempts to take control of both the federation and the provincial unions. Led by Amaury Fraginals and Fidel Iglesias, the Electrical Workers' Federation had been able to ride out the 1959 and 1960 storms by maintaining a militant revolutionary image while consistently opposing Communism.[9]

But as the final stages of the Castro revolution unfolded, the situation became increasingly tense. When the Cuban Power and Light Company was nationalized in August 1960, the differences between the Fraginals leadership and its Marxist opponents, supported by the Minister of Labor, came to a head. At an FSPE meeting, Fraginals accused the government-appointed administrator of trying to curtail previous benefits and seeking to undermine the position of the elected leaders. The Communists replied that Fraginals' allegations were only a fabrication intended to support counterrevolutionary rumors. A new meeting of the Federation endorsed Fraginals in his denunciation, but from that day on the electrical workers' leader was constantly accused in the government press of trying to wreck the labor unions.[10]

On November 29, 1960, saboteurs blew up five power terminals in Havana, blacking out several districts. Three nights later, anti-Castro elements raided the power company and stole $100,000, presumably for the underground struggle. The CTC-R called a general meeting of electrical workers to be held on December 9 to fix responsibilities for the sabotage and theft. On the day the meeting was going to take place, *Revolución* published a manifesto signed by 600 electrical workers condemning the sabotage, saying that it had been supported by the Executive Committee of the Federation and urging the revolutionary tribunals to mete out exemplary sanctions.[11] Almost simultaneously, the G2 political police issued a report with the names of the saboteurs, all of whom were electrical workers connected with the underground movement. While neither Fraginals' nor Iglesias' names were mentioned in the report, other persons belonging to their group did appear in the police investigation.

Probably impressed by these publications, and in view of the experience of previous meetings convened by the CTC-R, Fraginals decided to boycott the December 9 meeting. Instead of attending it he asked his followers to stage a demonstration to protest the attempt by Communist elements to seize control of the union. Some 1,000 men paraded through the streets of Havana en route to the Presidential Palace shouting "Fraginals and Cuba SI, Russia NO!" asking for free elections and waving banners.[12] In front of the Presidential Palace, the crowd demanded an audience from President Dorticós. The President said that he would receive the leaders only if the demonstration was dissolved. At the order of Fraginals, the crowd dispersed and an uneasy interview between four union officials and the President followed. Dorticós accused Fraginals of being a demagogue and of endangering the revolution. The electrical workers' leader replied that they were not fighting the Cuban Revolution but the Communist Revolution. He finally proceeded to enumerate their demands: respect for the terms of the collective bargaining agreement and no more hiring, firing or demotion by the government administrator or the CTC-R.[13]

Nothing positive came of the interview, but the subsequent government reaction provides additional indications of Castro's sensitivity towards any form of labor protest. The idea that a segment of organized labor, however small, was demonstrating against his government was regarded as an intolerable action calling for immediate countervailing measures. Fraginals and Iglesias were expelled *ipso facto* from the July 26 Movement and other electrical worker leaders were put on trial before the revolutionary tribunals. Apparently, however, such measures were not considered enough to erase the repercussions of the demonstration; the government thus decided once again to resort to mass mobilization techniques.

Trade unions and other labor organizations throughout the island held "lightning" meetings to discuss the crisis in the electrical union. Hundreds of telegrams poured into the CTC-R and the government denouncing the counterrevolutionary attitude of dissident electrical workers and condemning the sabotage; a number of telegrams included advice to electrical workers regarding the most effective ways of getting rid of counterrevolutionaries. A special meeting of the CTC-R, the various National Federations and all the Havana national unions was held on December 13 to pass judgment on the counterrevolutionary conduct of saboteurs and their accomplices. Press releases and trade union resolutions insisted that it was a duty of "all patriotic workers," regardless of their trade union affiliation, to condemn both the sabotage and the demonstration.[14]

The December 13 meeting approved a manifesto addressed to the nation condemning the allegedly criminal acts of November 29 and December 9 and appealing to the patriotism of electrical workers. The manifesto was signed by 31 of the 33 national federations. There was, however, another dissenting voice in addition to the Electrical Workers' Federation, namely the Federation of Food Workers (FORA), which declined to attend the meeting and refused to go along with the attacks against the electrical union. FORA was quickly denounced by the CTC-R in strong terms as an ally of the counterrevolutionary groups.[15] It is also noteworthy that the December 13 manifesto contained a paragraph addressed to all local and national unions urging them to define their position or stand the risk of being regarded as counterrevolutionaries.[16]

All these mobilization efforts reached their culmination two days later in a meeting of electrical workers convened by the CTC-R. While the meeting was intended only for electrical workers, groups of activists and sympathizers from other unions, as well as members of the University of Havana students' federation (FEU) were allowed to sit in certain sections of the CTC-R assembly hall. Special security measures were also taken in connection with the admission to the hall. The meeting agreed to expel dishonorably from the labor movement all those materially or intellectually connected with the sabotage and to depose the entire Executive Committee of the federation and the Havana electrical union. A provisional Committee was appointed to run the organizations and the trade union elections were called off until further notice. The relevant resolution was submitted by Jesús Soto, who asked if there were any votes against his proposal. When nobody expressed opposition, the motion was declared unanimously approved.[17]

The keynote speech was delivered by Prime Minister Castro. He began by saying quite bluntly that the electrical workers' problem did not come as a surprise to him as he knew that the rank and file of FSPE were confused and conditions were propitious for such a crisis.[18] Castro remarked that the crisis had not erupted in the sugar industry or in any other humble sector of labor; instead, he said, it broke out in one of the privileged sectors of labor, a sector in which the leadership had connived in the past with management to secure better working conditions at the expense of the public. There were other labor sectors, like the bank employees union, he added, which were also privileged in comparison with other workers, but fortunately these sectors had an intelligent leadership. In the electrical workers' union, he pointed out, the rank and file were predisposed towards counterrevolutionary activities and the leadership was poor. He then proceeded to launch a violent attack on Fraginals and his followers, saying that they had been willing to sell the birthright of the working class, its right to rule and direct the country, for a miserable pottage of special privileges. Castro also blamed bad labor leaders for fostering divisions within the working class, rendering labor impotent and preventing it from pursuing its real objectives. It was at this point that he put the following question to his audience:

> Do you know what is the first goal for which the working class should fight; the only goal for which the working class in a modern society should fight? For the conquest of political power.[19]

After insisting that labor represented the majority of the population and was the creator of all existing wealth, Castro declared that the workers were nevertheless doomed to a miserable life unless they took power from the hands of monopolies, landowners and foreign interests. Towards the end of his speech, he hammered away at the need to use drastic remedies and advised electrical workers "to shake the tree" immediately and effectively.

It should, finally, be noted that the crisis in the electrical workers union had a tragic epilogue. Three workers accused of sabotage by the G2 report, Guillermo Le Santé, Julio Casiellas and Orlirio Menéndez, were executed a few days later. Photos taken of the demonstration were circulated among law enforcement agencies and many of the demonstrators were identified and arrested. Fraginals managed to go underground and escaped to Mexico, but other anti-Communist trade unionists, including some women trade unionists, who were actively opposing the government plans, were sentenced to long prison terms.

Other Signs of Agitation

The explosion of the Cuban Electric Company's terminal power plant was not the only act of sabotage in which workers were involved. Immediately after the CTC-R meeting of December 14, radio and television employees set fire to the TV equipment of the CMQ broadcasting station. In December, two major department stores went up in flames, demolished by incendiary materials expertly placed by saboteurs; in these cases also, the blaze was attributed to employees within the establishment concerned. A month later, another fire destroyed tobacco leaves worth almost one million dollars and the Tobacco Workers' Federation authorized its governing body to accentuate its vigilance and to expel any counterrevolutionary element.[20]

The workers involved in these three cases were predominantly white-collar employees or skilled blue-collar workers. As Castro remarked in his December 14 speech, opposition to the government plans was more active within the "upper" sectors of labor, whose mentality was akin to that of the middle classes.[21] Electrical workers, commercial employees and radio and TV workers were in effect relatively well-off social groups before Castro came to power and had, consequently, much more to lose in the change to socialism than the lower sectors of the proletariat. But the explanation was not only an economic one, as Castro had suggested, using a simple Marxist approach. It is likely that another factor involved was directly related to the way in which Castro was proceeding to socialize Cuba. Workers belonging to the upper echelons of labor possessed enough schooling, political awareness and sophistication to grasp what was happening in Cuba; they may have felt that Castro had originally proposed a different kind of revolution and resented the abandonment of the democratic goals so clearly expounded before January 1959. Conversely, sugar workers and other sectors of the lower proletariat may have been more susceptible to radical propaganda and did not have the same concern for broken promises or ideological deviations.

Whatever the motivation of the groups involved, there is little doubt that opposition to Castro increased among various categories of the working population during the last few months of 1960. A number of workers joined clandestine organizations and participated in underground activities.[22] Most anti-Castro workers joined the November 30 Revolutionary Movement, but a number of leaders and trade unionists participated in the organization of the Movement for Revolutionary Recuperation (MRR), the People's Revolutionary Movement (MRP) and the Students' Revolutionary Directorate (DRE). There was also a

substantial number of workers who decided to go into exile. In the fall of 1960, for instance, the International Rescue Commission made a breakdown of the refugees arriv-
ing in Miami and found that between 50 percent and 60
percent were blue and white collar workers. Subsequent
estimates found that 20 percent of the total number of
refugees were skilled, semiskilled and unskilled workers.
Included among these exiles were scores of trade union
leaders. A book published in 1965, for instance, contains
a list of 54 top labor leaders who went into exile between
1959 and 1961.[23]

While underground activists and workers in exile were
still a minority in comparison with the size of opposition
to the government in other social sectors, the existence of
widespread and active workers' opposition served to highlight the fact that the split of the Cuban people caused by
the Castro revolution had penetrated to the lower levels
of society.

The government must have estimated that the situation
had become serious, for special precautionary measures
were adopted with regard to the holding of labor meetings.
Even before the electrical workers' demonstration, people
attending meetings began to be frisked, in spite of Castro's
remarks that such a practice was psychologically counterproductive.[24] Tight security measures were also extended
to workers' social clubs and youth organizations.

Two other measures were adopted in December 1960,
with a view to securing further government control of the
labor movement. One was a special Christmas bonus,
amounting to 50 million pesos, which was granted to two
million workers.[25] The other was a change in the utilization
of the funds levied through the 4 percent workers' contribution. The latter measure was approved by the
CTC-R following a recommendation made by Castro at a

labor meeting held on December 17, 1960 (precisely three days after the meeting of electrical workers). Castro's proposal indicated that in the future, one percent of these funds would be devoted to the promotion of workers' social clubs and the rest to industrialization; this change allowed the governmnent to announce immediately the construction of 300 social centers in sugar mills and small towns throughout the island.[26]

Though the Christmas bonus and the promotion of recreational centers ran counter to the established "productionist" line, both measures were prompted by the existence of critical circumstances in which the government wanted to reassure labor of Castro's continued concern for the workers' welfare. To dramatize further this concern, a few months later the government began to distribute among workers thousands of private houses, expropriated from the bourgeoisie or abandoned by their owners. The distribution was made through the CTC-R to its affiliates.[27] Government and labor unions were thus combining to distribute privileges in return for loyalty and conformity.

To be sure, these measures were coupled with other, more restrictive ones. The Food Workers' Federation (FORA) was drastically purged, and a new provisional committee headed by Jesús Soto and Rogelio Iglesias was appointed by the CTC-R to run the union's affairs.[28] Other purges were carried out in the typographical, commerce, construction and telephone industries; in the latter sector, the Secretary General of the Havana Provincial Union sent a letter to union members urging them to oppose government socialization plans, whereupon he sought asylum in a Latin American embassy.[29] Hundreds of employees working in the Cuban Electric Power Company were discharged in retaliation for their support of Fraginals. A number of employees in other enterprises, including the

Cuban Telephone Company, the Havana Transit Corporation and various department stores were also summarily dismissed. The experience of the electrical workers also led to the inclusion in a January statute of a new ground for dismissal, relating to "any counterrevolutionary activity engaged in by the worker concerned."[30] Dismissal in such case was, of course, authorized without prejudice to the criminal responsibility that might also be applicable.

The process of militarizing labor was also continued and pursued to its ultimate extent. In November 1960, Castro urged the workers to turn every undertaking into a military unit, and the CTC-R responded by adopting a series of resolutions designed to impede sabotage and to provide stricter vigilance over workshop activities.[31] So called "Comités de Vigilancia Revolucionaria" were created at the level of the undertaking to complement the work of the militia and the CDR.[32] As rumors of an impending invasion of Cuban exiles increased, the government launched a new revolutionary slogan: "from the workshop to the trenches and from the trenches to the workshop."[33] Military preparations, which had already included women workers, extended now to older workers. Lastly, in a speech delivered in March 1961, the Prime Minister warned labor organizations that the fight against saboteurs should be the responsibility of the workers themselves.[34]

All these measures contributed to consolidate Castro's hold over the labor movement as a whole, but they also pushed individual workers into the underground movement. As the possibilities of expressing anti-Communist views in public or speaking out in assemblies became nil, many dissident workers turned to direct action. Though the electrical workers' demonstration represented the last vestige of open resistance to the government, a complete liquidation of all signs of agitation did not come until April

1961, when the underground was smashed in the wake of the Bay of Pigs fiasco. Many underground workers were included in the quarter of a million people rounded up by the militia on suspicions of being disloyal to the regime. Other underground figures like Reynol González were apprehended in the ensuing months. A few fled to Latin American embassies, seeking asylum.

Even after the Bay of Pigs debacle, the government continued to regard any sign of opposition within trade union circles as a very serious matter. Penalties of rigorous imprisonment were imposed on workers brought before revolutionary courts under an extraordinary procedure laid down in an 1896 Act governing trials during the War of Independence. New crimes appeared in the law in respect of offenses against the authority of the state, acts against public safety or offenses against the unity and stability of the nation. Additional penalties imposed on all of the persons tried were suspension of civil rights, subjection to supervision by the public authorities for a period equal to the main prison sentence and confiscation of all their properties. Finally, the death penalty was specifically provided in 1961 for various crimes including arson and sabotage.

Many years after the capture of the Cuban labor movement, several union leaders who opposed Castro's aims were still imprisoned in Cuban jails. Although the exact number is not known, a petition submitted in April 1976 to the Cuban Embassy in Caracas by a delegation of Latin American and Venezuelan labor leaders[35] mentioned 19 former trade union officials who were still in jail and indicated that the list was incomplete and would be revised in due course.[36] At least one former trade union leader of major standing, Francisco Aguirre, who had also held important positions in the international labor movement, died in prison as a result of malnutrition and lack of medical care.

Other jailed trade union leaders were deprived of food and water, frequently exposed to simulated executions or kept in isolated dark cells.

Repressive measures have also continued to be taken as regards the control of the rank and file. For instance, two complaints filed with the International Labor Organization by the International Confederation of Free Trade Unions (ICFTU) and the World Labor Confederation (WLC) in 1983, i.e., more than 20 years after the emasculation of the trade union movement, referred to the case of a number of workers in the sugar and construction industries which were prosecuted for attempting to organize a union and declare a strike in order to press for the improvement of their condition of work. According to the complaints, five workers were sentenced to death (later commuted to life imprisonment) and the others to long prison terms.[37]

Protests before International Organizations

As protest inside Cuba became practically impossible, complaints relating to trade union rights began to pour into international organizations, particularly the Organization of American States (OAS) and the International Labour Organization (ILO). At the OAS, relevant complaints were transmitted to the Inter-American Human Rights Commission (IAHRC) which, after long investigations, issued various reports detailing numerous cases of incarceration, deportation and execution of Cuban citizens dating back to 1959.[38] One of these reports indicated that 112 complaints and 1,350 communications concerning alleged violations of human rights had been filed against the government of Cuba; some of these complaints dealt with workers, peasants and militiamen.[39] Though the IAHRC addressed 48 official communications to the Cuban Government, the latter replied to only 12 of them.[40]

In the ILO, two bodies were involved with the handling of cases concerning violation of trade union rights by the Cuban Government, namely the Committee of Experts on the Application of Conventions and Recommendations and the Governing Body Committee on Freedom of Association (FAC). The former Committee dealt with several cases of infringement or inappropriate application of international conventions ratified by Cuba and/or discrepancies between such international conventions and the Castro revolutionary legislation.[41] The Committee on Freedom of Association, in turn, was competent to deal with complaints specifically connected with trade union developments. Because of the more direct relation of the FAC reports with the capture of the labor movement special attention will be given to these reports in the following paragraphs.

In November 1960, the Second Plenary Congress of the Christian Democrat (COPEI) Workers' Party of Venezuela presented a complaint to the United Nations (later transmitted to the ILO) concerning allegations of infringements of the exercise of trade union rights in Cuba. This complaint was declared not receivable because it emanated from a political party and not from an occupational organization.[42]

The following year the International Federation of Christian Trade Unions (IFCTU) addressed to the Director General of the ILO a telegram containing a request for urgent intervention by the ILO on grounds that the Cuban trade union leader Reynol González was in imminent danger of execution. The Director General brought the contents of the telegram to the notice of the Prime Minister and the Minister of Foreign Affairs of Cuba and requested the Government to furnish as speedy a reply as possible. No reply was received from the government. For the following three years the ILO kept requesting the Government of Cuba to furnish its observations on this complaint without ever receiving a reply.[43]

Also in 1961 the Electrical Workers' Federation (in exile) submitted a complaint concerning the shooting in January 1961 of the three workers accused of the sabotage of the power terminal. The ILO asked the Cuban Government to state, *inter alia,* whether the death sentences had been pronounced by an ordinary court of law, and, if not, to give particulars as to the nature and procedure of the court concerned. The Cuban Government replied, after considerable delay, that the workers who were shot had been found guilty of sabotage and that "all workers spontaneously called for the shooting of those union members."[44] In its report to the Governing Body, the Committee on Freedom of Association stated that the explanation provided by the Cuban authorities was difficult to reconcile with the government's further indication that 314 workers had been suspended and that others had been given work only in places "where they cannot commit sabotage."[45] The Committee also recommended that the Governing Body request the government to furnish the text of the judgment given against the three workers involved. This request was never met by the Cuban Government. Over the following two years the Committee dispatched eleven reminders but they all remained unanswered. Finally, in 1963 the Committee decided to close the case, deploring the inexplicable attitude of the government and pointing out that "trade unionists accused of political or criminal offenses should be given prompt and fair trial by an independent judicial authority."[46]

Of more general character were the complaints presented by the Confederation of Cuban Workers in Exile and the Economic Corporations of Cuba in Exile. These complaints related to the detention of trade union officials, the dissolution of employers' organizations and the infringement of international labor conventions on freedom of association. Though most of these complaints were lodged after 1961, the findings of the competent ILO bodies throw some light on the nature of various pieces of legislation enacted during the period under review.

As regards the detention of trade union officials, the Committee on Freedom of Association recommended that accused trade unionists, like all other persons, should be entitled to the safeguards of normal judicial procedures. The Committee noted that detailed information on the situation of a number of trade union officials had not been supplied by the Cuban Government and invited it to cooperate more fully with ILO procedures.[47]

With respect to the dissolution of employers' associations, the Committee concluded that the provisions contained in the second Law respecting the Organization of the Ministry of Labor (Act No. 907 of 31 December, 1960) permitted the adoption of administrative measures for the control of employers' organizations, which led finally to their dissolution.[48]

Similar conclusions were noted in regard to the infringement of international conventions on freedom of association. The Committee concurred with an observation made by the Committee of Experts on the Application of Conventions and Recommendations that the provisions contained in the first Law respecting the Organization of the Labor Ministry of 1960, empowering the Minister of Labor to control occupational organizations when circumstances made it necessary, appeared difficult to reconcile with ILO Convention No. 87 on Freedom of Association (1948) ratified by Cuba.[49] It also pointed out that the 1961 Law of Trade Union Organization (which will be discussed in the next chapter) did not appear to be compatible with article 2 of the same Convention regarding the workers' right to join organizations of their own choosing without previous authorization.[50] Finally, the Committee drew attention to the fact that important aspects of conditions of work which fell under the regulatory powers of the Ministry of Labor were virtually excluded from the field of collective bargaining.[51]

Hardly any of the above noted conclusions brought about any changes in the government position concerning developments in the labor movement. The Committee on Freedom of Association of the ILO was established as a watchdog organ, with powers limited to moral suasion. Its decisions lack binding effects and its procedures are hemmed in by safeguards against public embarrassment of ILO member governments. It is, nonetheless, important to indicate that even those bureaucratic and bland procedures were systematically avoided by the Cuban Government during the critical period of the trade unions' capture. As noted above, the Cuban authorities refused for several years to furnish information on certain matters or provided it on a very limited basis.

It is also noteworthy that, for the first time since Cuba joined the ILO in 1919 the government did not send a delegation to the 1960 International Labor Conference. Either the Government felt insecure about the choice of the workers' and employers' delegates or it wanted to avoid an international debate about possible infringement of trade union rights. When it did send a delegation to the 1961

Conference, the workers' representation was given to Ursinio Rojas, a veteran Communist leader. Rojas delivered a virulent attack against the U.S. concerning both labor and non-labor problems. His language was so unusually inflammatory that the speaker had to be interrupted several times by the Chairman, who asked Mr. Rojas to confine himself to labor problems.[52] Although on that occasion the Bay of Pigs invasion provided ammunition for such an attack, the aggressive position taken by the Cuban workers' delegate in 1961 set a pattern which was to be followed in all subsequent international labor meetings.

NOTES

1. Joseph Morray, *The Second Revolution in Cuba* (New York, 1962), p. 78.

2. See *El Mundo*, January 8, 1960, p. A1.

3. See *El Mundo*, April 2, 1960, p. B6.

4. See Serafino Romualdi, *Presidents and Peons: Recollections of a Labor Ambassador in Latin America* (New York: Funk and Wagnalls, 1967), p. 208.

5. *Dos Discursos, op. cit.*, p. 61.

6. Rodríguez Quesada, *op. cit.*, p. 21.

7. See "En Cuba." *Bohemia*, Year 52, No. 14, April 3, 1960 and *El Mundo*, March 17, 1961, p. A1.

8. O'Connor, *The Origins of Socialism in Cuba, op. cit.*, p. 193.

9. That the FSPE had been closely associated with the anti-Communist campaigns may be seen by its willingness to sponsor in the summer of 1959 a TV program intended to point out the extent of the Communist threat. See Bethel, *The Losers, op. cit.*, p. 161.

10. See Monaham and Gilmore, *op. cit.*, p. 13; Draper, *Castro's Revolution: Myths and Realities, op. cit.*, p. 45.

11. *Revolución*, December 9, 1960, pp. 1 and 15.

12. See *New York Times*, December 10, 1960, pp. 1 and 4.

13. Monaham and Gilmore, *op. cit.*, pp. 14 and 15.

14. For a detailed account of these activities see the *Revolución* issues of December 10–15, 1960.

15. *Revolución*, December 15, 1960, p. 1.

16. *Ibid.*, pp. 1 and 13.

17. *Ibid.*, p. 13.

18. *Ibid.*, The text of Castro's speech also appeared in *Obra Revolucionaria.*, No. 32, December 15, 1960; excerpts were reproduced in *Trabajo*, No. 8, December 1960, p. 3. The following citations are from *Revolución*, December 16, 1960.

19. *Ibid.*

20. See the section "Un mes de acontecimientos laborales,"

in *Trabajo*, No. 2, February 1961, p. 88; and *Trabajo*, No. 3, March 1961, p. 88.

21. Castro's remarks coincided with Dudley Seers' observation that support for the regime was strongly correlated with former levels of income, though Seers added two other factors: skin color and age. See *Cuba: The Economic and Social Revolution, op. cit.*, p. 3.

22. References to workers' participation in underground activities can be found in Haynes Johnson, *Bay of Pigs* (New York: Grove Press, 1964), p. 40; Bethel, *The Losers op. cit.*, p. 273; Draper, *Castro's Revolution, op. cit.*, p. 45 and Howard Hunt, *Give Us the Day, op. cit.*, p. 217.

23. Mario Riera, *Historial obrero cubano, 1574–1965* (Miami: Rema Press, 1965), p. 303.

24. *Revolución*, November 9, 1960, p. 6.

25. "Un mes de acontecimientos laborales." *Trabajo*, No. 8, December 1960, p. 167.

26. See *Ibid.*, and *Revolución*, December 18, 1960.

27. "Una quincena de acontecimientos laborales." *Trabajo*, Year II, No. 10, 1st Fortnight, August 1961, p. 42.

28. "Un mes de acontecimientos laborales." *Trabajo*, No. 2, February 1961, pp. 93 and 94.

29. *Trabajo*, No. 3, March 1961, p. 42.

30. Law No. 924 of January 4, 1961, (*Official Gazette* of the same date).

31. See *El Mundo,* November 15, 1960, p. 1.

32. See *Trabajo*, No. 2, February 1961, pp. 89 and 90.

33. *Ibid.*, p. 63.

34. *Trabajo*, No. 4, April 1961, p. 126.

35. This delegation was headed by Rafael León, Secretary General of the Venezuelan Workers' Confederation (CTV) and Emilio Máspero, Secretary General of the Latin American Labor Confederation (CLAT).

36. "Libertad para sindicalistas cubanos." *Informativo CLAT* (Caracas), Year 1, No. 3, June 1976, p. 12.

37. See the 226th report of the ILO Committee on Freedom

of Association in International Labor Office, *Official Bulletin*, Vol. LXVI, 1983, Series B, No. 1. The two complaints gave rise to case No. 1198. In its reply the Cuban Government indicated that the workers in question had been tried and condemned for sabotage. See also *Le Monde* (Paris), June 28, 1983, p. 5.

38. See *Report on the Situation of Political Prisoners and Their Relatives in Cuba.* Approved by the Inter-American Commission on Human Rights at its session held on May 2, 1963 (OAS/Ser. L/V/II, 7, Doc. 4). See also *Report on the Situation of Human Rights in Cuba* (OAS/Ser. L/VIII, 4, Doc. 30) and *Second Report on the Situation of Political Prisoners and Their Relatives in Cuba* (OAS/Ser. L/V/II, 23, Doc. 6, rev. 1).

39. *Report on the Situation of Political Prisoners and Their Relatives in Cuba, op. cit.*, p. 1.

40. *Ibid.*

41. See, for instance, ILO, *Report of the Committee of Experts on the Application of Conventions and Recommendations*, Report III (Part IV), International Labor Conference, 46th Session, (Geneva, 1962), pp. 89–90.

42. See ILO, *Official Bulletin*, Vol. XLIV, No. 3, 1961, p. 227.

43. See a summary of this case in ILO, *Official Bulletin*, Vol. XLVI, No. 3, Supplement, July 1963, pp. 60–62.

44. See "58th Report of the Governing Body Committee on Freedom of Association," ILO, *Official Bulletin*, Vol. XLV, No. 1, Supplement, January 1962, pp. 104 and 105.

45. *Ibid.*, p. 107.

46. See "70th Report of the Governing Body Committee on Freedom of Association," ILO, *Official Bulletin*, Vol. XLVI, No. 3, Supplement 11, July 1963, p. 34.

47. See ILO, *Official Bulletin*, Vol. XLIX, No. 2, Supplement, April 1966, p. 47.

48. See ILO, *Official Bulletin*, Vol. LIII, No. 2, Supplement, 1970, p. 107.

49. *Ibid.* Convention 87 deals with freedom of association and protection of the right to organize.

50. *Ibid.*, p. 106.

51. *Ibid.*, p. 110.

52. See International Labor Conference, Forty-fifth Session, Geneva, 1961. *Record of Proceedings* (Geneva, 1962), p. 149.

XI

The Transition Comes to an End

Discontent: Latent and Visible

FOR ALL PRACTICAL PURPOSES, TRADE UNIONS CEASED TO EXIST as independent organs representing the workers in late 1960. In the twelve months that had elapsed between December 1959 and December 1960, the labor leadership had been purged, forced to emigrate, jailed, cowed or thoroughly indoctrinated, while the government had managed to retain the support of sizeable portions of the rank and file. To be sure, substantial segments of the work force, notably urban workers, remained opposed to socialism and assumed a sullen and uncooperative mood. For many of them, these feelings led to the decision to leave the island. As some observers have noted, the second wave of exiles who left the island in 1961 included a considerable number of skilled workers and representatives of organized labor.[1] A Cuban Democratic Revolutionary Labor Front was quickly set up in exile as one of the many organizations fighting for the overthrow of Castro. According to a Marxist-oriented writer, "an unknown number of its members infiltrated Cuba just before the Bay of Pigs invasion in order to lead a massive workers' uprising against the Revolution, which failed to materialize."[2]

For those who stayed in Cuba, the attitude of opposition was reflected mainly in the increase of absenteeism and the decline of productivity. In February 1961, for instance, Guevara visited a Havana metalworking factory with an Argentinian friend and noticed that many workers were absent, whereupon he asked for the payroll and other relevant documents and was able to verify that 25 per cent of the workers had been reported absent that day for sickness or other reasons.[3] This was approximately five times the normal acceptable rate of absenteeism and a considerable higher rate than the one that used to prevail in Cuba before Castro. Small wonder that a few months later, in September 1961, when he appeared before the First Plenary Session of Production Units of Greater Havana, Guevara bluntly recognized that absenteeism was reaching alarming proportions.[4] At about the same time, Lázaro Peña was decrying the workers of the largest textile enterprise in Cuba for their poor performance and sagging productivity trends. The government was obviously aware of this situation for it launched in October a vigorous campaign against absenteeism and in August 1962 issued a decree providing for harsh penalties for absentee workers. The first serious signs of what was to become a major problem of socialist production in subsequent years were thus detectable during the critical transitional period of 1960–61. It is interesting to note that nearly 20 years later, Raúl Castro was still denouncing the lack of discipline of the workers, their neglect of production efforts, persistent absenteeism, the abuse of breaks and the connivance of workers with foremen to elude the observance of production norms, as some of the factors accounting for the decline in labor productivity.[5]

The psychological effects of the Bay of Pigs debacle obviously contributed to consolidate Castro's grip on the country. For one thing, it fully dispelled any preconceived notions about the geopolitical significance of the "90 miles theory," i.e., the idea that a Communist regime could not survive in the backyard of the U.S. For another, it enhanced

Castro's image as a *macho* power, an image that was particularly appealing to certain sectors of the population. However, some spontaneous demonstrations of protest that took place over the following months served to spotlight the degree of opposition that Castro's plans had aroused. In September 1961, during celebrations of the Festival of Cuba's Patron Saint, crowds composed of workers and people of all walks of life shouted *Down with Communism* and booed Castro in Reina Street, near the very center of Havana. Several months later, a major outbreak of popular and workers' discontent took place in the city of Cárdenas on the north coast of Cuba. For almost two days, Cárdenas witnessed a violent and massive revolt against the Castro regime, staged by people of "humble" origin, wage earners, fishermen and housewives. According to an eyewitness, the protest demonstrations, which took place in practically all the streets of the city, were brutally quelled with use of tanks and planes.[6]

At the level of labor organizations, however, coordination of opposition activities became virtually impossible and Castro's control over the labor movement was practically unchallenged.

Having thus completed the final phases of the strategy to capture the labor movement, the stage was prepared for the establishment of a dictatorship of the proletariat. But before announcing formally that a "socialist republic existed in Cuba," there were still a few pieces to fit into place. In the field of internal union developments, it was necessary to finalize the process of merger of unions and modification of their structure and functions which had been begun in the fall of 1960. As regards international relations, it appeared opportune to formalize the CTC-R's entry into the Communist trade union world.

Trade Unions' Final Transformation

In early 1961, numerous discussions took place at various levels of the trade unions with a view to completing the reorganization of the labor movement. The telephone workers, for instance, merged with postal and telegraphic workers to form a larger telecommunications union. A united maritime and port workers' union was also established in Havana in place of 30 existing unions. Other unions in the airline and metal industries also decided to integrate themselves into bigger and more compact organizations.

Once enough ground had been broken in that direction, the CTC-R was asked, in March 1961, to discuss a draft new trade union statute. The draft, which had been prepared by the Ministry of Labor, contained some constitutional amendments and provided the basis for the readjustment of trade unions to the realities of a new socialist society. According to *Trabajo*, the proposed statute was unanimously and enthusiastically approved by the CTC-R national council.[7] Though it was supposed to become law in April, the Bay of Pigs invasion delayed its enactment until August 1961.[8]

The new organization of the labor movement followed closely the Soviet trade union structure. In every undertaking there was to be a branch union, in every industry only one union would be allowed and a single all-embracing central labor organization was to be established for the whole country. As in the Soviet Union, the right to organize was granted without distinction to private and public employees, including those engaged in the administration of the state and local government. Unions were to be constituted in the future on a semi-industrial basis; organization by craft was eliminated as it was regarded contrary to the traditional Communist stand regarding the composition of labor organizations. According to Communist theory, craft unions tended to split the workers into separate organizations which would often be bound to display a narrow, guildlike approach. Finally, a special provision of the 1961 law excluded members of agricultural producers' cooperatives from trade union membership. This provision followed a long standing practice in the USSR according to which workers in collective farms (kolkhozes) and producers' cooperatives (artels) were *de facto* placed outside the trade union structure.[9]

The total number of national unions or federations was limited to 25; the total number of members of the executive committees was reduced to a maximum of 13, which represented a substantial cut from the previous executive bodies composed of 30 to 40 members. According to the government press, the latter measure was intended to eradicate some of the shortcomings resulting from trade union "bureaucratism."[10]

In its internal composition, the new system provided that union sections in enterprises of a given industry affiliate with the regional and provincial bodies in that industry and with the appropriate national union. At the same time, each section was to affiliate with the CTC-R through its corresponding local, regional and the provincial bodies and national congresses of the national union.

The transformation was even more drastic with regard to the role assigned to trade unions. Workers' organizations ceased to be primarily concerned with the defense of sectional interests or with the promotion of particular demands.[11] Instead, the basic objective of the union was to assist in the fulfillment of the production and development plans of the nation, to promote efficiency, expansion and greater utility in the social and public services and to add to the betterment of administration in all fields. Other important objectives included organizing and carrying out political, physical and technical education activities and assisting the state in the formation of workers' social clubs.

These basic functions of trade unions were further developed when the new constitution of the CTC-R was approved by the Eleventh Congress held in November 1961. The duties of labor organizations as auxiliary organs of the state administration were spelled out in various sections of the constitution. There were, for instance, some references to the role of unions concerning the enforcement of labor legislation and social security measures, the allocation of housing facilities, the administration of nurseries and participation in economic planning.[12]

While the new statute recognized the workers' right to join or not to join a union and to engage in trade union and revolutionary propaganda, there were a few significant limitations. First, trade union pluralism and freedom of choice were excluded as workers had only one possible affiliation open to them. Secondly, the Minister of Labor and the CTC-R retained authority to accept or reject the application for recognition of new workers' organizations. Thirdly, propaganda activities were only permitted to the extent compatible with the interests of production, the state and public services. Fourthly, the CTC-R's constitution indicated that it was a duty of all affiliates to increase production and observe trade union discipline. Fifthly, the same constitution also made clear that all the resolutions adopted by the CTC-R top-level bodies were binding on the lower level labor organizations. Finally, people with a "counterrevolutionary background" were excluded from the governing bodies of the unions.

However, the 1961 trade union law fell short of recognizing the leading and overriding role of the Communist Party vis-à-vis the conduct of labor organizations, as it is recognized, for example, in the Soviet Constitution. True, the silence of the law did not prevent some trade union national congresses from accepting a few months later the guidance of the existing political apparatus, but the fact that this was not spelled out in the statutory regulation seemed to depart from the Soviet model. This difference may be explained, however, by the absence in 1961 of a unified, full-fledged Marxist-Leninist party, which was not set up in Cuba until 1962.[13] At the same time, the fact that doubts were expressed in 1961 about the raison d'être of unions and that some government officials considered that traditional labor organizations had become "outdated and useless,"[14] showed the extent to which some major trade union functions had been taken over by the government.

At the time the union reorganization law was adopted, the *Hispanic American Report* indicated that the reorganization was expected to expedite workers' cooperation in fulfilling production targets.[15] However, the reduction in the number of unions and trade union officials, the vertical type of organization created and the tendency to place authority at the top, also suggested that the new system was expected to facilitate control of the labor movement by the new hierarchy. It is also noteworthy that several months before the Eleventh Congress, various Communist leaders of the old generation, including Lázaro Peña and Blas Roca, were already submitting reports on emulation, absenteeism and productivity to the CTC-R Executive Committee and actually guiding its functions.[16] In the month of July, for example, Blas Roca delineated the future tasks of the trade unions by referring to the strengthening of the political consciousness of the back-

ward sections of the working class and the mobilization of
the workers for the increase of production and productivity. While he also mentioned the defense of the immediate
interests of the workers, Roca made clear that such interests would have to be sacrificed in case of conflict with the
objectives of the revolution.[17]

Changes in International Affiliations

In the field of international relations, the disaffiliation
of the CTC-R from ORIT was followed by an intensive
"anti-imperialist" campaign conducted by pro-Marxist
leaders throughout Latin America. Cuban trade union
leaders toured Central and South America immediately
after the Tenth Congress with a view to promoting a purely
Latin American organizational structure and to excoriating
ORIT and panamericanism. Contacts were made with the
Chilean CUTCH, the Bolivian COB and other Marxist-
oriented national organizations in Uruguay and Venezuela, with a view to creating a new Latin American confederation.[18] ORIT reacted in December 1959, by observ-
ing that the labor policies of the Cuban Government were
actually serving the interests of the Kremlin.[19] The ORIT's
statement did not elaborate, but one might assume that it
was referring to the rise of PSP leaders in Cuba and the
promotion of a separate Latin American group in the Western Hemisphere.

No open move mas made, however, to affiliate the
CTC-R to the Communist-controlled World Federation of
Trade Unions (WFTU). The government apparently
wanted first to defuse the ORIT charges and to bid for

some additional time. Starting in January 1960, however, numerous trips were organized to send CTC-R leaders to socialist countries, especially East Germany, the USSR, China and Czechoslovakia. Included in these trips were not only the well-defined Marxist leaders of the CTC-R, but also some formerly independent or middle-of-the-road officials. Articles also began to appear in the government press extolling the progress achieved by the labor movement in socialist countries.

Visits and articles were coupled with meetings designed to foster greater affinity with Communist-sponsored movements. As mentioned in Chapter IX, a Latin American Congress of Young Trade Unionists held in July, 1960, gathered in Havana an array of Maoist, Trotskyist and pro-Moscow participants who seemed to share a common hatred of "imperialist" policies. In October of the same year, the CTC-R invited the Secretariat of the International Trade Union Committee for Solidarity with the Workers and People of Algeria to meet in Havana. WFTU organizations and a large contingent of pro-Communist Latin American, African and Asian trade union leaders attended the meeting, which was regarded as a demonstration of the effectiveness of neutralist and Soviet bloc working relations in the international trade union field.[20] A few months later, Havana also hosted a plantation workers' conference which served as a forum to disseminate revolutionary teachings and to establish a rival to the ICFTU plantations organization.[21] The bonds of sympathy and mutual understanding between WFTU and its affiliates and the CTC-R were further reinforced through various exchanges of solidarity messages. In November 1960, for instance, the WFTU sent a message to the CTC-R condemning American aggression and praising the patriotism of Cuban workers.[22] In February 1961, the CTC-R and the East German trade union federation signed a joint statement on the exchange of information and delegations.

At the level of industry-wide organizations, steps were taken to affiliate individual Cuban federations to the corresponding WFTU trade departments. This was done first in July 1960, with the metal workers' federation and continued with the railway unions. By the fall of 1960, almost all the ICFTU international trade secretariats had pulled out of Cuba and were being gradually replaced by the WFTU departments.

The situation became accordingly ripe for a closer rapprochement of the CTC-R with the higher bodies of the WFTU. Cuban observers attended WFTU meetings on an informal basis and in February 1961, Fausto Calcines and O. Alvarez de la Campa represented the CTC-R officially at a regular meeting of the WFTU. When they returned from Prague, they brought along a WFTU delegation which toured the island and reached final agreement on the affiliation of the Cuban labor movement to the Communist world labor organization. This affiliation was ratified by the national unions concerned in November 1961. Strangely enough, however, the Eleventh Congress did not consider it necessary to discuss this point and devoted its relevant "international" resolution to the organization of a Latin American Trade Union Conference.[23] But a month after the Congress, i.e., in December 1961, Lázaro Peña, the new Secretary-General of the CTC-R, was elected Vice-President of the Communist World Federation of Trade Unions.

The National Union Congresses

Following the reorganization of the unions in August 1961, union elections were held throughout Cuba in October. Each industrial sector elected both a union section committee and delegates to the coming national union congresses, to be held in November, and for the Eleventh Congress of the CTC-R. The latter was billed in the government press as the culminating point of the restructuring of the trade union movement.

According to Cuban government sources, about two million workers participated in the elections. Balloting was secret and candidates were nominated by the groups of workers concerned. However, it is not certain how much freedom there was in the choice of candidates. The CTC-R publication *Vanguardia Obrera* urged editorially that the workers show their revolutionary solidarity by nominating a single candidate for each post.[24] *Trabajo* subsequently indicated that in 98 per cent of the cases the single slate had been unanimously elected.[25] The pattern of Communist elections was thus dutifully respected.

On November 22, 23 and 24, the twenty-five national unions held their congresses in Havana. The meetings took place in the premises of large hotels and workers' social clubs which, as mentioned earlier, were now installed in what used to be the hotels and clubs of the middle and upper classes. The sugar workers, for instance, met at the Havana Hilton, while the metal workers held their sessions in the former Havana Yacht Club.

More than 10,000 delegates were on hand for the meetings. The delegates were treated with the utmost attention by the government; an elaborate program of banquets, concerts, ballet performances, floor-shows and films was

organized and occupied a substantial part of the time al-
lotted to the congresses. Cabinet ministers and other high-
ranking government officials made special efforts to attend
the congress meetings, particularly those specifically connected with the business of their departments. Each national congress meeting also benefited from the presence
and advice of fraternal observers from other socialist
countries.[26]

The twenty-five national congresses gave first priority
to the ways and means of meeting the targets set down in
the national development plans prepared by JUCEPLAN.
After three years of revolutionary mobilization, most delegates were responsive to government exhortations and
this may explain the adoption of resolutions aimed at over-
fulfillment of the targets, stimulating productivity, cutting
down production costs, eliminating absenteeism and promoting socialist emulation. One after the other, the national congresses also agreed to relinquish certain social
benefits liable to hamper production efforts, such as the
automatic payment of nine days' sick leave, the Christmas
bonus and the fixing of hours of work below the eight
hours standard.[27] Many congresses agreed to revise whatever clauses of collective bargaining agreements could be
regarded as excessively costly or contrary to productivity.
According to a prominent PSP delegate, such austerity
measures were intended to ameliorate the country's budg-
etary situation and to reinforce capital formation.[28]

Other items discussed by the delegates attending the
national congresses related to further improvements in the
revolutionary national militias, the stepping up of vigilance
at the workshop, the strengthening of the Committees for
the Defense of the Revolution, the reactivation of grievances committees and technical advisory councils, the al-

location of housing to the most needy people, improvement of workers' social clubs, promotion of cultural and sports activities and eradication of illiteracy.[29]

The new mentality of the Cuban labor leaders was also discernible in the resolutions approved by the sugar workers regarding shipment by bulk and by the port workers with respect to mechanization of port operations. Both measures had been strongly opposed in the past as inimical to employment maintenance and job creation policies. It was also significant that the various national congresses adopted a slogan aimed at producing "today more than yesterday, tomorrow more than today."[30] As Carlos Fernández pointed out, there was no doubt that the resolutions of the national congresses "marked the triumph of revolutionary notions over the narrow and opportunistic ideas of business unionism."[31]

There were also other resolutions dealing with political questions. Some national congresses decided to accept the guidance and orientation of the recently-created ORI (Organizaciones Revolucionarias Integradas) political mechanism.[32] The miners' congress voted to send a message to Nikita Khruschev, greeting him as "the first miner of the world."[33] Other congresses preferred to salute in more general terms the Communist Party Congress then being held in Moscow. The usual condemnation of yankee imperialism appeared in various resolutions but was particularly resounding in the one adopted by the textile workers' congress.

One common characteristic of all the proceedings was the fact that all the resolutions, regardless of their nature, were unanimously approved by the delegates. Not a single dissenting vote was cast; not a single dissenting view was expressed. The phenomenon was indeed so remarkable

that in his speech before the Eleventh Congress the Secretary General of the PSP, Blas Roca, recommended that
some discussion be encouraged before approving a resolution and that a vote should be taken in every case.[34]

The Eleventh Congress of the CTC-R

Immediately after the national union congresses, nearly
ten thousand delegates (9,560 to be exact) met for the
holding of the Eleventh Congress of the CTC-R. A few
weeks before its opening, another deliberately ignited fire
had partially destroyed the Workers' Palace, but a government appeal to construction, electrical and metal workers
had made possible the reconstruction of the assembly hall
in time for the opening ceremony. This was hailed in the
press as another victory of the revolution.

Attending the congress were 200 fraternal delegates,
mostly from socialist countries. Included among them were
top level representatives from the USSR, Bulgaria, East
Germany and Czechoslovakia. Messages from socialist dig-
nitaries were read and the International Anthem was played
at the opening ceremony. All the top hierarchy of the
government, including eight ministers, also made a point
of mingling with delegates and participating in the work
of the congress.[35]

Having thus taken care of all the preliminary details,
the stage was now set for the nomination of Lázaro Peña
as chief of the Cuban labor movement. On November 29,
after nearly fifteen years outside the trade union leadership, the veteran Communist leader was elected for the
post of Secretary General on the strength of a single list

of candidates. Peña's election was not an easy decision for Castro. Though the PSP leader was a dedicated and honest labor leader who had participated in the founding of the CTC, he also represented the past, the old association between Batista and the Communist Party. The fact that he was also the instrument chosen by the government to implement the tough productionist line probably contributed to his declining popularity. Three years after the Eleventh Congress, a pro-Castro Argentine author observed that "the one leader who enjoyed the unanimous opposition of [Cuban] workers was Lázaro Peña."[36] He was, however, familiar with the application of Marxist principles and could exhibit a one hundred per cent loyalty record to the Communist cause.

Along with Lázaro Peña, various members of the "old guard" also rose to power within the labor movement. Castro, however, did not allow a full takeover of the CTC-R by the seasoned Communist leadership. His unwillingness to grant too much power to a potential competitor was once again manifested here. Although he had no doubt decided since the beginning to radicalize the revolution, and to introduce Communism in Cuba, there is little doubt that he wanted to do so on his own terms and without endangering his personal power. Moreover, there were during the first months of 1959 and on other brief occasions some mutual misgivings and divergences between Castro and a few top leaders of the PSP.[37] Such tensions were prompted by tactical differences or personal jealousies and were never due to the PSP being opposed to Castro's moving towards a radical transformation of Cuban society.[38] Now, after three years of personal rule, most of these apprehensions had disappeared due to the unconditional acceptance of Castro's leadership by the PSP. The Prime Minister was therefore willing to place the expert

Communist leaders in command of organized labor. Yet to avoid any possible challenge to his absolute power, he was also determined not to confer upon them full control of the working class structure.

A glance at the composition of the Executive Committee elected at this Eleventh Congress reveals, in effect, the presence of three different groups sharing control of the CTC-R. There was, first of all, the "old guard" group represented by five members of the PSP: Lázaro Peña, Carlos Fernández, Ursinio Rojas, Fausto Calcines and Héctor Carbonell. Next, there was the group of opportunistic and adaptable leaders who, under the flag of the July 26 Movement, had so effectively been in charge of the transition. Jesús Soto, José María de la Aguilera, Rogelio Iglesias, Octavio Louit and Odón Alvarez de la Campa made up this group.[39] Finally, there were three representatives of the new breed of "true revolutionary leaders," those who were products of the revolution and owed allegiance only to Castro. These were: María de los Angeles Periu, Vicente Valdés and Waldina Restano.

But the Eleventh Congress was a momentous one not only because it marked the return of the Communist leadership. It also served to ratify the voluntary renunciations made previously by the national congresses of various privileges and rights that the Cuban working class had secured during the previous 25 years. This abrogation comprised legal as well as contractual provisions. Regarding the former, the congress agreed, for instance, to relinquish the practice of paying an employee at the end of the year the nine days' sick leave prescribed by law, even if he had not been sick. Another resolution provided for the discontinuation after 1962 of the Christmas bonus which constituted in fact part and parcel of the basic remuneration. The delegates also decided on a 48 hour work week instead of the maximum of 44 hours (with 48 hours of pay) established in the 1940 Constitution; this measure, which entailed an increase in hours of work and a 9.09% reduction in wages, applied to all industries except those involving dangerous or unhealthy conditions. Furthermore, the congress decided that overtime remuneration for extra hours worked during the 1962 sugar harvest should be given up.[40] Finally, on Lázaro Peña's proposal, the delegates agreed that workers should continue to contribute 4 per cent of their remuneration for industrialization, but without receiving any interest on these contributions. Past interest and dividends were also specifically abandoned by the congress, on behalf of the workers.[41]

As to the contractual benefits, the congress resolved to do away with any form of profit-sharing, feather-bedding, or make-work practices contained in existing collective agreements. It further authorized the Minister of Labor and the parties concerned to revise all clauses of collective agreements which might hinder the development of production, the growth of productivity and the progress of socialism.

The foregoing renunciations were preceded by direct exhortations from high-ranking government officials. In delivering the opening speech, President Dorticós told the congress that the objectives of the working class no longer were to obtain piece-meal economic demands or partial "social conquests" but to make the new society advance along the path of socialism.[43] Dorticós made some critical remarks about the "false leaders" who betrayed the cause of the workers' liberation and declared that the Cuban revolutionary process, "which has gone through sad moments of backward steps, is tied to the development of the Cuban workers' movement."[44]

Minister of Industry Ernesto Guevara announced that by the end of 1961, 90 per cent of all industries would be in the hands of the working class and that the goal was nothing less than 100 per cent worker control of the economy.[45] "We are already owners of virtually all the means of production," he said, "but this entails some responsibilities."[46] He then proceeded to impress upon workers the need to improve their political and technical abilities and to increase productivity. A special paragraph was devoted to the old collective bargaining agreements which were, in his view, unsuited to socialist production norms and new production patterns. Though he recognized that labor leaders were placed in a difficult position in asking workers to relinquish some benefits, he made it clear that the workers' resistance to accepting the new, modified agreements would not be tolerated. Towards the end of his speech he predicted that differences between manual and non-manual or intellectual work, between the city and the countryside, would gradually disappear and that a new classless society would emerge as the society of the future.

Less concerned with future developments was the statement of the Minister of Labor, who indicated that the congress closed one stage and opened a new one and explained the new tasks assigned to both labor leaders and his department.[47] Martínez Sánchez recommended that the word Confederation be changed to Central (Central de Trabajadores de Cuba Revolucionaria), since the structure of the labor movement had been transformed and national federations no longer existed. He said that the Eleventh Congress was not the result of chance but "the result of the tireless efforts of a group of comrades who appeared to be a minority but enjoyed the support of the majority of the people." He referred to the developments of the

Tenth Congress and introduced a colorful note in his recollections by saying:

> Those traitors and rascals who opposed the unified labor
> movement and who stood in the aisles yelling "¡Melones!
> ¡Melones!" are no longer here. And we shall always be here,
> because we shall always be melones—green outside but red
> inside."[48]

Almost all the speakers referred to the conquest of political power by the working class and the fact that the
future was in its hands, but only one speaker, Blas Roca,
noted that not a single worker had yet been appointed to
the Cabinet or to a Cabinet-level position.[49]

Castro's Closing Speech

As usual, the keynote address was delivered by the Prime
Minister. His was a long-winded and fiery speech filled
with the customary denunciations of imperialists and counterrevolutionaries. The day before the closing of the congress, a peasant and a militia man had been killed by guerrillas in Las Villas Province and this event prompted Castro
to devote the first part of his speech to the denunciation
of such actions using the kind of emotional oratory that
he so effectively mastered.

But the special circumstances of the first labor congress
held under a socialist regime and the contrast between its
quiet atmosphere of unamimity and the turmoil of the

Tenth Congress also lent themselves to some retrospective accounts. Only three days later, Castro was to deliver his famous Marxist-Leninist speech containing a most candid account of the origins of the revolution. Now, before an assembly of ten thousand cheering workers' delegates, he also felt in the mood to reveal some aspects of the successful strategy he had used to introduce socialism in Cuba.

As a point of departure, he stated once again that the Cuban Revolution was nothing more and nothing less than the government of workers and peasants, though on previous occasions he had characterized it in a more elliptical way as "the Revolution of the humble, for the humble and by the humble."[50] He also expressed satisfaction over the fact that there was not a single turncoat or enemy among the ten thousand delegates.[51]

Castro then proceeded to indicate how the revolution had been forced to advance cautiously at the beginning, because the structure of power in Cuba in 1959 was substantially different. "The balance of power was such at that initial moment," he said, "that the working class was placed in a perilously weak position." "Few members of the working class could visualize at that moment," he added, "the bright future that was ahead for it." This explained, to his mind, the myopic view of some leaders who, by contenting themselves with securing specific demands, were renouncing the goal of abolition of the propertied class and giving up the workers' right to replace the employers as the ruling class of Cuba.[52]

The Prime Minister next went on to praise the "instinct" of certain sectors of the working class, who understood from the beginning the nature of the revolution and had faith in his government. He referred in particular to the sugar workers and the four-shift demand presented in January 1959. "Had we accepted that demand," he said, "we would have irrevocably impaired our economic future with costly working conditions liable to drain the national resources." For that reason, he added, we pleaded with the sugar workers to leave aside such demands and to accept the other terms and conditions offered by the government. Though the mills were not yet nationalized, he said, the sugar workers accepted the government proposal and thereby evinced an admirable understanding of our intentions. "We only suggested at that time that in due course we would make appropriate use of the savings of the bourgeoisie, because we were not yet in a position to launch the nationalization drive. And the working class understood the message and trusted the government."

The Prime Minister pointed out that at the outset of the revolution it had been necessary to be patient and to wait for the right moment. The revolution had not yet been sufficiently strong to engage in major battles and it had first been necessary to operate a change in the balance of power between conflicting social forces. He asked his audience what would have happened if the government had met all the various demands made by the people. "Fortunately," he said, "we were able to avoid most of the major social and economic burdens implicit in those demands, but we could not eschew all of them." A few small burdens had to be accepted at that time; they were not fundamental or decisive but they were rather significant. These "liabilities" were an inevitable by-product of the first stages of the revolution. It was against that background, he said, that the working class, already in control of the government, was proceeding to eliminate, of its own free will, those "liabilities" inherited from the first stages of the revolution, as well as the others inherited from previous administrations. These liabilities represented roadblocks in

the path to socialism which the workers were then re-
moving because they were the owners of the economy.[53]

Only a revolutionary working class fully aware of its
responsibilities under the new political conditions, he observed, could undertake to rectify past errors and to do
away with costly social benefits. "Some of these benefits,"
he insisted, "represented absurd payments which the revolution could not afford to absorb." Consequently, he proceeded, it was only through abandonment of such benefits
that it would be possible to develop the national wealth
that now belonged to workers and peasants. The workers
were not depriving themselves of anything, they were just
clearing the path of roadblocks.

He finally alluded to the future and once again drew a
vivid picture of affluence. He cited the experience of the
Soviet Union and said that according to his information,
in 20 years' time, Russia would be producing double the
output of all the non-socialist countries put together. This
experience, he pointed out, should encourage Cubans to
carry on with enthusiasm and determination. Cuba was in
the advantageous position of profiting from the experience
of the Soviet Union. The Russians, he contended, had been
forced to chart their own course without any help, while
Cuba had been following from the outset a familiar road.[54]

NOTES

1. Nelson Amaro and Alejandro Portés, "Situación de los grupos cubanos en el exilio." *Aportes* (Paris), No. 23, January 1972, pp. 10–11.
2. Hobart S. Spalding, Jr., *Organized Labor in Latin America. Historical Case Studies of Workers in Dependent Societies* (New York: New York University Press, 1977), p. 241.
3. Ricardo Rojo, *Mi amigo el Che* (Buenos Aires, Editorial Jorge Alvarez, S.A., 1968), p. 117. This book is also available in English: *My Friend Che* (New York, Grove Press, 1969).
4. *Revolución*, September 25, 1961, p. 2.
5. R. Castro, "Discurso con motivo del Acto Central por el XXIII Aniversario del Levantamiento del 30 de Noviembre," *Granma*, December 1, 1979, p. 2.
6. C. Franqui, *Retrato de familia con Fidel, op. cit.*, p. 287.
7. *Trabajo*, No. 4, April 1961, p. 122.
8. Law No. 962 of August 1, 1961 (*Extraordinary Official Gazette*, August 3, 1961).
9. See for instance ILO, *The Trade Union Situation in the USSR* (Geneva, 1960), pp. 42–43.
10. See *Revolución*, November 22, 1961, p. 1.
11. Although provision was still made in the law for the conclusion of collective bargaining agreements and the representation of individual and collective interests.
12. See *Revolución*, November 24, 1961, pp. 1 and 6.
13. An interim organ designed to pave the way for a united socialist party was set up in July 1961, under the name of Integrated Revolutionary Organizations (ORI). It was replaced in 1962 by the United Party of the Socialist Revolution (PURS). The Central Committee of the Cuban Communist Party was not established until October 1965. It should be added that the guiding and commanding role of the Communist Party was later enshrined in the Constitution and Declaration of Principles of the CTC-R. See the resolutions adopted by the Thirteenth Congress of the CTC-R in *Granma*, 19 November 1973, supplement).

14. See *Trabajo*, Year II, No. 15, October 1961, p. 47.

15. *Hispanic American Report*, Vol. XIV, No. 8, August 1961, p. 694.

16. See "Una quincena de acontecimientos laborales," in *Trabajo*, No. 11, August 1961, p. 45 and No. 13, September 1961, p. 89.

17. *Hoy*, July 20, 1961, p. 1.

18. See CTC-R, "La CTC Revolucionaria y la ORIT," *Boletín Internacional con noticias de Cuba* (Havana), No. 5, December 1959, p. 2.

19. See *Diario de la Marina*, December 18, 1959, pp. A1 and A2.

20. George Linchtblau, "Communist Labor Tactics in the Colonial and Former Colonial Countries," in Everett M. Kassalow, ed., *National Labor Movements in Postwar World* (Evanston, Ill., Northwestern University Press, 1963), p. 91.

21. See "La primera conferencia de plantaciones." *Trabajo*, No. 3, March 1961, p. 95.

22. See *Revolución*, November 5, 1960.

23. See *Los 25 congresos nacionales de industrias y el XI Congreso Nacional de la CTC-R* (Havana: Suplemento de Trabajo, n.d.), pp. 3, 8 and 12.

24. *Vanguardia Obrera*, October 7, 1961, p. 2.

25. "Un mes de acontecimientos laborales." *Trabajo*, No. 17, November 1961, p. 121; see also Jaime Gravalosa, "Los trabajadores en el poder." *Trabajo*, No. 19, December 1961, p. 69.

26. See *Revolución*, November 21 and 22, 1961.

27. *Los 25 congresos nacionales de industria, op. cit.*, pp. 2 and 3.

28. Carlos Fernández, "El XI Congreso Nacional de la CTC," *Cuba Socialista*, Year II, No. 6, February 1962, p. 52.

29. *Los 25 congresos nacionales de industria, op. cit.*, pp. 2 and 3. See also *Revolución*, November 24, 1961, pp. 1 and 6.

30. *Revolución*, November 25, 1961, p. 6.

31. Carlos Fernández, *op. cit.*, p. 52.

32. *Revolución*, November 25, 1961, p. 6; see also *Los 25 congresos nacionales de industria, op. cit.*, p. 2.

33. *Revolución*, November 25, 1961, p. 6.

34. *Revolución*, November 28, 1961, p. 5.

35. *Revolución*, November 27, 1961, pp. 1 and 5.

36. Adolfo Gilly, "Inside the Cuban Revolution." *Monthly Review* (New York), Vol. 16, No. 6, October 1964, p. 13.

37. See Draper, *op. cit.*, pp. 83–84.

38. For a similar view see Farber, "The Cuban Communism in the Early Stages of the Revolution," *op. cit.*, p. 78.

39. Alvarez de la Campa, however, defected in 1965 and later settled in the U.S.

40. Since all those extra payments had with the passage of time become an integral part of wages and since they were taken into account in the determination of workers' remuneration, it is clear that those relinquishments entailed a substantial reduction of yearly earnings. As a result of this reduction and concurrent economic factors, René Dumont holds that the standard of living stagnated in 1961 and fell perhaps 15 to 20 per cent in 1962. See René Dumont, *Socialisme et Développement* (Paris: Editions du Seuil, 1964), p. 91.

41. *Revolución*, November 29, 1961, p. 4.

42. "Un quincena de acontecimientos laborales." *Trabajo*, No. 19, December 1961, p. 22.

43. *Revolución*, November 27, 1961, p. 1.

44. *Ibid.*

45. *Revolución*, November 29, 1961, p. 3.

46. *Ibid.*

47. *Revolución*, November 27, 1961, p. 2.

48. *Ibid.* Also in *Trabajo*, No. 19, 1961, p. 21.

49. *Revolución*, November 28, 1961, p. 3.

50. *Revolución*, November 29, 1961, p. 7; see also "Los 25 congresos nacionales de industria," *op. cit.*, pp. 12–17.

51. *Revolución*, November 29, 1961, p. 1.

52. *Ibid.*, p. 7.

53. *Ibid.*, p. 8.

54. *Ibid.*

XII

The Conspiracy Theory Revisited

The Picture Reconsidered

THE PICTURE THAT EMERGES FROM THE PRECEDING PAGES DOES not appear to endorse Castro's pre-1959 version of the origins of the revolution. Nor is it in accordance with the views expressed by those who feel that the establishment of a Marxist-Leninist regime in Cuba was simply an accident of history, an unwanted departure from what was intended to be a social democratic revolution. There are many important elements of the 1959–61 revolutionary process which conflict with the vision of a liberal, democratic and progressive government: the instant urge to radicalize the revolution, early opposition to the bourgeoisie, the fostering of class conflict, gradual abolition of private property, the virtual elimination of non-Marxist political parties, newspapers and interest groups as well as the promotion of the leading role of the working class. The very tempo and crescendo of the revolution also seem to indicate that Castro was not "reacting" or "learning from experience" but rather applying from the beginning some preconceived ideas about the nature and final destination of the revolution. Not to be overlooked either is the fact that the overwhelming majority of the events discussed in previous chapters are of a purely domestic nature and thus totally independent from U.S. policies or actions.

A retrospective analysis also shows that the events discussed above, and particularly those dealing with the capture

of the Cuban labor movement, are not isolated or unconnected episodes. They constitute on the contrary a pattern
of actions, a comprehensive and consistent form of behavior
that can only be explained with the help of a previously
established design or a supporting ideology. If Marxism had
not yet been declared the official ideology in January 1959,
it was no doubt the underlying force which guided and animated the whole initial stage of the revolution.

As far as labor relations are concerned, hardly any of the
objectives expressed by Castro in his 1959 version came into
being during the period under review. Neither the workers'
right to participate in the profits of industrial, commercial
and mining undertakings, nor the guarantee of the right to
strike or the system of six hour shifts in the sugar industry
was ever implemented. One could always argue, on the other
hand, that the appointment of the Provisional Executive
Committee of the CTC-R and the holding of free trade union
elections in the first part of 1959, seemed to fulfill Castro's
promises to re-establish trade union democracy. However,
these initial measures were taken by the "liberal" Cabinet
which under the shadow of Castro ruled Cuba during the
first six weeks of 1959. In accepting the recommendations
of the "liberal" Cabinet, Castro may have felt that political
power was not yet fully consolidated in his hands and that
the first chaotic months of the revolution were a transitional
period in which certain concessions had to be made. These
concessions included the temporary appointment of some
progressive minded non-Communists to the leading positions in the labor movement. The provisional leadership of
the CTC-R was thus intended to perform exactly the same
role as the one played by the liberals appointed to the Cabinet. They were going to provide a semblance of trade union
freedom during the first critical months of the revolution
and to support the first package of populist and redistributive

measures which the Castro regime adopted in 1959. Like the "liberal" Cabinet, the non-Communist leadership of the CTC-R was however a short-lived arrangement destined to last only a few months.

The position is somewhat different with regard to the other version presented in Chapter I, namely that Castro had envisaged from the outset the socialization of Cuba and that for tactical reasons, he had decided to hide his real intentions. To begin with, none of the indications relating to this version (as disclosed *inter alia* in the speeches made on November 28 and December 2, 1961, in 1973 and in 1975) has ever been withdrawn or rejected by the Cuban Prime Minister. Castro simply preferred, on some other occasions, to play down his admissions or to refer in more ambiguous terms to the origins of the revolution. Furthermore, the analysis of the events leading to the capture of the labor movement tends to support the post-1961 version of the rationale of the revolution. When Castro's retrospective references are placed in the context of historical developments, they do not appear to be irrelevant or out of place. This is the case with such general statements as the identification of socialism as the major objective of the revolution, the need to proceed cautiously in unfolding the real goals of the leadership, the relations between the old and the new Communists, the steps taken to avoid a premature clash with the bourgeoisie and the necessity to use astuteness and flexibility in order to accomplish the revolutionary objectives. This is also the case with other more specific statements, such as the references to the general strike, the political mobilization of the masses and the promotion of class struggle. Both kinds of statements seem to match the actual development of facts and thereby give credibility to the post-1961 version. To suggest that the December, 1961, speech was only an *ex post facto* attempt by Castro to gain credentials as a Marxist-Leninist, clearly underestimates the interconnections between developments in the labor field after January 1959 and the tenor of Castro's statement.

The Four Basic Elements of the Communist Takeover

At the same time, the description of the 1959–61 period has served to identify other efforts and tactics which also fit in the same revolutionary strategy. These efforts and tactics can be reduced to four basic elements: inducement, indoctrination, deception and intimidation. The four elements had as a common denominator the relationship between Castro and labor and the interconnections between means and ends. The Communist dictum that the end justifies the means permeates all of them.

The strategy included first some inducement schemes intended to motivate and please workers in order to attune them with the revolution and pave the way for the subsequent teaching of new principles and beliefs. Inducement tactics were addressed to the workers by means of promises of undreamed wealth and through some tangible, albeit ephemeral, improvements of their conditions of work and life. From the FNTA speech of January, 1959, to the closing speech at the Eleventh Congress (November 1961), Castro endeavored to entice workers with expectations of prosperity and intimations of a grandiose future. While a superficial analysis of the revolutionary process might regard Castro's tactics as inconsistent in view of his initial emphasis on immediate improvements and his subsequent rejection of redistribution-oriented approaches, it is clear that these two policies correspond to different stages of the revolution. Consumptionist policies were linked to the seizure and consolidation of power; productionist policies aimed at the establishment of a socialist regime. New levels of aspiration were also subtly introduced through the constant mobilization of the masses and government attempts to convince workers that they were already sharing political power.

Indoctrination meant continuous efforts at massive ideological persuasion. New ideas and beliefs were disseminated to question the validity of capitalism, to criticize the operation of market economies and to introduce the basic tenets of Marxism. Castro's considerable persuasive powers were used to erode the major pillars of the old social order, so that people could be prepared for new patterns of socialization. Castro's ability also consisted in turning sizeable segments of his 1959 mass of followers into unconditional supporters of his views as a preliminary step to the establishment of a Marxist constituency. He could profit in this regard from his magnetic power of attraction, the ingrained tradition of "caudillismo" and the importance that leadership and personal influences had always had in Cuban politics. Here again, Castro's efforts were geared chiefly towards converting to his views the largest possible number of workers and peasants. This explains his frequent appearance at labor rallies, his long speeches, his simple dialectic and his repetitive argumentation.

Deception was employed to avoid dangerous, premature confrontations and to manipulate Castro's following. Given the extent of anti-Communist feelings before the revolution, there is little doubt that deception tactics had to play a vital role in the over-all Castro strategy. The original project had been so emphatically expounded by the "supreme" leader before 1959 that it amounted to a moral commitment entered into by the revolutionary elite and

the national community. In departing from it, Castro was
forced to proceed gradually and in the most secret and
furtive manner. Hence, the necessity to hide the real objectives of the revolution through the appointment of re-
spectable, unsuspected and easily disposable personalities
for the top government positions and the need to spread
"disinformation" and to mask the real meaning of certain
government actions. The frequent denials of Marxist leanings, the rationale provided by the government for the
seizure and nationalization of enterprises, the justification
of the changes in labor-management relations and the
reasons invoked for the purges, are examples of the decep-
tive tactics used by the revolutionary leaders to achieve
their own objectives. Castro's much publicized 1959 "humanist" philosophy was also part of the scheme as it turned
out to be short-lived and nothing less in fact than a fake
and a subterfuge.

   To a great extent, deception was also used to depict the
Cuban people as a backward, illiterate and poverty-stricken
one, where workers were exploited and most enterprises
were controlled by U.S. interests. In fact, deception was
used even before the revolution when Castro invoked the
name and ideals of Eduardo Chibás, a well-known anti-
Communist, as a means of advancing his own personal
goals. Small wonder that some authors have asserted that
misrepresentation, conscious or unconscious, as well as
constant manipulation of popular support were definitely
part of Castro's policies.[1]

   Not to be forgotten either was the exploitation of the
new, nationalist fervor that permeated Cuba from the beginning of 1959. Comtemporary history shows that nationalist sentiments are often intertwined, paradoxically,
with the advent or consolidation of Communist regimes.

As the rest of the Cuban people, the labor movement was fired upon Batista's downfall by a revival of patriotism and an upsurge of civism and hero worship, which Fidel Castro shrewdly used to further his own objectives. Mass mobilization campaigns relied heavily on nationalistic and chauvinistic appeals. Castro's frequent calls to the workers to support his government against alleged threats by foreign powers, were again a demonstration of his political skills, but also of his ability to twist and divert the original attitude of the labor movement and the population at large.

Elements of intimidation were also discernible throughout the transitional period of 1959–61. Intimidation appeared during the purges at the end of 1959 and have thereafter continued as one of the trade-marks of the revolution. It adopted various forms and originated in many different sources but was for the most part related to the position of trade unionists as citizens and workers. Trade union unity, national defense and the need to fight counterrevolution were some of the reasons invoked to coerce workers into accepting the ideology of the revolutionary leadership. Other more individualized threats related to job security, possible loss of economic benefits, transfer of employment, deferment of promotion, withdrawal of rationing coupons and low priority in the allocation of houses. No aspect of life was in fact so deeply affected by intimidation as the employment dimension. Government control of job opportunities, unpaid voluntary work and the control of absenteeism, together with the measures adopted in 1964 against vagrancy, became in effect the pillars of a vast and insidious system of forced labor.

And there was also fear, physical fear of Castro, his power and his methods. As a former terrorist and guerilla leader, Castro was capable of taking the most drastic action without the slightest hesitation or inhibition. At the very

314 *Efrén Córdova*

outset of the revolution, he gave clear indications of his
implacable resolution to move ahead with his plans when
he ordered the execution of hundreds of active supporters
of Batista, set aside *res judicata* verdicts that he considered
insufficiently punitive[2] and fomented sentiments of revenge and vindicitiveness among the populace. Later in
1959 while making his way towards absolute power, he
managed at times to present a more benign and peaceful
image. But once he reached his goal and became an all-
powerful leader he manifested again his ruthless determination to quell all signs of opposition as witnessed by
the execution of three electrical workers, the harsh sentences meted out to dissenting labor leaders, the incarceration and inhumane treatment of internationally prominent trade unionists, the persecution of opposition groups
and the violent repression of the Cárdenas riots. Disagreement with his policies entailed enormous risks and
called for highly exceptional qualities of courage and brav-
ery. In the context of a totalitarian regime of typically
Stalinist features, resistance to an unforgiving and pitiless
ruler of Castro's dimension amounted in fact to a choice
between martyrdom, exile and prison.

The Chronological Development

Even if Castro had not provided his own candid account
of the origins of the revolution, the analysis of the 1959–
61 period would lead to similar conclusions. The account
presented in the previous chapters shows, in effect, that a
number of actions were carried out from the beginning
with a view to undermining the old social order and fa-

cilitating the introduction of socialism. These actions reveal a unity of purpose and a deliberate design characteristic of the existence of a previously conceived strategy.

The first year of the revolution was devoted to consolidating Castro's personal power and to preparing the ground work for the introduction of a Marxist totalitarian regime in Cuba. Every possible effort was made to identify the aims of the revolution with the needs and aspirations of the working class. Not only was work promoted but care was taken to enhance constantly the role of labor in the revolution. The revolutionary leaders also endeavored to impress upon the workers the idea that criticism of the revolution came only from the representatives of the foreign and privileged interests. They further strove consistently to create the atmosphere of hostility and class consciousness that was necessary for the inception of Communism. And they systematically sought to undermine the position of employers and to weaken the power of the propertied classes.

During this period, the Prime Minister voiced hints on various occasions as to his real intentions, though he took pains to do this in rather subtle and mysterious terms. It is quite likely that these hints were aimed at reassuring other members of the inner circle about his Marxist objectives, encouraging PSP affiliates to support the revolutionary government and whetting the appetite of opportunists willing to join the revolutionary bandwagon. At any rate, they were invariably accompanied by statements of attachment to democracy and followed by denials of his Marxist leanings. In line with Lenin's teachings, Castro was not afraid of ambiguities and even contradictions when they seemed to him politically useful. Such ambiguities, denials and contradictions played a significant role in the establishment of socialism as they served to befuddle critics and to stymie potential opponents. This explains, for instance, the assurances given to employers at the beginning of 1959, the acceptance in May of the invitation to attend the banquet offered by businessmen at the Havana Hilton and the authorization granted to the American Society of Travel Agents (ASTA) to hold its Congress in Havana in the month of October.

Once the Prime Minister felt that his position was secure and that conditions were propitious for the unfolding of his plans, he proceeded, in 1960, to carry out drastic institutional changes. He smashed the anti-Communist opposition within the labor movement and completed its capture in a few months. Trade unions' original aims were quickly diluted and their much touted independence proved illusory. He nationalized all large and medium-sized enterprises and wiped out employers and employers' associations from the national scene. He did away with freedom of the press, freedom of association, judicial safeguards including the *habeas corpus* and other features of democracy. All these steps were taken in a typically determined and implacable fashion without the slightest concession to conventional political arrangements. In the context of his long term objectives, Castro's capture and emasculation of the labor movement were obviously only part, albeit an important one, of the over-all strategy to introduce Communism. Castro's denial of freedom of association should thus be seen as paralleling similar developments in the larger society—his failure to fulfill earlier promises regarding political rights, a pluralist society and the holding of elections within an eighteen-month period.

It is important to note that, in 1960, three spokesmen of the revolutionary regime (Raúl Castro, Guevara and Aguilera) clearly indicated that the government was already engaged in the implementation of Marxism. Fidel

Castro, however, remained silent on the subject and limited himself to the same cryptic allusions to the role of labor in the new emerging society.

The third year witnessed the official proclamation of the socialist republic, the formal incorporation of trade unions as organs of the state and the promotion of the Communist leaders to the top hierarchy of the labor movement. In 1961, all rights of speech, assembly, free representation and criticism were already openly denied. Opposition to the regime was deemed as a capital offense and a reign of permanent terror began to engulf the country. While it is true that the manner and the tone of some of these developments may have been influenced by external events, the outcome would probably have been the same regardless of the state of U.S.-Cuba relations. U.S. political pressures only served in fact to restrict opposition activities and to give Castro a pretext for accelerating certain actions. The Castro regime also used American economic sanctions to explain the 1961 economic decline and food rationing, and to consolidate power by fomenting anti-U.S. feelings among the general population.

As soon as the takeover of the propertied classes and the labor movement was consummated, there was no need to continue with double-talk tactics. In fact, it was evident in 1961 that the revolution could have no other end but the establishment of a totalitarian regime; the process which had started in 1959 had reached its culmination and the government needed no further excuses to acknowledge the obvious facts. As President Dorticós put it in June, 1961, "we just put a name to the facts that had already taken place."[3]

In retrospect, Castro's major achievements during the first three years of the revolution were: (1) his quick assertion of personal supremacy over a highly factionalized anti-Batista Movement. (Ironically, the Prime Minister became the undisputed leader of the July 26 Movement at a time when he was paving the way for its destruction); (2) his capacity to surmount a critical stage in his design to capture organized labor by transferring his personal leadership to the interior of the labor movement and by mercilessly crushing the opposition; (3) and, perhaps most important, his ability to convey one impression to one constituency (a touch of Marxism for the members of the PSP, the landless peasants and the lower strata of urban labor) and another to others (a heavy dose of nationalism and democracy to the bulk of the population). A final achievement consisted in disguising his strong authoritarian approach under the mantle of consensus politics and direct approval of the people.

Similarities with the Soviet Revolution

There is also the question of the contacts and similarities between the Cuban and the Soviet Revolutions, i.e., what Castro called the "familiar path." In developing his revolutionary strategy during those three years, Castro followed closely the experience of the Soviet Revolution. Though he was more Leninist than Marxist, in the sense that he was more familiar with the techniques for the seizure of power than with the application of the economics of Marxism, he had enough grasp of the latter to be able to apply the general lines of Communist theory. His interest in Marxism-Leninism extended to the prerequisites of socialism including industrialization and class relationships and covered the whole range of socio-political aspects

THE CONSPIRACY THEORY REVISITED

regarding the establishment of a dictatorship of the proletariat. True, some strains of Maoism also slipped into
Castro's thinking and vocabulary at the beginning of the
revolution. Rural workers, for instance, were lifted to the
category of major protagonists of the revolution and moral
incentives were given high priority. However, the upgrad-
ing and adulation of rural workers which reflected the Sierra Maestra mythology and the initial disappointment
with urban workers, were soon counterbalanced by the
urge to industrialize the country and later replaced by the
recognition of the role played by workers in general. Moral
incentives also gave way in due course to a more balanced
mix of stimuli in accordance with Marxian teachings
about material and economic factors.

Castro's adherence to the more orthodox Soviet version
of Marxism involved in fact both techniques and sub-
stance. Mass mobilization techniques, the elimination of
private ownership, the worker-peasant alliance, socialist
emulation, the elimination of free collective bargaining,
central planning—these were all basic elements of both the
Soviet and Cuban Revolutions. Substantial similarities are
also discernible in respect of such important matters as the
trade union structure, the extent and exclusions of the
right to organize and the dicouragement of economic
strikes. Even in matters of lesser significance, such as the
promotion of voluntary work, payment by results, workers'
contributions, labor conscription, the use of militias, the
coining of discipline-oriented slogans, and the discontinuation of the check-off system, the approach followed by
the Cuban Revolution paralleled, *mutatis mutandis*, similar
developments in the Soviet Union. The use of trade unions
for military purposes, for instance, was recommended by
Lenin in an article written in 1921 and advocated by Castro

in several speeches delivered in 1960. Castro's 1959 description of the one thousand towns that he intended to build bore a close resemblance to the system of interfarm cooperatives and concentration of agricultural undertakings which had been favored in the Soviet Union after the death of Stalin. Finally, some of the forms used in Cuba to promote voluntary work, including work on Sunday, can trace back their origins to the "subbotnicks" practice of the Russian Revolution.

One could always argue that some of these similarities obtain also in non-Communist revolutions. But it is the pattern of steady and consistent coincidences that makes the Cuban Revolution so closely related to the Russian experience. The big difference lies in the fact that in Russia, the application of Marxism was made in the name of a Bolshevik Revolution and in Cuba, it was introduced by an alleged nationalist, democratic and non-Communist regime.

Castro's knowledge of Marxism-Leninism included the need to control, at an early stage, the trade union movement. The survival of an independent and free trade union movement represented a challenge to the political authority of a dictatorship of the proletariat. How could such authority be reconciled with the fact that large portions of the labor sector remained independent or assumed an attitude of opposition? A genuine totalitarian regime could not afford to tolerate the existence of an autonomous intermediary power between government and the working class. There was also the problem of a possible incompatibility between a consumption-oriented labor movement and the economic plans of a new socialist government. All this explains Castro's early efforts to capture and dominate the whole structure of Cuban trade unions.

The Cuban Revolution profited in this respect from previous socialist experience and was placed in an even better position than the Soviet Revolution. When the Bolsheviks took power in 1917 no precise definition of the role of trade unions in a Communist society had been formulated. Marx had been rather vague on the determination of the functions of trade unions under the dictatorship of the proletariat. Lenin's views had emphasized the supremacy of the party of professional revolutionaries over trade unions but had not spelled out the role of labor organizations. It was only a few years after the triumph of the revolution that Lenin was able to write that trade unions of a socialist country lose their original raison d'être, namely class economic struggle, though they were not deprived of their other objectives, i.e., supervision and correction of the bureaucratic distortions of the Soviet apparatus.[4] It was probably because of this delay that a workers' opposition led by Tomsky gained momentum in the USSR and was not completely eliminated until 1927. It was also because of these uncertainties that the Soviet Revolution had to wait four years to have some concrete indications about the role of trade unions in a socialist society. At the Tenth Congress of the Communist Party held in 1921, Aleksandra Kollontai raised her voice in favor of independent labor organizations, but her efforts were unsuccessful: other more powerful leaders, including Trotsky, had already decided to suppress all possible forms of opposition.

What emerged from the Soviet trade union debate of the 1920s was a model of a monopolistic, state-controlled and production-oriented union, mainly concerned with mobilization, labor discipline and the fulfilment of development targets. While unions were also supposed to serve their members by protecting workers against bureaucratic arbitrariness and by running various welfare services, they

were weak in interest articulation and their main functions
were essentially macrosocial ones. These functions gradually led the unions towards their transformation into
transmission belts between the party and the masses; they
also meant that other activities were to be rigidly demar-
cated by the recognition of the leading role of the party.
All other alternatives, premised on the existence of autonomous organizations, were quickly rejected as they entailed
a dispersion of political power and a threat to the totalitarian nature of a Communist regime.[5]

This model was transplanted to Cuba *in toto*. Other Communist countries have tried to make some adaptations in
the model (witness Yugoslavia since 1950, Hungary since
the late 1960s and Poland in 1981), but the Castro regime
subscribed to it unconditionally and without reservations.
Castro and his associates thus knew from the beginning
the goal to be pursued in this respect. To capture, emasculate and transform the labor movement represented from
the outset an essential element of the strategy aimed at
establishing a Marxist regime in Cuba. The revolutionary
leaders learned from the Russian experience that there
simply was no room in Communist Cuba for an autonomous trade union power and consequently developed an
early determination to place workers' organizations under
government control. They knew that the fate of a free
trade union movement in a Communist society is to disappear and that the surviving labor organizations were to
become government instruments primarily concerned with
increasing production, administering certain social services
and disciplining the labor force. The Cuban trade union
movement consequently did not have the slightest chance
of retaining its independent character in the face of the
revolutionary march towards socialism.

The fact that the Cuban labor movement was so rapidly

and effectively controlled by the Revolutionary Government may also be explained by the critical significance attached to the wielding of political power in a less developed society. As mentioned in Chapter II, the Castro regime enjoyed full political power almost from the outset of the revolution. At the same time, the power of resistance of Cuban society had been greatly undermined by the frustration caused by repeated political failures, the ruthless Batista dictatorship and the vacuum created by its downfall. The revolutionary elite was thus able to complete in less than two years what would have required a longer period of time under normal circumstances or in a more developed society. They could also profit in their endeavours from Castro's charismatic personality. Both elements — the influence of political factors and the paramount significance of Castro's charisma — point out the need to combine a Weberian approach with the conspiracy theory in order to achieve a better understanding of the dynamics of the revolution. Needless to add that neither charisma nor conspiratorial action has anything to do with the changes in the infrastructure of society and the requirements of production forces that were so frequently invoked by the American scholars who formulated the other theories mentioned at the beginning of the Introduction.

Dispelling Confusion

It is suggested, in the light of the above findings and considerations, that there has been some confusion about the origins of the Cuban Revolution. To maintain, for instance, 16 years after the triumph of the revolution, that its Marxist-Leninst nature was "an accident of history, a forced response to a complicated mass of internal and external events and pressures" is indeed the utmost of naïveté.[6] Even a Cuban-born writer who is familiar with many aspects of the Cuban experience has failed to grasp the significance of Castro's manipulations when he states that "the first stage of the revolution, 1959–60, lacked a defined ideology."[7] This seems to imply that it was only in 1961, i.e. after the Bay of Pigs operation, that the revolutionary elite leaned towards Marxism.

There has also been a tendency to discard out of hand the conspiracy theory without adequate consideration of its real meaning and historical context. It is not enough to say that "the conspiracy theory offends common sense and displays an attitude towards the Cuban people bordering on contempt."[8] It is necessary to investigate the magnitude of the vacuum that existed in Cuba after Batista's downfall and to appreciate the extremes of shrewdness, duplicity, lack of scruples and masterly use of misinformation and double talk tactics that were employed by the Prime Minister and his associates. The transition to a Communist society, against the will of the majority of the Cuban people and in a country situated in the very heart of the American sphere of influence, entailed enormous difficulties. The fact that Castro was able to overcome them indicates that both the capture of the labor movement and the introduction of Communism were exceptionally well executed operations. True, not all the details of the blueprint for socialization were previously thought out, but intuition, careful attention to tactics, capacity for swift and expeditious action, periodic appraisals of the balance of forces and full commitment to the basic objectives of the revolution made up for any possible lack of planning. There were probably moments of exasperation and some outbursts of impatience prompted by the relatively slow attainment of the revolutionary goals. Guevara in particular is known to have been impatient with the tempo of the revolution and to have argued for a quicker realization of its objectives. But Castro was always in full control and it was he who determined the pace and momentum of the takeover; it was he who decided when to cajole and when to threaten, when to move ahead and when to slow down. He was particularly skillful in profiting from the traditional weakness of Cuban politics and in turning to his advantage the tensions with the U.S. As Theodore Draper put it, Fidel Castro and his inner circle leaped at one pretext or another to do what they wanted to do, they incessantly increased their power by taking the initiative against their enemies and relentlessly pressing the advantage.[9]

The Roots of Castro's Communism

Opponents of the conspiracy theory have pointed to Castro's recognition, in the Marxist-Leninist speech, that he had read only 347 pages of *Das Kapital* as an indication of the lack of seriousness of his claim that he was already a Communist in 1959. They forget, however, that Castro's knowledge of all the details of Marxist theory was unnecessary since he was able to count, from the Sierra Maestra days, on the advice of Cuban Communist Party's ideologue, Carlos Rafael Rodríguez. Moreover, Castro's reading of the Marxist-Leninist literature was much more extensive than suggested in the speech and was definitely not limited to *Das Kapital* (which is not, incidentally, an easy book to read). On other occasions, even before 1959, he referred to his study of other publications of Marx, including *The Communist Manifesto, The 18 Brumaire of Louis Bonaparte* and *The Civil Wars in France.* Suffice to cite in this respect his letters from prison and in particular the one written on 4 April 1954.[10] As mentioned before, however, he was in fact more adept at reading Lenin for whom he doubtless felt genuine admiration. One of his closest collaborators indicated, for instance, that from his student days Castro always carried a volume of Lenin under his arm.[11] Another recalled how Castro recommended the study of "Marxist material" to some of his companions of the Moncada attack.[12] Not to be overlooked either is the fact that in the same Marxist-Leninist speech Castro also alluded to his readings of Lenin and the selected works of Marx and Engels since the Moncada days.

Apart from this evidence of Castro's familiarity with the Marxist-Leninist literature, one is entitled to wonder about the importance of the role played by classic Marxist works in the process of Castro's conversion to Communism. The question could, in fact, be raised with regard to any other revolutionary leader and present-day Communist ruler. Are they actually persuaded to accept Communism as a result of reading Marx's *Das Kapital* or Engel's *Anti-Duhring* or Lenin's *State and Revolution?* It is suggested that in many cases the generating causes of an individual's spousal of Communism go well beyond the purely intellectual sphere and may relate to emotional and personal factors. To bring to light the complex process of motivation, frustration and perhaps resentment by which one becomes a Communist (or a "true believer" in general), and which may differ substantially from person to person, would require endless investigations and analysis. Is a person intellectually persuaded by Marxist reasonings? Are Marxists emotionally attracted to Communist tactics and goals? Or are they motivated by the rejection of capitalism or the failure to function within the existing system or some traumatic experience or the ostracism created by social or ethnic origin? One could surmise, for example, that Fidel and his brother Raúl having been born as illegitimate children, they probably suffered for several years (until their father legitimized his relationship with Lina Ruz) the social stigma that was frequently associated to that condition. One could also speculate that the social origin of their mother and the economic position of their father may have inclined the Castro brothers to identify themselves with the underdogs and to spurn the rich and powerful. Given the prejudices prevailing at the time of Castro's childhood, it is not likely that such circumstances may have left a trace of resentment in his personality. However, this is an elusive area where no causal link can effectively be established and which belongs at any rate to the domain of psycho-historical analysis.

One thing is nevertheless certain, namely, that activists and agitators of the Fidel Castro type would certainly be influenced by reasons considerably different from those that would affect university professors or literary people. The Marxist education of some present-day Communist leaders shows that it stemmed in fact from a few basic elementary sources.[13]

To probe into remote causes seems on the other hand useless when more immediate and tangible indications are available. These indications relate to Castro's well-known personality traits, the analysis of which throws light on his decision to spouse Communism as well as on his behavior before and after that decision. Three major reasons were probably instrumental in this respect. The first relates to his visceral, compelling need to wield absolute power for an indefinite period of time. A limited and fixed-term exercise of power would have been incompatible with his personal goals and ambitions. Only the Communist theory could provide him with the ideological justification to stay permanently in power. Other totalitarian ideologies might also have provided similar possibilities in the past but in 1959 they were obviously outdated and lacked the force and appeal of Marxism. Traditional or populist Latin American dictatorships were also less attractive and far more devoid of potentialities than the exercise of full, permanent power on behalf of the working class. Marxism offered a ready-made theory and a coherent political program which emphasized the vital role of the dictatorship of the proletariat and preached the capture of the entire power of the state by the Communist Party. As Mario Llerena put it, "without Communism Castro would never have gained the only kind of power that satisfies him."[14]

Castro's second motivation concerns the Communist advocacy of class struggle, violent seizure of power and world domination. This again fitted well into his own personal traits and vocation which had pushed him in the past to become a member of a terrorist organization, to participate in the Colombian "Bogotazo," the Cayo Confites expedition, the assault on the Moncada military barracks, as well as to continuous action, militant pursuits and deep-seated antagonisms. Castro's militaristic mind and his penchant for weapons, secret operations, uniforms and constant preparations for war, led him almost naturally to promote bellicose endeavors. To rule peacefully and quietly a small, developing country would have been enormously boring and frustrating to him. He needed, on the contrary, to maintain the heroic tempo of the revolution and he could only do this after the triumph of the July 26 Movement by promoting subversion and agitation in the Third World and by committing himself to a state of perennial confrontation with the U.S. This in turn, required some ideological justification which he found in the Marxist-Leninist ideology. Communist aims and philosophy regarding the establishment of a dictatorship of the proletariat, first, and the subsequent fight against imperialism, were precisely the kind of activity for which Castro was particularly motivated and qualified.

Communism, finally, represented for Castro a worldwide platform from which he could develop his enormous ambition and almost pathological vanity. Any other kind of nationalist, populist or socio-democratic revolution would have condemned him to act within the limits of the small Cuban stage. Marxism-Leninism opened up, on the contrary, broader horizons. It gave him the opportunity to champion Latin America against the U.S. or to lead the Third World against the rich countries, to become, in short, a world-wide personality. All this constituted an irresistible attraction to him.

But if Castro used Marxism to advance his own personal ambitions, he was also no doubt fascinated well before the revolution with the theory and practice of Marxist-Leninist teachings. Even the most cursory reading of his correspondence from jail and the Sierra Maestra would show Castro's strong attraction and admiration for socialist principles. His statements during the transitional period serve in turn to show Castro's familiarity with the tactics expounded by Communist thinkers as regards the capture of political power. All this seems to indicate that Castro's fascination with Communism did not derive only from certain features of his personality but reflected a more profound intellectual spousal of Marxist principles. True, Castro's interest in the workers and the labor movement was more instrumental than substantive, more egotistical than altruistic. He was fascinated by the role that the working class was supposed to play in a Communist takeover and quickly understood its potentially vast implications for the future of his revolution. He may have been sympathetic to workers' problems and complaints, but his main concern related to the utilization of organized labor and the working masses as a tool for the conquest of political power. Other, long-term problems dealing with the well-being of the workers largely escaped his attention. At times during the first years of the revolution, he seemed to be more interested in inspecting cows or agricultural projects than in evaluating social services or verifying possible improvements in conditions of work and life. Except for the coverage of social security, which was undoubtedly expanded, few improvements can be registered in respect of workers' rights and benefits.

Castro did not evince special interest in institutionalizing workers' rights as a whole or in including new principles thereon in the Constitution. Unlike leaders of other socialist countries, he attached such a low priority to the adoption of a labor code that it was only in 1985 that a code dealing with conditions of work and labor relations came into effect. He has never tried to enlarge workers' participation in decisions within undertakings or to search for new participative schemes. Moreover, his much publicized encounters with workers and peasants turned out to be rather patronizing exercises marked by an exchange of banalities ("Are you happy with the revolution? Do you approve the nationalization of enterprises? How were you treated before the revolution?").[15] The energy, audacity and imagination of which he has made ample use in his foreign ventures and political affairs were completely absent with regard to labor relations. His approach has simply been one of full adherence to the Soviet model with a minimum of adaptations and alterations.

Castro never saw himself as a servant or interpreter of the workers' needs but rather as a domineering leader who chose for them unanticipated functions, visualized on their behalf objectives and goals, indicated tactics, admonished the weak, punished the dissenter and was always demanding increasing sacrifices. Workers were of interest to him only as a group and as long as they constituted a political force.

While Castro was thus determined from the outset to transform Cuba into a Communist country, he was not a typical card-carrying member of the Communist Party. Although he served his country on a silver platter to the USSR, the Cuban dictator was probably right when he stated in the Lockwood interview that he was not, in 1959, a disguised or infiltrated agent of the Soviet Union. Castro represented, on the contrary, a new breed of Communist dictator: the action-oriented, unscrupulous, ruthless, despotic and ambitious leader who was attracted by Marxism not only because of its socioeconomic tenets but also on account of its enormous political potentialities. He was indeed the first leader of the developing world to demonstrate that Communism represented both a far-reaching revolutionary ideology and a convenient means of wielding absolute, personal power for an indefinite period of time.

NOTES

1. See, for instance, Samuel Farber, *Revolution and Reaction in Cuba, op. cit.*, p. 224.

2. This happened for instance with the trial of several members of the Air Force in the month of April, 1959.

3. *Verde Olivo*, June 25, 1961, p. 29.

4. See V.I. Lenin, *Oeuvres*, Vol. 32 (Moscow: Editions du Progrès, 1965), p. 79.

5. See Alex Pravda, "Trade Unions in East European Systems" *International Political Science Review* (Geneva), Vol. 4, No. 2, 1983, pp. 244 and 245.

6. Herbert Mathews, *Revolution in Cuba, op. cit.*, p. 6.

7. C. Mesa Lago, *Cuba in the 1970s: Pragmatism and Institutionalization* (Santa Fe: University of New Mexico Press, 1974), chapter 1.

8. James O'Connor, *The Origins of Socialism in Cuba, op. cit.*, p. 4.

9. Theodore Draper, *Castro's Revolution: Myths and Realities, op. cit.*, p. 106.

10. See *Diario de la Revolución Cubana, op. cit.*, p. 325.

11. See the testimony of Juan Almeyda in Carlos Franqui, *The Twelve* (New York: Lyle Stuart Inc., 1968), p. 23.

12. See the testimony of Melba Hernández in *Diario de la Revolución Cubana, op. cit.*, p. 303.

13. Deng Xiao Ping's early spousal of Communism, for instance, was the outcome of reading *The ABC of Communism* and a few other booklets and pamphlets. See *China Review*, Vol. V, No. 1, 1983.

14. *The Unsuspected Revolution, op. cit.*, p. 202.

15. Cited in C. Franqui, *Retrato de familia, op. cit.*, p. 514, supra, p. 18.

Index

About the Author

Born in Havana, Cuba, and an American citizen since 1966, Efrén Córdova holds a Doctor of Law degree from the University of Havana and a Ph.D. in industrial and labor relations from Cornell University. He taught labor law and labor relations at the universities of Havana and Puerto Rico (Río Piedras). In 1967 he joined the International Labour Organization (ILO), where he was chief of the Labor Law and Labor Relations Branch for several years and served in 1984-1985 as chief technical advisor in Brazil. A member of various professional associations, Dr. Córdova was until 1984 secretary of the International Industrial Relations Association; in 1986 he was elected member of the Iberoamerican Academy of Labor Law and Social Security. Professor Córdova has written extensively on labor law and labor relations in general and Latin America in particular. His latest publications include: *Industrial Relations in Latin America* (Praeger, 1984), "Strikes in the Public Service. Some Determinants and Trends", *International Labor Review* (Geneva), April 1985 and *Inflación, política salarial y relaciones de trabajo* (Mexico, Trillas, 1986).

DATE DUE

JUL 20 2007			

GAYLORD

PRINTED IN U.S.A.